The Chapters of Mary and *Ṭā Hā*

The Chapters of Mary and *Ṭā Hā*

Sūrah Maryam & Sūrah Ṭā Hā

from

The Immense Ocean
(*al-Baḥr al-Madīd fī Tafsīr al-Qurʿān al-Majīd*)
A Thirteenth/Eighteenth Century
Quranic Commentary
by

Aḥmad ibn ʿAjība
(d. 1224/1809)

Translated and Annotated by
Mohamed Fouad Aresmouk and
Michael Abdurrahman Fitzgerald

FONS VITAE

First published in 2021 by
Fons Vitae
49 Mockingbird Valley Drive
Louisville, KY 40207
http://www.fonsvitae.com

Library of Congress Control Number: 2021946511

ISBN 978-1941610-862

This book was typeset by Neville Blakemore, Jr.

Printed in USA

Contents

بسم اللّــــه الرحمن الرجيم
وصلى اللـــــه على سيد محمد وعلى آله

Translators' Note and Acknowledgements

This present work is, to some extent, a companion volume to our first translation of a portion of Ibn ʿAjība's monumental Quranic commentary, *al-Baḥr al-Madīd fī tafsīr al-Qur'ān al-Majīd*, published by Fons Vitae under the title *The Immense Ocean* in 2009. Following the appearance of that work we were encouraged by the kind words and messages of thanks we received from many far-flung places in the world as well as by the revived interest in the writings of Ibn ʿAjība we saw shown by the appearance of several new translations of his works and even some study groups in the UK and Australia devoted to his *tafsīr*. The present humble effort is offered in gratitude to those who found something for their hearts in that previous publication and as part of a continued effort to make available to Anglophone readers some of the beauty of the spiritual tradition of Islam.

This work has been a journey that has lasted a number of years and we would like to thank a number of people who have been our companions and helpers along the way. First of these is Virginia Gray Henry, the inspiration behind and director of *Fons Vitae*, for her encouragement, enthusiasm, and vision. We would also like to thank our dear friends and colleagues at the Center for Language and Culture, Brahim Zoubairi and Hamza Weinman, for their suggestions, help, and support along the way. We are grateful to the following students of Arabic: Zakaria Gangat, Saffiya Ghaffar, Mohamed Faizan Hakim, Isma Kouser, Halima Limbada, Jafar Marcelo Cipola, Brandon Merrifield, Anjum Saad, Mahyar Sajadi, and Imaan

Tarapuri. These students, most of whom were preparing to enter the Cambridge Muslim College, were kind enough to meet with us weekly during the first half of 2020 to read a portion of this translation together and offer their suggestions. In the same vein, we are very grateful to the people of the Kutubia Centre in Orgiva, Spain, who arranged for us to give a reading of a portion of this work in 2017 and gave us much appreciated encouragement to complete this project. Last but in no way least, none of this work—indeed, nothing in our lives—would have been possible without the love, patience, and support of our spouses, may God bless them always.

Mohammad Fouad Aresmouk
Michael Abdurrahman Fitzgerald
Marrakesh, Morocco, Spring, 2021

Guide to Transcription	
SYMBOL	ARABIC REPRESENTED
ṭ ṣ ḥ ẓ	ظ ح ص ط
a i u *a* pronounced like the *a* in "and" *i* pronounced like the *ee* in "free" *u* pronounced like the *ou* in "you"	ُ ِ َ
ū ā ī = the vowel sound is sustained twice as long as the normal vowel sound: *qulūb* (= "quluub"), *mā* (= "maa"), *fī* (= "fii").	قُلُوب ، مَا ، فِي
ʿa ʿu ʿi	عِ عُ عَ
aʾ iʾ uʾ = the presence of a *hamza* (the glottal stop) as in *shāʾ*, *jiʾta*, *muʾmin*	شَاء ، جِئْتَ ، مُؤْمِن
The combination *aw* is pronounced to rhyme with the English word "now." The combination *ay* is pronounced to rhyme with the English word "day."	أَوْ ، أَيْ
dh as in the English "*th*at" *sh* as in the English "*sh*ow" *th* as in "wi*th*" *gh* no exact equivalent in English, but close to the sound of G in "gale."	ذ ش ث غ
The raised point (·) indicates that there is a syllable break, as is the word *aṣ·ḥāb* ("companions").	أَصْحَاب

The following Arabic terms have been left in their transliterated form:

sūrah, *sūrahs* = a chapter of the Qur'ān, of which there are a total of 114.
ḥadīth, *ḥadīths* = a saying of the Prophet Muḥammad ﷺ.

imām = one who leads the congregational prayer, often used to designate a great spiritual leader.
tafsīr, *tafsīrs* = a commentary of the Qur'ān.
faqīr, *fuqarā'* = literally, "needy one(s)," used by Sufis to denote someone who is part of a Sufic order, or simply an aspirant to the Way.
ṭarīqa, *ṭarīqas* = a Sufic order.
zāwiya = literally, "a corner," used to refer to a place where Sufis gather.

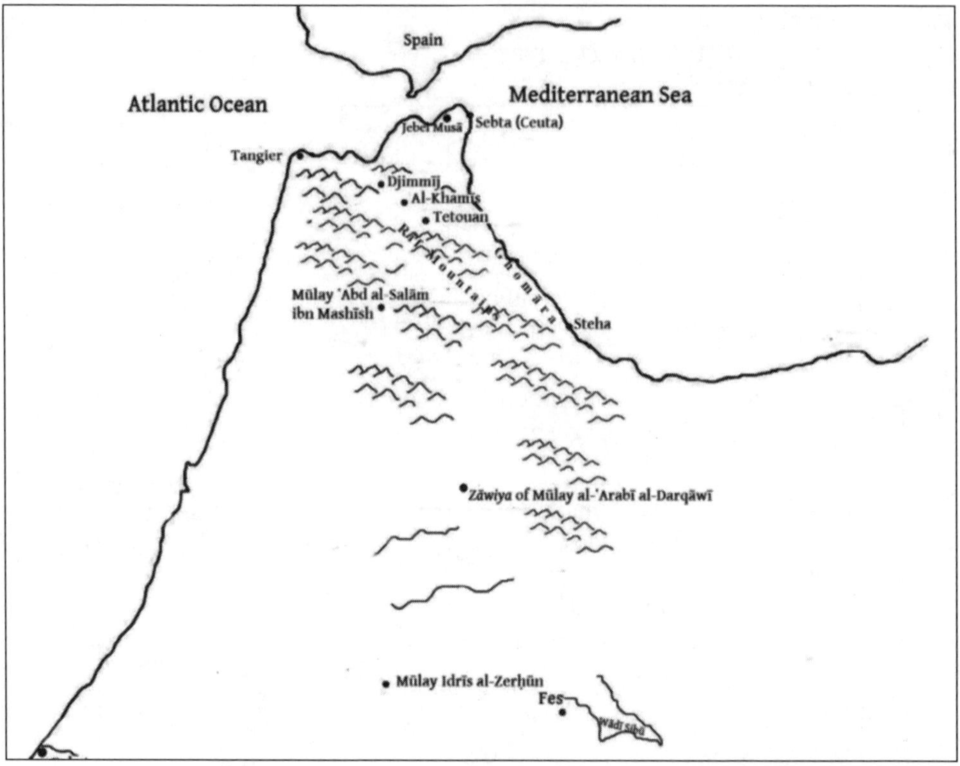

Map of Northern Morocco showing some places mentioned in the text

A view of Jebel Mūsā from Gibraltar by José Rambaud

Introduction

The Land between the Two Seas

Abū al-ʿAbbās Aḥmad ibn ʿAjība al-Idrīsī al-Ḥasanī, best known as Ibn ʿAjība or, in Morocco, as "Sīdī Binʿajība," was one of the first recognized scholars to become affiliated with the Darqāwī Sufi order that appeared in northern Morocco in the latter half of the 13th/18th century. Given the vital role that geography has always played in the history of Morocco, before speaking of the author himself, we would first like to mention something about the Jbāla region where he was born, lived most of his life, met his spiritual mentors, and wrote the Quranic commentary of which an excerpt is translated in the pages which follow.

According to a number of early Quranic *tafsīrs*, *the junction of the two seas* (*majmaʿ al-baḥrayni*) mentioned in *Sūrat al-Kahf* [18:60] at which the prophet Moses ﷺ was to find his spiritual teacher, al-Khiḍr, is where the Mediterranean Sea and the Atlantic Ocean merge off the coast of Tangier.[1] This is also the point at which the Rif mountain range, which occupies over 13,000 square miles be-

1. Mentioned in the commentaries of al-Ṭabarī (d. 310/922), al-Baghwī (d. 510/1116), al-Qurṭubī (d. 671/1272), ibn Juwzayy al-Kalbī (d. 741/1340), and others, all of whom attribute this explanation to Muḥammad ibn Kaʿb al-Quraẓī (d. ca. 120/737).

tween Morocco's Mediterranean and Atlantic coasts, meets the ocean in the imposing sight of Jebel Mūsā, identified by the ancients as one of the Pillars of Hercules.

If such places are endowed with special power and blessing, then the mountainous land between those two coasts must have received some portion of it. For one thing, it is among the most physically beautiful places in all of Morocco, covered by extensive groves of cork oak which give way to pine and, at the higher altitudes, cedar forests. Here, too, falls the most rain of anywhere in the country—over 78 inches a year in some places—and where the higher peaks become blanketed by heavy winter snows which feed into the springs, streams, and rivers that seem to flow everywhere. In the lower hills and plains where the Berber and Jbāla tribal peoples who have inhabited this region for centuries farm the land, olives, almonds, stone fruits, vineyards, and grain crops thrive.

The geographical location of this region also made it the place where many of those who came to "the furthest west"[2] from the outside first arrived. Mūlay Idrīs I, who was the great grandson of Ḥasan, grandson of the Prophet Muḥammad ﷺ, and who is considered the spiritual founder of Morocco, undoubtedly passed through this region in the late 8th century in his westward flight from the strife of Abbasid Baghdad, and when he and his progeny intermarried with local Berber women, they conferred upon the area its Sharifian lineage.[3] It was also here that Muslims and Jews, fleeing the Spanish Inquisition from the late 15th century on, found refuge after managing to make the nine-mile crossing of the Straits, bringing with them, besides the meager possessions they could carry in a boat, the knowledge, ideas, and skills of 700 years of Andalusian civilization, a civilization that had begun in 711 when a Muslim army crossed the Straits of Gibraltar from Septa (Ceuta), the most northerly point on the African continent, and arrived in Spain.

THE SHĀDHILĪ *ṬARĪQA* IN MOROCCO

This mixture of beauty, ethnicities, and history also made this

2. *Al-maghrib al-aqṣā*, "the furthest west," is the traditional Arabic name for Morocco.

3. *Sharīf* is literally "noble." In Morocco, this term is applied to one descended from the Prophet Muḥammad ﷺ.

area a fertile ground in which Sufism, the mystical dimension of Islam, could germinate, grow, and flourish. It could almost be said that for every spring in those mountains, there is a *zāwiya* or shrine dedicated to a saint. Principal among these, on a mountain top near the geographic center of this region, is the tomb of Mūlay ʿAbd al-Salām ibn Mashīsh (d. 624/1227), considered by many to have been *quṭb al-zamān*, the spiritual axis of his time. It was here that he was born and lived his entire life, and it was here that his one and only disciple, Abū'l-Ḥasan al-Shādhilī (d. 656/1258), born only a few miles away in the region of Ghomāra, received from him both his blessing and his teachings which Abū'l-Ḥasan took with him when he traveled east, first to Tunisia, where they were transmitted to a circle of students over a period of about 20 years, and then to Egypt where they became formalized into what became known as *al-Ṭarīqat al-Shādhiliyya* (the Shādhilī order) and later recorded in such works as *Laṭā'if al-Minan*, *al-Tanwīr fī isqaṭ al-tadbīr*, and *Kitāb l-Ḥikam*, all written by Shadhili's second successor in Egypt, Tāj al-Dīn ibn ʿAṭā'illah (d. 708/1309). When these books then made their way back to Morocco, they would be taught first in Fes by the saintly scholar and *imām* of the Qarawiyyan Mosque, Ibn ʿAbbād al-Rundī (d. 792/1390), who would eventually produce what remains the greatest and most widely-read commentary on *Kitāb al-Ḥikam*.[4] From Fes these teachings would spread throughout Morocco, taking on different hues and methods, but never losing their essential connection to what had begun on Jebal ʿAlam, equidistant from the two coasts and "*the junction of the two seas*."

It is not surprising, then, that four hundred years later, in the mid-13th/18th century, a new and vital branch of the Shadhiliyya tree would appear in this same fertile region, first in the person of the charismatic teacher, Mawlay al-ʿArabī[5] al-Darqāwī, who began calling people to a spiritual way which he said would "give new life to God's servants and to the land (*yuḥyi al-ʿibad wa'l-bilād*),"[6] and then through the life and works of one of his most gifted disciples, Sīdī Aḥmad ibn ʿAjība.

---

4. *Ghayth al-mawāhib al-ʿalīyya fī sharḥ al-Ḥikam al-ʿAṭā'iyya*, which Ibn ʿAbbād humbly referred to as *al-Tanbīh*: "Remarks."

5. Pronounced in Morocco "Mūlay Lʿarbī."

6. Al-Maʿāskarī, 8-9.

SĪDĪ AḤMAD IBN ʿAJĪBA AND HIS JOURNEY

Before his meeting with Shaykh al-Darqāwī, which took place around 1207/1793 in the Shaykh's *zāwiya* in Banī Zarwal, Ibn ʿAjība had led a life fairly typical for the son of a well-to-do, learned family in that area. Born in al-Khamīs, a village about 13 miles northwest of Tetouan, around 1161/1748, his earliest education consisted in memorization of the Qur'ān, which he completed before the age of 10, then the study of the essential texts (*mutūn*) which still constitutes a traditional Islamic education in some parts of Morocco to this day. From his autobiography, we can gather that he was a person who truly loved learning and by the time he had reached his late twenties, he was well on his way to becoming the epitome of the traditional Moroccan *ʿālim*, living a comfortable life of books and teaching, respectable and respected by all around him.

This situation would begin to change, however, after he was given a copy of the *Ḥikam* of Ibn ʿAṭā'illāh along with the commentary mentioned above by Ibn ʿAbbād al-Rundī. This one book and its commentary, which itself is a compendium of Sufi teachings from the time of the Prophet ﷺ on, made such a deep impression on him that he was ready to give up everything and spend the rest of his life as a recluse on top of Jebal ʿAlam near the tomb of Ibn Mashīsh about 37 miles southwest of Tetouan, but a vision at the shrine of one of the saints of Tetouan convinced him to persevere a little longer with the acquisition of formal knowledge.

Over the next ten years, Sīdī Binʿajība would become a husband, father, and one of the most respected scholars of Tetouan. Judging from the writing he completed during those years—commentaries on the *Burda* and *Hamziyya* of al-Buṣīrī, *al-Ḥizb al-Kabīr* by Imām al-Shādhilī himself, and the *Waẓīfa* of Aḥmad al-Zarrūq,[7] to name just a few—even though he had not renounced his life in the workaday world, he had nonetheless become a man whose heart was turned towards the teachings of the Sufis and especially of the Shādhiliyya. Then, at the age of about forty-seven,[8] he decided to take a detour on his way back from Fes to Tetouan up into the Banī Zarwal tribal region to meet Shaykh al-Darqāwī, whose *Ṭarīqa* by this time had become known throughout the region from

7. Michon, *The Autobiography*, p. 182
8. According to his own account, this took place in 1208/1793.

Fes to Tangier and beyond.[9] There he met not only the Shaykh but also his charismatic representative (*muqaddam*), Sīdī Muḥammad al-Būzīdī, who was to become his guide through the early years of the Way. In his autobiography, Sīdī Binʿajība writes:

> When I presented myself to them, they both received me and looked upon me insightfully. I initially met Sīdī Muḥammad and one of the first things he said to me was "May God make you like Junayd with fourteen thousand in patched cloaks following you!" Then he took me to Mūlay al-ʿArabī and in the course of visiting him, (Mūlay al-ʿArabī) said, "May God make you like Jilānī!" Sīdī Muḥammad then said, "I said to him, 'Like Junayd!' to which Mūlay al-ʿArabī responded, "God willing, he will combine them both!" .... I stayed with them for three days, during which time we spoke of knowledge and the mysteries of Divine Unity... I did not, however, ask the Shaykh to impart to me the litany for I had heard in Fes that Sīdī ʿAlī Jamal [Mūlay al-ʿArabī's shaykh] did not have any litany except companionship.[10]

This seems to have been a misunderstanding on the part of Ibn ʿAjība and he would eventually be given permission to recite the litany through the hand of Sīdī Muḥammad, whose home in Steha, a village about 44 miles south of Tetouan along Morocco's Mediterranean coast, was a much shorter and easier journey than to the mother Zāwiya in Banī Zarwāl. According Ibn ʿAjība's own account, al-Būzīdī and some other *fuqarā'* came to Tetouan to formally receive him into the order and upon doing so, al-Būzīdī said to those present, "Sīdī Aḥmad is a person of asceticism (*al-zuhd*), dependence upon God (*al-tawwakul*), scrupulousness (*al-warʿa*) , patience (*al-ṣabr*) ..." and went on to mention nearly twelve stations of the way. "I said to him," writes Ibn ʿAjība in his autobiography, "'O Sīdī, this is Sufism!'" And he said, "This is *outward* Sufism. There is yet an *inward* Sufism which you will come to know, God willing."[11]

The road towards that knowledge would begin with the process known as *kharq al-ʿawā'id* ('breaking habits'). In practice, this consisted in the disciple being assigned what were considered at the time demeaning tasks aimed at producing a break with the

9. The *zāwiya* that Sīdī Benʿajība visited had been built in 1778.

10. *Al-Fahrasa*, p. 45.

11. *Al-Fahrasa*, p. 46.

ego. In Ibn ʿAjība's case, it would also allow him to experience a level of humility that would have been otherwise next to impossible for a man of his social rank in Morocco at the time.[12] The first of these tasks was to trade his fine clothes for a coarse woolen jellaba and to enter the city of Tetouan on foot with other *fuqarā* chanting the *haylala.*[13] Such a procession, which would undoubtedly attract the attention of many people in the city, amounted to a public declaration that he was affiliated with the *Ṭarīqa*. In the days that followed, Sīdī Binʿajība was instructed to sweep the marketplace, wash the other *fuqarā's* clothes, and, finally, to the extreme consternation of those who knew him, to beg at the doorway of the mosque on Friday. This was eventually followed by his leaving the city along with a fairly large group of other *fuqarā'* and journeying on foot through the mountains around Tetouan, chanting as they walked, and calling upon the village dwellers to renew their faith through the remembrance of God and companionship in the *ṭarīqa*. In some cases, he writes, whole villages—men, women, and children—would enter the Way, and in other cases, they would be greeted by volleys of stones...[14] Predictably, such a movement eventually attracted the attention of certain of the authorities in Tetouan and resulted in some of the *fuqarā*, including Ibn ʿAjība, being arrested and briefly imprisoned for actions deemed disrupting to the general order.

Upon their release, Shaykh al-Būzīdī instructed them to travel outside the Jbāla area completely and make their way towards Sale and Rabat, which would have been several days' journey on foot to the north along the Atlantic coast. This began a period of spiritual travel (*siyāḥa*) that would last about five years and become a time for Ibn ʿAjība not only of intense practice, companionship, and teaching but also of writing. Thus, it was during these years that, at the behest of his shaykh, he completed or began work on most of the writings for which he is best remembered: esoteric commentaries on works such as the *Ḥikam* of Ibn ʿAṭā'illāh, the *Khamriyya* of Ibn al-Fāriḍ, the *Taṣliyya* of Ibn

12. This, in fact, was the most common approach for the Darqāwiyya at the time. Shaykh al-Darqāwī himself mentions how he had experienced his initial spiritual opening (*fatḥ*) after his shaykh, Sīdī ʿAlī al-Jamal, had bade the *fuqarā* to transport baskets of mulberries on their shoulders. See *Letters of a Spiritual Master*, p. 11.

13. That is, chanting the words *lā ilāha illa Llāh* in unison.

14. See Michon, *Autobiography of a Moroccan Soufi*, pp. 90-91.

Mashīsh, and at least the beginning of his magnum opus, *al-Baḥr al-Madīd fī tafsīr al-Qur'ān al-Majīd.*

The very end of the 1700s was also a time when the plague reappeared in northern Morocco, afflicting the city of Fes in 1799, causing hundreds of deaths every day.[15] The disease spread north to Tetouan and the surrounding region, and eventually claimed the lives of several of Ibn ʿAjība's children. Shortly after that, in November of 1809, Ibn ʿAjība himself, just past his 60th year, succumbed to the disease as well, making *al-Baḥr al-Madīd* one of the last works he completed before his death. It was his destiny to be outlived by both his own spiritual mentor, Sīdī Muḥammad al-Būzīdī, as well as Shaykh Mūlay al-ʿArabī al-Darqāwī, who lived on into his 90s and finally passed away in 1823.

The tomb of Ibn ʿAjība, a humble domed structure a few hundred feet up the mountain from the ruins of the house in Djimmīj where he lived those last years of his life and completed work on his *tafsīr*, remains a place of visitation as well as the site of a large yearly *mawsam* which attracts hundreds of *fuqarā'* from the region and beyond.[16] On clear days, you can see the Mediterranean in the distance and "the meeting place of the two seas," a view which the shaykh must have looked out upon often as he neared the completion of his own journey as well as of his *tafsīr*, *al-Baḥr al-Madīd.*

Ibn ʿAjība's Approach to *Tafsīr*[17]

According to Michon's summary of his works, Ibn ʿAjība wrote *al-Baḥr al-Madīd* in four volumes over the period from 1216/1801 to 1221/1806. If this chronology is correct, it means that he started writing it during his years of travel and completed it after he had returned to the Jbāla region and the house he had built in Djimmīj.[18]

15. The Great Plague of 1799-1800 peaked between the months May and November, 1799. According to the estimate of an eye-witness, it killed two-thirds of the population of the country. See Jackson, *An Account of Timbuctoo and Housa*, p. 187.

16. A *mawsam* is a seasonal yearly gathering, often associated in Morocco with the shrine of a saint. The one at Ibn ʿAjība's tomb has been fixed for many years to take place in mid-August.

17. For an overview of the history and forms of *tafsīr*, see the introductory pages of our previous translation, *The Immense Ocean.*

18. It is unclear both from his autobiography and other sources how Ibn ʿAjība was able to consult and copy from the books he used in his *tafsīr* during his trav-

As the editor of the 1999 printed edition, Dr. Jawda Abū Yazīd al-Mahdī, points out in his introduction, in composing *al-Baḥr al-Madīd*, Ibn ʿAjība was careful to observe the traditional format found in most classical Quranic commentaries. At the beginning of each *sūrah*, he mentions the place where it was revealed, the number of verses it contains, its relationship to the *sūrah* which precedes it, and the circumstances of its revelation. He then treats the verses in paragraph-like groups, and for each group he usually begins by a brief explanation of its lexical or syntactical features,[19] then proceeds to an exposition of their meaning based on the Qur'ān itself, *ḥadīth*, and other narrations pertaining to them, including what certain earlier *tafsīrs* have said. In explaining a certain Quranic phrase, he sometimes uses one of the most common words in *tafsīr*, "*ay*," which is roughly equivalent to the abbreviation in English, "i.e." = "that is," or "in other words," but at other times he simply re-phrases it as if it were a quotation. If there is more than one explanation of the meaning of a particular verse, he includes them, generally joined by the word "or" (*aw*), and then states his own judgment as to which of the explanations he finds most acceptable based on the context and his own extensive knowledge of the Book. He also mentions any variant recitations of words in the verse which could give variations in meaning, and which of the Companions ﷺ is associated with a particular variation.

When he quotes a *ḥadīth*, he generally does so without its chain of transmission (*asnad*), but if it is known it to be part of the two Sound Collections (*ṣaḥīḥayn*), he mentions that fact, and then the wording of the *ḥadīth*.

In addition, he sometimes mentions so-called *Isrāʾīliyyāt*, narrations that the Companions had heard from Jews or Christians concerning certain persons or events which appear in both the Qur'ān and their own scriptures. Although an extensive treatment of this subject is beyond the scope of this introduction, suffice to say that Ibn ʿAjība was well aware of the conditions which apply to such narratives according to the words of the Prophet ﷺ: "Do not

---

els. It is hard to imagine his carrying rather delicate manuscripts with him, but it may have been the case that he borrowed them from others or that books he needed were brought to him on a pack animal.

19. We have usually omitted this *tafsīr lughawī* our translation, as explained below.

confirm what the people of the Book relate nor deny it, but rather, say *We believe in what has been sent down to us and what has been sent down to you* [29:46]. *Our God and your God is one, and to Him do we submit,*"[20] and also "Convey (what you hear from me) to others even if it is only a single verse, and report what you hear from Children of Israel without being troubled. Whoever tells a lie about me intentionally makes his place in Hellfire." In practice, this means that the exegete may quote these narratives unless they explicitly contradict the Qur'ān, and all the classic *tafsīrs* contain them, usually marked by the words "and it has been said" (*wa qīl* or *wa yuqāl*) or "it has been related that..." (*wa ruwiya an...*).

These same words, however, may precede a passage quoted from an earlier *tafsīr*, sometimes by the name of its author, but often without attribution. The editor of the 1999 edition, al-Mahdi, has identified eight *tafsīr* sources most quoted by Ibn ʿAjība:

1. *Al-Kashf wa'l-bayān ʿan tafsīr al-Qur'ān*, by al-Thaʿlabī (427/1035).
2. *Al-Muḥarrir al-wajīz fī tafsīr al-kitāb al-ʿazīz* by Ibn ʿAṭiyya (542/1147).
3. *Anwār al-tanzīl wa asrār al-ta'wīl* by al-Bayḍāwī (685/1286).
4. *Mudārik al-tanzīl wa ḥaqā'iq al-ta'wīl*, by al-Nasafī (710/1310).
5. *Al-Tashīl li ʿulūm al-tanzīl*, by Ibn Juzzāy al-Andalūsī (741/1340).
6. *Irshād al-ʿAql al-salīm*, by Abū al-Saʿūd (982/1574).

To which we would add:

7. *Laṭā'if al-ishārāt*, by Imām al-Qushayrī (465/1072).

In addition to these, he refers to two *ḥāshiyāt* (marginal notations on previous commentaries):

8. *Nawāhid al-abkār wa shawārid al-afkār*, better known as *Ḥāshiyat al-Suyuṭī ʿalā tafsīr al-Bayḍāwī*, by Jalāl al-Dīn al-Suyūṭī (911/1505).
9. *Al-Ḥāshiya ʿalā tafsīr al-Jilālayn*, by ʿAbdurraḥmān al-Fāsi (1096/1685).

Ibn ʿAjība's Approach to *Ishāra*

Besides traditional Quranic exegesis, Ibn ʿAjība's *tafsīr*, at the behest of both Shaykh al-Būzīdī and Shaykh al-Darqāwī, contains for each group of verses being explained a section labeled in Arabic, *al-Ishārah*. This term, which is derived from the verb *shawwara*—"to point or make a gesture towards something, to indicate, or to al-

20. *Ḥadīth* found in Bayhaqī, *Shuʿab al-īmān*, 4842, and in Bukhārī, 4485, with slightly different wording, and several other principal sources.

lude to," is used by the Sufis to refer to the symbolism or allegory which might be discovered in the literal meaning of a text, generally either in the Qur'ān or *ḥadīth*. In the context of *al-Baḥr al-Madīd*, these sections were directed particularly to disciples following the Darqāwī path at the time or else to those who might be attracted to it, but in their broader application, they are keys to anyone trying to come nearer to the divinity in his or her life. They include both Ibn ʿAjība's own personal insights into the Way as well as quotations from other Sufi sources such as Ibn ʿAṭā'illāh's *Kitāb al-Ḥikam*, *Laṭā'if al-Minan*, and *al-Tanwīr fī isqāt al-tadbīr*, al-Qusharī's *Laṭā'if al-ishāra*, and a source referred to as "al-Wartajibī," who, as we pointed out in our previous translation from *al-Baḥr al-Madīd*, is actually the Persian mystic Ruzbahān al-Baqlī (606/1209), author of the mystical *tafsīr* called *ʿArā'is al-bayān fī ḥaqā'iq al-qur'ān*.[21] Sīdī Binʿajība, who by the time he started work on this *tafsīr* was extremely well-versed in all the religious sciences of Islam, took special care to insure that these *ishāri* sections were clearly separated from *tafsīr* proper and also included in his introduction (translated below) a careful explanation of the difference between *the two*.

THE HISTORICAL PLACE OF *SŪRAHS* MARYAM AND *ṬĀ HĀ*

In the pages that follow, we have translated Ibn ʿAjība's commentary on the 19th and 20th chapters of the Qur'ān, *Sūrah Maryam* and *Sūrah Ṭā Hā*. According to the two chronologies given in al-Suyūṭī's *al-Itqān*, these *sūrahs* were the forty-fourth and forty-fifth in order of revelation, just after *al-Fāṭir* and before *al-Wāqiʿa*[22] and figure among those revealed during the middle Meccan period.[23] In a *ḥadīth* found in Bukhārī, the Prophet ﷺ said of the five *sūrahs*—*Banī Isrā'īl*, *al-Kahf*, *Maryam*, *Ṭā Hā*, and *al-Anbiyā'*—"They are among the first of the ancient and beautiful ones (*al-ʿitāq al-awwal*) and they are my

21. We would again like to acknowledge the contribution of Dr. Alan Godlas of the University of Georgia, for being the first, to our knowledge to point this out. We would add that all references Ibn ʿAjība makes to "al-Wartajibī" are within passages he quotes from the *Ḥāshiya* of ʿAbdurrahmān al-Fāsī (see reference 9 above). Needless to say, all books that existed in Morocco before the 20th century were copied by hand and so the attribution "al-Wartajibī" could have been the name of the scribe who had written the copy that al-Fāsī used.

22. *Al-Itqān*, I:43 and I:97. These are 35th and 56th in the standard arrangement of Quranic chapters.

23. *Al-Itqān*, I:61.

legacy."[24] Of these five, *Mary* and *Ṭa Ha* are distinguished from the other three by the fact that they both begin with separated letters (*al-muqaṭṭaʿāt*)[25] followed by long, continuous narrative sections. In *Sūrah Maryam*, this consists of the next thirty-six verses recounting the birth of Jesus ﵇, focusing mainly upon his mother, and in *Ṭā Hā*, after seven verses of introduction, ninety verses recount the story of Moses ﵇ leading to his encounter with Pharaoh's sorcerers. Thus, at the hearts of both these *sūrahs* are the stories of the most important figures of Judaism and Christianity.

Although there are a number of traditions that speak of the special qualities of each of these *sūrahs*, we would like to mention here only the role they played in the early history of Islam.

Concerning *Sūrah Maryam*, the biography of the Prophet ﷺ by Ibn Hisham (d. 218/831) recounts that in the fifth year of the Prophet's mission a group of the poorer Muslims from Mecca emigrated to Abyssinia to flee persecution. When they came before the Negus, the king of that ancient Christian land, Jaʿfar ibn Abī Ṭālib described to him what their life had been in the *jāhiliyya*[26] and the religion to which the Prophet ﷺ had called them. The Negus then asked Jaʿfar if he could recite some of the revelation, and he chose to begin with these verses from *Sūrah Maryam*.

> And remember Mary in the Book, when she withdrew from her family to an
> Eastern place. And she veiled herself from them. Then We sent to her Our Spirit
> and it assumed for her the likeness of a perfect man ....[27]

It is recorded that when the Negus heard the recitation, he wept until his beard became damp with tears, as did his bishops, and said to those around him, "This and what Jesus son of Mary brought are lights from the same lamp..."[28] He then granted the Muslims refuge in his land.

Apart of this historical note, *Sūrah Maryam* is the only place in

---

24. Bukhārī, 4994.

25. In the case of *Sūrah Maryam*, these letters are *Kāf, Hā, Yā, ʿAyn,* and *Ṣād*, the longest grouping of *muqaṭṭaʿāt* in the Qur'ān, and in the case of *Ṭā Hā*, the two letters which give the *sūrah* its name.

26. Literally, "the time of ignorance," referring here to pre-Islamic Arabia.

27. *Sūrah Maryam*, verses 16-17.

28. Ibn Hishām, Abū Muḥammad ʿAbd al-Mālik, *al-Sīrat al-Nabawiyya*, ed. by Ṭaha ʿAbd al-Ra'ūf Saʿd, Dār al-Jīl, Beirut, 1998, II:189 ff.

the Qur'ān where a woman is mentioned by name, and the chapter of the Qur'ān which contains the most occurrences of God's Name *al-Raḥmān* ("the All-Merciful"). Indeed, nearly one third of all instances of this Divine Name in the Qur'ān, other than in the opening *basmalah* formula, are in *Maryam*.

Also in Ibn Hisham is recounted the story of the role *Sūrah Ṭā Hā* played in the conversion of ʿUmar ibn al-Khaṭṭāb, which marked a turning point in the early history of the religion. ʿUmar, a powerful man among the Meccans, began as a staunch enemy of the new religion, which he feared would cause a rupture in their society and way of life. Deciding that the only way to restore order was to slay the Messenger ﷺ, he had set out one morning armed with his sword for that purpose. On the way, however, he encountered someone who told him that he would be better advised to first correct his own family, for his sister, Fāṭima, and her husband Saʿd had already secretly embraced the new faith. Hearing this only added to ʿUmar's rage, and he turned towards their house instead to confront them. At that same moment, a friend of theirs and fellow Muslim, Khabbāb ibn Aratt, was reciting to Fāṭima and Saʿd from a page with *Sūrah Ṭā Hā* written on it, but when they heard ʿUmar's voice, Fāṭima hastily placed the page under her robe and Khabbāb hid in some corner of the house. When ʿUmar came in, he demanded to see the page on which "the gibberish" he had heard was written, and moved to attack his brother-in-law. Fāṭima intervened to protect her husband and in the struggle that ensued ʿUmar inadvertently struck her so hard that it drew blood. When he saw his beloved sister's face bleeding, he was brought back to his senses and asked again, more calmly, to see the page. She said she could not give it to him since he was impure from idolatry, so he agreed to wash and then began to read from the page:

> Ṭā Hā. *We have not revealed this Qur'ān to you to cause you distress but only as a reminder to anyone with reverent fear, a revelation from the One Who created the earth and the heavens sublime, the All-Merciful established upon the Throne. To Him belong what is in the heavens and what is in the earth, and what is between, and what is beneath the soil. And if you speak aloud, He knows what is secret and what is more hidden. Allāh! There is no god except Him. His are the most beautiful Names.*[29]

29. *Sūrah Ṭā Hā*, verses 1-8.

When he had finished, ʿUmar said, "How beautiful and noble is this speech!" and then asked Khabbāb to take him to the Prophet ﷺ so that he could formally embrace Islam.[30]

About this Translation

In the pages that follow, we have sought to produce a text that is both readable and rich for a speaker of English while maintaining as closely as possible the meaning and tone of the original. To help achieve this end, we have made the following modifications and additions to the original Arabic text:

1. Ibn ʿAjība's brief grammatical explanations at the beginning of each section of commentary, usually quite technical in nature, have been omitted except in cases where they explain a variation of meaning that is comprehensible in English. In this latter case, the explanation is usually included as a footnote.
2. Quranic verses, phrases, and words are italicized, while Ibn ʿAjība's re-phrasing is indicated by single quotation marks ('___').
3. Where Ibn ʿAjība supplies an Arabic synonym for a given word that is already self-evident in the translation of the Quranic verses themselves, this synonym has been omitted, usually marked by three points (...).
4. Following the Arabic editions of *al-Baḥr al-Madīd*, the portions on spiritual allusion (*ishārā*) have been set apart from the *tafsīr* by the words "Spiritual Allusion" at the beginning of the block of text.
5. The grouping of verses being commented on follow Ibn ʿAjība's divisions in the original text but with the addition of their numbering according to modern printings of the Qur'ān. For the sake of clarity, we have repeated these verse numbers at the beginning of the section of text pertaining to that verse.
6. For the basic translation of the Qur'ān, we have relied mainly on *The Study Qur'ān* (2015), but have replaced the older English forms (thou, thy, ye) of that edition with their modern forms. In the rare cases where Ibn ʿAjība's commentary defines a word or phrase differently from *The Study Qur'ān*, we have modified the translation to be in accordance with his usage. All Quranic citations of verses other than those being commented on are followed

30. II:188-189

by the number of the *sūrah* and verse in brackets.

7. We have sought to include sources for all the *ḥadīth* quoted and, in some cases, have also footnoted the source Ibn ʿAjība is quoting. In noting *ḥadīth*, we have used the following abbreviations:

Bukhārī : *Ṣaḥīḥ al-Bukhārī*
Muslim: *Ṣaḥīḥ Muslim*
Tirmidhī : *Sunan al-Tirmidhī*
Nasā'i: *Sunan al-Nasā'ı*
Abū Dāwūd: *Sunan Abī Dāwūd*
Mālik: *al-Muwaṭṭa'*
Ibn Mājah: *Sunan Ibn Mājah*
Aḥmad: *Musnad Imām Aḥmad ibn Ḥanbal*
Bayhaqı: *Shuʿab al-īmān*
Al-Ṭabarānī: *al-Awsaṭ: al-Muʿjam al-awsaṭ*
or *al-Kabīr*: *al-Muʿjam al-kabīr*
Ḥākim: *al-Mustadrak ʿalā ṣaḥīḥayn*
Ibn Ḥibbān: *Ṣaḥīḥ ibn Ḥibbān*

Other *ḥadīth* sources are cited by complete title.

In addition to *ḥadīth*, because of Ibn ʿAjība's numerous direct or indirect references to the *Kitāb al-Ḥikam*, we have included the number of the particular aphorism in brackets according to the system followed in the Victor Danner translation (see bibliography) and have largely depended on that translation, with minor exceptions, for the wording of the aphorisms themselves.

8. We have supplied four indices to the text: one of Quranic verses cited; one of *ḥadīth*s cited; a biographical index of all persons mentioned in the body of the commentary and a general index.

9. In references to the Divinity, the use of the masculine pronoun is a convention of the Arabic language and by no means a sign of gender which would be anathema to all the Qur'ān says about God's uniqueness and incomparability.

10. In a few places—generally in the *ishārī* portions—we have substituted the pronoun "you" or "we" for "the servant," and "he." Besides making the text easier to read in English, these portions were very much addressed to those either following the spiritual path or interested in doing so and have a personal tone which is better expressed in English by the first or second person.

The Translation

بسم اللّه الرحمن الرحيم
وصلى اللّه على سيد محمد وعلى آله

Ibn ʿAjība's Introduction to *al-Baḥr al-Madīd*[1]

In the Name of God, the All-Merciful and Compassionate
May God bless our beloved master Muḥammad and his People and Companions and give them salutations of peace....

You we praise Who unveils Himself to His devotees by way of His Speech[2] in the perfection of His beauty and splendor, Who loosens the tongues of sages to bring forth there from Its pearls and gifts, Who lets flow from their hearts the springs of Its wisdom, strengthened by Its principles and design, and Who allows them to gather the benefits of Its singularities and repetitions[3] when they dive into its currents, that by Its dazzling signs and verses and Its evident proofs they might refute what is false. It is both a fathomless ocean and a verdant garden from which no blossom is lacking. And how could it be otherwise, when It is the Word of our Lord, the Knower of all that is hidden, all that was, all that is, and all that shall ever be.

May blessings and salutations be upon our master Muḥammad, the manifestation of all-mercifulness brought forth with miracles and light, and upon his People and Companions, the fountains of clemency and magnanimity and the unshakeable mountains of certitude when crises and distress loom large.

1. From *al-Baḥr al-Madīd*, v. 1, p. 49.
2. By which he means the Qur'ān.
3. *Farā'idihi wa mathānīhi.* This is a reference to [15:87], *And We have given you the seven oft-repeated verses (Sūrat al-Fātiḥa) and the Immense Qur'ān*, as well as *God has revealed the fairest of discourse: a book (containing) that which is repeated and which has inner resemblance* [39:23]. That is, there are some verses which are unique and others which reappear, as it were, throughout the Qur'ān but in slightly different forms.

Of all the religious sciences, the science of *tafsīr* is the greatest and the most excellent object of thought and understanding. None, however, should approach this vast undertaking other than an accomplished scholar who has achieved a profound knowledge of the exoteric sciences of the religion and has then directed thought and meditation towards the Qur'ān's beautiful meanings. In other words, to explain the Qur'ān, one must first have mastered, under the tutelage of the learned, the Arabic language, its morphology, semantics, and rhetoric, then jurisprudence (*fiqh*) and *ḥadīth*. If one then becomes immersed in the science of Sufism and attains therein a genuine spiritual taste (*dhawq*), then state, and then station through companionship with experienced people of the Way,[4] (it is permissible to mention as well the Qur'ān's inner meanings), but if not, then it is better to remain silent concerning them and limit oneself to the exoteric dimension.

For the immense Qur'ān has an outward dimension for the people of the outward and an inward dimension for the people of the inward, and commentary by these latter cannot be [fully] understood or experienced except by people of the inward, nor is its mention even permissible except after having affirmed [the Qur'ān's] literal and outward meaning. Only then [is it permissible] to indicate the esoteric by means of subtle references and allusions. And if one's understanding has not reached the level of being able to grasp such mysteries, then one should at least acknowledge they exist and not hastily deny them. For the science of gnosis lies beyond the mountain of discursive thought and is not to be reached by mere repetition of texts.

[In *Laṭā'if al-Minan*] Ibn ʿAṭā'illāh wrote:

> Know that commentaries by the [Sufis] upon the Word of God and the words of His Prophets through meanings which are rare and strange in no way alter the literal meaning of the text. The literal meaning is what is understood from context and usage, while the inward meanings of either a [Quranic] verse or prophetic saying are those which are understood by someone whose heart God has opened. Even so, did the Prophet say, "Every verse has an outer

4. "The Way" (capitalized) refers throughout the translation to *al-Ṭarīqa*, which may refer to a Sufic order in particular or the path of approaching God in general.

> aspect and an inner, a limit and a vantage point."[5] Do not, then, let yourself be turned away from these spiritual commentaries by inveterate polemicists who say to you, "This will detract you from the literal meaning of the Word of God Most High and the word of His Messenger ﷺ!" Such would be the case if the mystics said that a given verse had no other meaning except an esoteric one, but they do not say this. Rather, they take the literal meaning in its literal sense, purpose, and context, and then realize from God whatever else He allows them to realize...

The Prophet's saying, "Every verse has an outer aspect and an inner, a limit and a vantage point"[6] thus means that *the outward* is for those such as the grammarians, the experts in language and declension. *The inward* is for those concerned with the meanings of words, the commandments and prohibitions, parables and narratives, the affirmation of God's oneness, and other like teachings of the Qur'ān, such being the domain of the exegetes. The *limit* is for the juridical scholars (*al-fuqahā'*) who are concerned with the derivation of rules from the verses, who come to a verse and then carry its arguments as far as possible but without addition. The vantage point (*al-muṭṭalaʿu*) is for the people of spiritual truths among the greatest of the Sufis, where, from the outward meaning of a verse, they look down, as it were, into its inward meaning. Then are unveiled to them, through reflection upon the verse, its mysteries, teachings, and mystic sense.

Literally, *muṭṭalaʿu* means any place from which one may look down upon something from its highest to lowest point and this word is mentioned in a sound *ḥadīth* referring to the "terror of the vantage point"[7] by which is meant a place of approach from which one will look down upon the events of the Last Day. Thus too can it be said [in Arabic], "Where is the vantage point of this question?" meaning its point of approach, which is literally an elevated point from which something may be seen from its highest to lowest limits. In a like manner do the people of spiritual truth look down

5. Ṭabarānī, *al-Kabīr*, 8587. See footnote 111 for the explanation of this term.

6. Ṭabarānī, *al-Awṣat*, 777; Tirmidhī, *Manāqib*, 3255; Ibn Mājah, *Faḍā'il al-aṣḥāb*, 93.

7. Aḥmad, 14037; Bayhaqī, 10193. The complete wording of the *ḥadīth* is "Do not wish for death, for verily the terror of the vantage point is mighty, and a part of happiness is for God to prolong the life of a servant and provide him with the means of turning back to Him (*al-ināba*)."

from the outward meaning of a verse into the mysteries of its inward dimension and then plunge into the depths of its ocean. And God Most High knows better.

I have been requested by my Shaykh, Sīdī Muḥammad al-Būzīdī al-Ḥasanī, as well as his Shaykh, the *Quṭb*,[8] Mūlay al-ʿArabī al-Darqāwī al-Ḥasanī , to set down in writing a commentary that would combine both exoteric explanation and esoteric allusion, and I have responded to their request...in hopes that this work will benefit many and be a joy to the heart as well as to the ear.

For each verse, I have first treated the important grammatical and linguistic features, then the literal meaning of the phrases, and finally the spiritual allusions, while trying to keep to a moderate length—all this in hopes that the treasures of God, Most Generous and Forgiving, might be opened to me thereby—and have named it *The Immense Ocean of Commentary on the Glorious Qur'ān*. I ask God to clothe it in the raiment of His acceptance, and bring about its desired purpose. He is the One Who is Able to Accomplish whatsoever He wills and the best from whom to hope for an answer. There is neither strength nor power except through All-Mighty God. May God bless our master Muḥammad and his People and Companions and give them salutations of peace....

8. The *Quṭb*, literally, "axis" or "pole," is a term applied to the greatest spiritual master in a given time or place.

The Chapter of Mary
(*Sūrah Maryam*)

This *sūrah* was revealed in Mecca and comprises ninety-eight verses. It responds (in part) to Christians who claim that Jesus 🌸 shares divinity with God and it is thus like a completion of the last words of the *sūrah* which precedes it: (*So whosoever hopes for the meeting with his Lord, let him perform righteous deeds) and make no one a partner to his Lord in worship* [18:110].

> 1. *Kāf, Hā, Yā, ʿAyn, Ṣād* 2. *A mention of the mercy of your Lord to His servant Zachariah, 3. When he called out to Him in secret. 4. "O Lord! The bones of my body have grown frail and the hair upon my head is blazed with white, and O Lord I have never been wretched in calling upon You. 5. Truly, I fear those who will follow me and my wife is barren, 6. So bestow upon me a successor from Your presence who will inherit from me and inherit from the family of Jacob. And make him, O Lord, pleasing."*

[1] *Kāf, Hā, Yā, ʿAyn, Ṣād*. It has been said that these letters stand for Names of God Most High—*kāf* from *Kāfin*, the One Who suffices, *hā'* from *Hādi*, the One Who Guides, *yā* from *Yamīn*, the One Who blesses, *ʿayn* from *ʿAlīm*, the Knowing One, or *ʿAzīz*, the Mighty, and *ṣād* from *Ṣādiq*, the Veracious. This is mentioned by al-Harawī quoting Ibn Jubayr who attributes it to Abū'l-Haytham...[1]

Thus, when facing any extreme difficulty, ʿAlī (may God ennoble his countenance) would supplicate God beginning with these

---

1. There are wide-ranging explanations of these and the other sets of separated letters (*al-ḥurūf al-muqaṭṭaʿat*) which begin 29 of the 114 suras of the Qur'ān. In many cases, the exegetes say only God knows their meaning, but some of the earliest commentaries, quoting Ibn ʿAbbās and other Companions, relate that particular divine names or qualities are attached to each letter.

Concerning the name *Yamīn*, al-Harawī notes that the verbal root YMN, which means "to augur well, to be fortunate or blessed," gives the noun *al-yamīn*, which may mean both "the right hand" and "the One who blesses."

words: "O *Kāf Hā Yā ʿAyn Ṣād*! I seek refuge in You from sins which require Your retribution; I seek refuge in You from sins which remove us from grace; I seek refuge in You from sins which rend [the veil of] Your protection; I seek refuge in You from sins which hold back the rain; I seek refuge in You from sins which strengthen our foes. Help us against those who oppress us." This could mean that his supplication to God was by way of the (five) Divine Names signified by those letters or else by the letters taken together as one Name. Some have even said that *Kāf Hā Yā ʿAyn Ṣād* is the Supreme Name of God.[2]

They can also be understood as symbols which refer to the interaction between God Most High and those He loves. The *kāf* refers to the sufficiency (*kifāya*) He grants them, the *hā'*, to the guidance (*hidāya*) by which He brings them into His Presence, the *yā'* to the blessings which come to them and to any who are connected to them, the *ʿayn* to the protection and care (*ʿināya*) He bestowed upon them in His eternal knowledge, and the *ṣād* to His veracity (*ṣidqihi*) in fulfilling His promise of generosity and grace. And God Most High knows better.

It has also been said that these letters stand for names of the Messenger ﷺ: "O you who suffices us (*yā kāfī*), who guides us (*hādī*), who is blessed (*maymūn*), who is the source of all sources (*ʿayn al-ʿuyūn*), who is truthful (*ṣādiq*) and worthy of trust (*muṣaddaq*)." Māḍī ibn Sulṭān, the disciple of Abū'l-Ḥasan al-Shādhilī (may God be pleased with them both), once saw himself in a dream speaking with some jurists (*fuqahā'*) about the meaning of the letters *Kāf, Hā, Yā, ʿAyn, Ṣād, Ḥā, Mīm* [and] *ʿAyn, Sīn, Qāf*.[3] "I said to them, 'These are intimate secrets between God Most High and His Messenger ﷺ. By the *Kāf*, it is as if God were saying to him, 'You are the sheltering cave (*al-kahf*) of existence towards which all creatures turn,' and by the *Hā*, He is saying, 'We have bestowed upon you (*habnā laka*) the earth and made ready for you the celestial domains,' and by *Yā ʿAyn*, He is saying, 'O source (*yā ʿayn*) of all sources!' and by *Ṣād*, He

2. This saying is attributed to al-Suddī in *Tafsīr al-Qurṭubī*. In respect to the Supreme Name of God, (*ismu-Llāhi al-aʿẓam*), al-Suyūṭī wrote a short treatise in which he lists twenty different possibilities (see *al-Durr al-Munaẓẓam fī ismi Llāhi al-Aʿẓam*) and the Yemeni scholar al-Shawkānī states there are as many as forty (see *al-Tuḥfatu'l-Dhākirīn*).

3. These letters appear towards the beginning of Imām al-Shādhilī's "Litany on Land" (*Ḥizb al-Barr*).

is indicating the attributes *(ṣifāt)* of God expressed in His words, *Whoever obeys the Messenger obeys God* [4:80], and by *Ḥā'*, He is saying, 'We have made you beloved (*ḥabbabnāka*),' and by *Mīm*, 'We have given you dominion (*mallaknāka*),' and by *ʿAyn*, 'We have taught you (*ʿallamnāka*),' and by *Sīn*, 'We have disclosed to you secrets (*sārarnāka*),' and by *Qāf*, 'We have brought you near (*qarrabnāka*).'" But they disagreed [with my explanation] and would not accept it, so I said to them, 'Then let us go to the Prophet ﷺ so that he can settle it.' So we left that place and came to the Messenger of God ﷺ and he said to us, 'What Muḥammad ibn Sulṭan says is the truth.' [Following this interpretation], the letters stand for divine actions.

[2-3] God Most High ﷻ says: 'What We recite to you in this *sūrah* is *a mention of the mercy of your Lord to His servant Zachariah when he called out to his Lord* from the prayer niche (*al-miḥrāb*) and asked Him for a son. [This prayer is described as being] *in secret* (*khafiyya*) either because he said it in a place that was hidden from his family, or because he was offering it in the middle of the night, with the deepest sincerity so that no one could know about it except God. In offering it thus, Zachariah was following the best practice, deepest in sincerity, and least likely to become the object of people's gossip about why he was asking for a son at a time of life when he was well past his prime. There were also those among his family whom he feared.

[4] He said in his prayer ﷺ: *O Lord! The bones of my body have grown frail ...* That is, 'My body is weak and my strength is gone,' for the bones are the pillars of the body and its support and if they grow frail and weak, the whole body grows frail and weak... This was due to his old age, which some *tafsīr*s have said was seventy or seventy-five, and others, a hundred or more.[4]

And the hair upon my head is blazed with white. Its turning white with age is compared to flames from a fire, for just as the whiteness of age spreads through the hair, so do flames spread through wood and finally turn it all ablaze... *And O Lord, I have never been wretched in calling upon You.* 'During all the years of my long life, whenever I prayed to You, I was never disappointed; every time I called to You, You answered me...' Thus, he begins his supplication by ask-

4. Al-Fāsī mentions in his notation on *Tafsīr Jalālayn*, I:472, that Jacob ﷺ was a hundred and twenty years old and his wife ninety-eight when he made this prayer.

ing for God's mercy upon him in his old age and weakness, then invokes all the goodness that God has shown him in the past, and only then does he ask his Lord to intervene in his life once again, repeating the name "Lord" (*Rabb*) twice in hopes that the fervor of his supplication might move the chain of Divine response. About this, it has been said, "If you wish your prayer to be answered, call upon God by those of His Names and Attributes which correspond to your need."[5]

[5] *Truly, I fear those who will follow me and my wife is barren...* The successors he feared were his relatives, the sons of his paternal uncle, who were the worst of the Children of Israel, and his fear was that they would act unjustly with his community. For this reason does he ask God (be He glorified) for a pious son as an heir (*mawālī*) to succeed him as the leader of his people. This word may also be understood in the sense of "an authority" (*al-walāya*), in which case the phrase means that he feared that the authority that would come into power [after his death] would be oppressive.

[6] *So bestow upon me a successor from Your presence...* [Zachariah's] wife had not borne a child since she was young, so he says to God, 'Give me [a child] purely by way of Your all-encompassing grace and astounding power.' The phrase *from Your presence* (*min ladunka*), implying extreme directness and proximity, signifies that this will be a miraculous act, and the particle *fā'*[6] marks an order between what is before it and what is after it: that is, that Zachariah's عليه السلام age and the barrenness of his wife precluded any hope of their having a son by normal means. Also implicit in [this prayer] is the fact that he had already witnessed something miraculous in respect to Mary, referred to in the verse which begins, *Then did Zachariah pray to his Lord* [3:38]....[7] That it is not mentioned again here is an example of revelatory succinctness (*al-nukta al-tanzīliya*).

Who will inherit from me and inherit from the family of Jacob ...That is, '[Grant me a successor] who will inherit from me knowledge, religion, and prophecy,' for the prophets عليهم السلام have no heirs to their

5. This arises from the mystery of the Divine Names. Thus, someone who is ill might call upon God by His Name *al-Shāfī*, the One Who heals.

6. Translated above as 'so' in the phrase, *so bestow upon me*.

7. *Each time Zachariah went into [Mary] in the sanctuary, he found there was food and he asked her, "From where does this come to you?" She answered, "It is from God. Verily God provides for whomsoever He pleases without measure"* [3:37].

material possessions, as a *ḥadīth* states: "We, the prophets, do not leave [material] inheritance."[8] It has also been said that this means [his successor would inherit] the rabbinate, since Zachariah ﷺ was a rabbi, and would also inherit from the family of Jacob prophecy, authority, and wealth. Most of the commentaries say that the Jacob mentioned here is Jacob, son of Isaac, but al-Kalbī and Muqātil say he was Jacob son of Māthān, the brother of ʿImran, father of Mary. Zachariah's wife was Mary's aunt, while Māthān was from the lineage of Soloman ﷺ. The family of Jacob were thus the maternal uncles of John. According to al-Kalbī, "The people of Māthān were the kings and chiefs of the Children of Israel and Zachariah was head rabbi of that time. Thus, he wished for a son who could inherit from him the rabbinate and from the Banī Māthān wealth."

And make him, O Lord, pleasing. That is, 'Make him someone with whom You are pleased and who is thus pleasing to You...' The word *raḍiyya* may also be understood to mean "content."[9] The heir for whom he prayed would be someone who was content with God's decrees and laws, content with his knowledge of God, and content with [bearing the] responsibilities [that would be placed upon him]. And God Most High knows best.

Spiritual Allusion

It is permissible [for a shaykh] to pray for a spiritual heir who will inherit from him both his teachings and his state so that his benefit to others might continue after his death, but it is said that to remain silent and accept whatever God decrees is preferable, and is what is implied in the *ḥadīth*, "May God be merciful to our brother Zachariah concerning his heir."[10]

In respect to God's words, *A prayer in secret,* it is said that for the Sufi, supplications, invocations, and all other devotional practices are better done in secret, except in the case of the perfected masters who merit being emulated, for whom [the best practice] is whatever appears for a given time.

And as for His words, *O Lord I have never been wretched in calling upon You*, these compare what remains to what has passed: that

8. Related in the collection of al-Nasāʾī.

9. This echoes the words *God is content with them, and they are content with Him* which occur in 5:119 and 98:8.

10. Al-Ṭabarī mentions this *ḥadīth* in his commentary on this verse in *Jāmiʿ al-bayān* and Ibn ʿAsākir narrates it from him in *al-Tārīkh.*

God, Who has always been good to you in the past, will be good to you in the years that remain. This is one of the ways we can strengthen our good opinion of God (*ḥusna al-ẓann bi-l-Lāh*). Higher than this, however, is the state of someone whose good opinion of God Most High is based on the qualities with which God describes Himself: His perfect power, generosity, excellence, kindness, and mercy. The former way is based on experience, while the latter arises from a vision and consciousness of the Source of all grace. In the words of the *Ḥikam* [39]: "If you have not improved your thinking of Him because of His ineffable nature, improve it because of His treatment of you. For has He accustomed you to anything but what is good? And has He conferred upon you anything but His favors?"[11]

> 7. *"O Zachariah! Truly We bring you glad tidings of a boy whose name is John; We have not given this as a name to any before him."* 8. *He said, "My Lord! How shall I have a boy, when my wife is barren, and I have grown decrepit with old age?"* 9. *He said, "Thus shall it be. Your Lord says, 'It is easy for Me, even as I created you before when you were nothing!'"* 10. *He said, "My Lord! Appoint for me a sign." He said, "Your sign shall be that you shall not speak with men for three nights, [even while you are] sound."* 11. *So he came forth from the sanctuary to his people, and signaled to them that they should glorify morning and evening.*

[7] God, the Truth ﷻ says by the intermediary of the angel: "*O Zachariah! Truly We bring you glad tidings* and We are answering your prayer [with the promise] *of a boy whose name is John*, (Yaḥyā), so called because he would give life (*yuḥyī*) to the barrenness of his mother. But while God answered Zachariah's prayer in a general sense, it was by the Divine will that it not be answered in every detail. For he had prayed for both a son and a successor, and while he was granted a son, he was not granted a successor, since it is

11. Ibn ʿAjība says elsewhere in his commentary upon this *Ḥikma*: "In having a good opinion of God, people are of two categories: the elect and the generality. For the elect, their good opinion of God is founded on their perception of His beauty and their vision of His perfection, and so it is not changed by whether they are confronted by His beauty or His rigor... because they know that at the heart of it is God's perfect grace and all-encompassing mercy. As for the generality, their good opinion of God is based on His treatment of them and the favor He bestows upon them. So when hardship befalls them, they look back towards His goodness in the past... and gauge by that what will come." *Īqāẓ al-himam*, p. 88.

generally acknowledged that John died before his father (may peace be upon them both), or according to some, a short time after him...

God's mention of Zachariah's future son's name was both an affirmation of His promise and an honor, and that this name had never been given to another added to that honor; indeed, to be given a unique name is surely a distinction for the one who receives it. It has been said that the word *samīya* (*named*) can also mean "equal in favor and honor," as in God's words, *Do you know any who is His equal?* (*hal taʿlamu lahu samīya*) [20:65]. Indeed, in many respects there had never been anyone before quite like John ﷺ, for he never once considered committing a sin, he was the son of an aged man well past his prime and a barren old woman, and he remained chaste his entire life. Such were qualities no one else before him had ever been given.

[8] *He said, "My Lord! How shall I have a boy when my wife is barren, and I have grown decrepit with old age?"* That is, 'From where and in what manner will a son come to me?' Here the word *ʿutīyan* (*decrepit with old age*) literally means 'emaciated and dry in limbs and sinews.' When he uttered these words, it has been said that he was one hundred and twenty years old and his wife was ninety-eight, but as we have already mentioned, there is disagreement concerning this. He said this even while his prayers in the past had been answered, his certitude was strong, and he had already witnessed the miracle mentioned in *Āli ʿImrān*,[12] so these words were not really a question, as much as an expression of awe at the power of God Most High, a way to count the many blessings he had been given, and also to clearly acknowledge that this would be purely by God's

---

12. That is, the miracle mentioned in note 7 above. In his commentary on this verse, Ibn ʿAjība says:

"When Mary was put in the care of Zachariah, he built for her a room and provided her a nursemaid. Then, when she matured, he built for her a sanctuary (*miḥrāb*) in the mosque and made a door in the middle of it. No one could reach this room except by a ladder, and only Zachariah ﷺ went up to her. He would take her food and drink every day, and then, when he left, he would lock her in with seven doors. But whenever he entered the sanctuary to bring her food, he would find provision already there: fruit out of season, that is, winter fruit in summer and summer fruit in winter. [When he first saw this], he said to her, 'O Mary, how do you have this?' meaning, "Where does this provision come from when it is not even its season and all the doors are locked?" And *she said, "It is from God. Truly God provides for whomsoever He will without reckoning."* [4:37]

generosity and grace and impossible by any other means. Thus, some commentators have said that his words were uttered in astonishment and joy, others that he was asking to understand how [this miracle] would take place, and others that sixty years had passed between the time he made his supplication and the time he received the glad tidings of its being answered, and that in the interim, he had forgotten that he had made such a prayer. This latter explanation, however, seems least likely.

[9] *He said, "Thus shall it be. Your Lord says, 'It is easy for Me..* That is, 'What Zachariah عليه السلام says concerning his old age and the barrenness of his wife are true, but in Our power, it is still something easy.' The phrase *ka dhālika* has also been said to refer to God's words which follow it: '*It is easy for Me...*'

Even as I created you before means 'Even as I brought into being your progenitor, Adam, from nothingness and then brought you forth from his loins *when you were nothing*.' Related to this, Abū'l-Saʿūd said that the creation of Adam عليه السلام and his form contained within it the creation of all Adam's progeny, and so these words are similar to the words of God elsewhere: *We have created you* [*all*] *and We have given you forms* [7:11].

[10] *He said, 'O my Lord! Appoint for me a sign.'* That is, 'Give me a sign which will show me that what I have hoped and prayed for—that my wife may conceive a child—has come to pass, so that I might receive this immense blessing with gratitude from this very moment and not have to wait until the time when [the birth] actually happens.' In all likelihood, he asked God for this sign just after having received the news of a son, for it has been related that John was six months or as many as three years older than Jesus (may peace be upon them both),[13] but there is no doubt that Zachariah's prayer referred to in God's words [in *Āli ʿImrān*], *Then did Zachariah pray to his Lord* [3:38] was made when Mary was still young, for according to some she gave birth to Jesus عليه السلام at the age of ten, or according to others, thirteen.[14] It is also possible that the appearance of the sign [for which Zachariah prayed] did not occur until Mary عليها السلام was near maturity.[15]

---

13. This is still according to the *tafsīr* of Abū al-Saʿūd, quoting Ibn ʿAbbās رضي الله عنهما.

14. In *Sūrat Āli ʿImrān*, the prayer of Zachariah عليه السلام is mentioned immediately preceding mention of Mary's conception of Jesus عليه السلام.

15. *Al-bulūgh* roughly corresponds to the age of puberty.

"Your sign will be that you will not speak to people ..." That is, 'You will only be able to invoke God, not speak to people, for three nights' and three days, as *Sūrat Āli ʿImrān* states,[16] 'even while you will be otherwise in good health and not afflicted by muteness...' During those [three] days [and nights], his speech would only be words of gratitude and invocation.

[11] *So he came forth from the sanctuary to his people ...* That is, he left the place of prayer, which he had locked from within. [Here] the word *miḥrāb* is usually understood to mean 'a place for worship.'[17] Some *tafsīrs* have said that he had been in a chamber behind the *miḥrāb* and that people had been waiting for him to open the door to them so that they could go in and offer their prayers. When he came out, his color had changed so much that they hardly recognized him and asked, 'What ails you?' *And [he] signaled to them* by gestures or, according to some, by writing upon the earth: 'Glorify your Lord in prayer *morning and evening*,' that is, at the times of the *fajr* and the *ʿaṣr* prayers, for those were most likely their two times of worship.[18] These words may also be understood to mean, 'Exalt your Lord at the two ends of the day,' for he himself had been commanded to glorify God at those times in gratitude, and so he commanded his people to do the same. And God Most High knows best.

Spiritual Allusion

A supplication is answered on the condition that it be made with complete and pressing need. God Most High says: [He is the One] *Who answers the one in pressing need when he calls out to Him* [27:62], and as it is stated in the *Ḥikam* [129], "Nothing pleads on your behalf like extreme need nor does anything speed gifts to you quicker than lowliness and want." If you pray to your Guardian Lord in pressing need, He will surely answer your prayer, but in the way He wants, not in the way you want, and in the time He wants, not in the time you want. So do not despair nor lose patience. *God knows*

16. In Q. 3:41 it is said to Zachariah ﷺ ...*You shall not speak to the people for three days, save through signs.*

17. In the context of Islam, *al-miḥrāb* refers to the niche in the *qibla* wall of a mosque which indicates the direction of Mecca and where the imam stands to lead the prayer.

18. Al-Rāzī mentions in his commentary that the verb SBḤ, usually translated as "to glorify" (as in the words *subḥān Allāh*), is used in a *ḥadīth* as a synonym for the verb ṢLLĀ, "to offer the prayer."

and you know not [2:216]. And when you see your Lord has answered your prayer, make all your speech gratitude and invocation, and empty your moments of everything apart from bearing witness to His generosity and goodness. And in God is all success.

> 12. *"O John! Take the Book with strength!" And We gave him wisdom as a child,* 13. *And a tenderness from Our Presence, and purity; and he was reverent,* 14. *And dutiful toward his parents. He was not domineering, rebellious.* 15. *Peace be upon him the day he was born, and the day he dies, and the Day he is raised alive.*

[12] God, the Truth 🌿 says: *"O John! Take the Book with strength!"* These words resume a narrative of many things which had happened before them, including John's birth 🌿 and his early life up to the moment revelation came to him. *The Book* is generally understood to mean the Torah, though some say it was a book sent especially to him, which would make this verse proof that John 🌿 received [his own scripture and law]. According to the *tafsīr* of Ibn al-'Arafa, John 🌿 was a messenger like Jesus. *Take the book with strength* has been said by some exegetes to mean 'with diligence and effort,' and by others to mean, 'by acting upon what it contains.'

And We gave him wisdom as a child... Ibn 'Abbās says, "Wisdom (*ḥukma*) in this context means prophecy (*nubūwa*), which John 🌿 was granted at the age of three." That an infant could be a prophet (*nabī*) is rationally possible and a majority of the learned accept is as a possibility. As for his being a messenger (*rasūl*), that is also rationally possible, and according to al-Fakhr, it actually happened, which would mean that both John and Jesus (may peace be upone them both) were messengers in their infancies.[19] Ibn Marzūq, in his commentary on al-Bukhārī, says, "Generally speaking, the prophets are given their prophecy after the age of forty," for it is at that age that they attain full strength, "but it is said that John and Jesus (may peace be upone them both) were brought forth as messengers (of God) in their infancy." According to Ibn al-'Arabī,[20] it is permissible [to believe that scripture and law could come to a

---

19. Fakhr al-Dīn al-Rāzī, in his *tafsīr* on this verse, holds that if we accept the possibility of miracles, that should include the possibility of an infant being the bearer of scripture.

20. He is referring the Andalusian scholar and exegete, Qāḍī Abū Bakr Muḥammad ibn 'Abdallah ibn al-'Arabī al-Mu'āfirī, in his *tafsīr Aḥkām al-Qur'ān,*

child], but it never happened. So the words of Jesus ﷺ, *Verily, I am a servant of God. [He has given me the Book ...]*[21] announce what was destined to happen in the future, not what had already taken place.[22] It is, in fact, doubtful that a child could be given scripture and law because that would entail [legal] responsibility, and a condition for this is to have reached puberty, about which the religious laws do not differ." See the marginal notes of al-Fāsī concerning this.[23]

The most likely explanation is that John and Jesus (may peace be upone them both) were given prophecy as children but [were not given scripture and law] until they had reached puberty, and God Most High knows best.[24] It has also been said that the word *ḥukma* means "understanding of the Torah and knowledge of the rules of religion." And it is related that some children once called John ﷺ to play, and he answered, "It is not for play that I was created."

[13-14] *And [We gave him] a tenderness from Our Presence...* John ﷺ was given a deep sense of compassion from God's sacred presence. This may also be understood to mean the affection that people had for him, for ʿAwf said, "*Ḥannān* means 'beloved.'" *And [We gave him] purity (zakātan)*, meaning that he was pure of faults and sins, or '[*We gave him*] as charity (*zakāt*) to his parents,' or that God accorded him the means by which to give charity to others. *And he was reverent (taqiyyan)*, obeying God and avoiding sin, *and dutiful to his parents,* treating them with kindness and goodness, *and he was not domineering, rebellious*, that is, proud and disobedient. *Al-jabbār* is a person who tries to persuade or even force people (*yujbiru al-nās*) to be like him. It is also said these words mean that [John was not] someone who rejected advice or was rebellious to God Most High.

[15] *Peace upon him...* means God's protection and safety, on *the day he was born*, from the Devil's temptations, *and the day he dies* from the punishment of the grave, *and the day that he will be raised alive,*

not to be confused with the Sufi, Ibn ʿArabī al-Ḥātimī (d. 638/1240). See also biographical notes.

21. Verse 30, below.

22. This is one of the many cases in Arabic in which an absolute truth may be expressed using the past tense of the verb.

23. Al-Fāsī, *al-Ḥāshiya*, I:473.

24. The distinction being made is between a prophet (*nabī*), who is someone given knowledge of eschatological realities and future events, and a messenger (*rasūl*), who is given, in addition, a scripture that contains a law.

from the calamities of Judgment Day and the torments of hell.

It has been related that John and Jesus (may peace be upone them both) met and John said to Jesus, "Ask God to forgive for me, for you are better than I." And Jesus ﷺ replied, "No, you are better than I, for I asked for peace and safety upon myself, while God granted it to you [without your having asked]."[25]

Spiritual Allusion

To *take hold of the Book with strength* means that we read it with fervor and diligence, detached from all else as we do so, with our attention directed towards it and away from anything else. When a servant's recitation is like this he can be said to be "taking hold of the Book... with strength." According to al-Wartajibī, "*The Book* is God's eternal speech, and to *take hold of* it with strength means with God's eternal strength, such that the reciter becomes effaced from himself, and speaks and hears by way of his Lord." Such is the state of those brought near, and God Most High knows better.

> 16. *And remember Mary in the Book, when she withdrew from her family to an eastern place.* 17. *And she veiled herself from them. Then We sent to her Our Spirit, and it assumed for her the likeness of a perfect man.* 18. *She said, "I seek refuge from you in the All-Merciful, if you are reverent!"* 19. *He said, "I am but a messenger of your Lord, to bestow upon you a pure boy."* 20. *She said, "How shall I have a boy when no man has touched me, nor have I been unchaste?"* 21. *He said, "Thus shall it be. Your Lord says, 'It is easy for Me.'" And [it is thus] that We might make him a sign to mankind, and a mercy from Us. And it is a matter decreed.*

[16] God, the Truth ﷻ, says: *And remember*, O Muḥammad, *Mary*, in the Qur'ān, especially in this noble *sūrah*, which begins with the story of Zachariah ﷺ and is followed by the story of Mary because of the similarities between the two. *When she withdrew from her people* and went to a place facing east, which has been said to mean either some place in Jerusalem or else a place in her house where she could be alone to worship. It is for this reason that Christians take the east as their prayer direction (*qibla*). It has also been said that she had gone to a watering place in order to bathe after menstruation....

25. This refers to verse 33 below.

[17-18] *And she veiled herself from them... Then We sent to her Our Spirit.* While she was bathing, veiled from people, Gabriel ﷺ came to her in the human form of a beardless youth with a radiant face. He is referred to in the verse as "Our spirit" (*rūḥanā*) in honor of the sublimity of his station, but in some recitations this word is read as *rawḥanā*, meaning "Our relief," because of the rest and comfort he brings to God's servants who receive the guidance he bears. There is also a reference here to the provision given to those who are drawn near, according to God's words, *Then, if he be of those Drawn Near—Rest* (*rawḥun*) *and Satisfaction* [56:88-89]. Gabriel appeared to her as a perfect human being, lacking not a single feature of human beauty. It has also been said that he appeared in the form of a youth whom she knew named Joseph, one of the servants of the Sacred House of Jerusalem, sent to her in that beautiful form so that he might approach her and convey to her from God what he had to convey, for had he come to her in his angelic form, she would have fled in fear unable to bear his awesome presence.

There have been those who said that the beauty of Gabriel's human form was to awaken in her physical desire so that ovulation could take place, but this is an enormity arising from the school of [rationalist] philosophy, taken by someone from the pages of their books.[26] It is also belied by the words of Mary which follow, *"I seek refuge from you in the All-Merciful One if you are reverent*, proof that there was nothing resembling desire within her. In fact, there was quite the opposite.

Abū al-Saʿūd said, "Yes, it is possible that [the angel] was sent to her in that extraordinarily beautiful human form as a trial and test of her purity, in which case what she showed in response was the highest degree of chastity and detachment. Her mention of God in His Attribute of all-encompassing mercy (*al-raḥmāniya*) also shows the degree to which she sought that particular form of Mercy in which there is protection (*al-ʿiṣma*) from whatever might cause fear. Her words *if you are reverent* (*in kunta taqīyya*) mean 'If you have reverent fear of God, then my seeking refuge in Him will mean something to you.'"

[19] *He said: I am only a messenger of your Lord...* That is, 'I am not

26. This notion is mentioned in passing in the commentary of Abū'l-Layth al-Samarqandī (d. 321/933) on 3:44 and was subsequently transmitted by al-Bayḍāwī (d. 685/1286) and a few others. It is quite possible that al-Samarqandī, known principally as an orthodox Ḥanafī jurist, came into contact with Muʿtazilite thought.

someone who could commit any evil you might imagine, but rather a messenger from the very One in whose all-encompassing mercy you seek refuge, and as a means by which the gift of this son will come to you....'[27] The words "your Lord" (*Rabbuki*), which join the possessive "your" to God's Name "Lord," are a way of honoring Mary ﷺ, gladdening her heart, and showing her the sublime source of this decree, for the gift to her of a son was to be one of the stages of her [spiritual] training.[28] [This son is described as] *zakīyya*, which may be understood to mean "a pure child free of faults," or else someone whose states will become ever purer as he develops from childhood to maturity.

[20] *She said, "How shall I have a boy...?"* That is, how could she conceive a child when no mortal had touched her in wedlock, nor was she a wanton woman (*baghīyya*). The angel answered, *Thus shall it be*, that is, 'It will come to pass as I have said to you.' *Your Lord says, 'It is easy for Me.'* That is, 'To endow you with a son without your ever having been touched by a man is something easy to do in Our power, even if it is something impossible by normal means, for We have no need of secondary causes or intermediaries. Rather, Our command is between the *kāf* and the *nūn*.[29] And We have done this in order *that We might make him a sign for mankind,* to show them the perfection of Our power,' and here the shift in person to the *We* of majesty expresses God's omnipotence and might.[30] 'This is also in

27. Here Ibn ʿAjība adds the linguistic note that there is a recitation in which the verb *ahaba* ("*that I may bestow*") is read as *yahaba* which would mean, "*in order that He may bestow...*"

28. Ibn ʿAjība is referring to a perspective found in several *tafsīr*s according to which all that happened to Mary ﷺ during her life—being dedicated to the temple as a female, having provision come to her in a locked chamber in the temple (in 3:33-37), her conception of Jesus ﷺ without human intercourse (mentioned in 3:45-47 as well as here), and her returning with the baby who spoke to her people (mentioned in verse 27 below)—were all part of her own personal spiritual journey and education.

29. There are seven verses throughout the Qur'ān which state that when God decrees that something exist, He says to it *kun* (be!) and it is. The saying, "His command is between the *kāf* and the *nūn*," (which spell the word *kun* in Arabic) occurs in several very old commentaries as well as in verses of poetry, as a way of expressing how immediate and easy it is for something God decrees to come into existence.

30. At this point, the divine discourse, which began in the first person singular (*It is easy for Me*), shifts to first person plural (*That We may make him a sign from Us*).

order that We may make him an immense mercy *from Us* to human beings through the guidance and direction he will bring.' *And it is a matter decreed* in eternity when, by God's power and determination, it was inscribed in the Guarded Tablet.[31] 'So what is happening to you was inevitable.' This may also be understood to mean that it was actually happening at that moment as an expression of God's perfect wisdom and mystery. And God Most High knows best.

Spiritual Allusion

The fruits and mysteries [of the Way] do not appear until we have withdrawn from the company of the sinful, and from everything else that distracts our heart from the invocation or from the vision and awareness of God. Then, when we are secluded in *a place facing east*, near to where lights and secrets dawn by virtue of its being close to the people of light or [by having] their permission (*idhn*) in the Way, God sends to us a holy spirit, that is, divine inspirations which give new life to our spirit, soul, heart, and body, and we are endowed with a knowledge from His presence that will be *a sign* for those who come after us and a mercy for those who wish to be like us and follow us [in the way]. And in God is all accord.

> 22. *So she conceived him and withdrew with him to a place far off.* 23. *And the pangs of childbirth drove her to the trunk of the date palm. She said, "Would that I had died before this and was a thing forgotten, utterly forgotten!"* 24. *So he called out to her from below her, "Grieve not! Your Lord has made a stream to flow beneath you.* 25. *And shake toward yourself the trunk of the date palm; fresh, ripe dates shall fall upon you.* 26. *So eat and drink and cool your eye. And if you see any human being, say, 'Verily I have vowed a fast to the All-Merciful, so I shall not speak this day to any man.'"* 27. *Then she came with him to her people,*

31. "The Guarded Tablet" (*al-Lawḥ al-Mahfūẓ*) is mentioned at the end of *Sūrat al-Burūj* [Q. 85:22]. It is also referred to in a *ḥadīth* found in Ṭabarānī, *al-Kabīr*, where it is reported that according to Ibn ʿAbbās, the Prophet ﷺ said, "Verily, God created a Guarded Tablet of white pearl. Its pages are red coral, and its Pen is light. Every day, God looks upon it three hundred and sixty times. He creates, provides, causes some to die, gives life to others, exalts some, abases others, and He does what He wills." In the commentary of al-Qurṭubī on this verse, he adds that the Guarded Tablet is also "the Mother of the Book (*umm al-kitāb*) from which the Qur'ān and [other sacred] books were copied," and thus identical to "a hidden book" (*kitābin maknūnin*) mentioned in Q. 56:78.

carrying him. They said, "O Mary! You have brought an amazing thing! 28. O sister of Aaron! Your father was not an evil man, nor was your mother unchaste." 29. Then she pointed to him. They said, "How shall we speak to one who is yet a child in the cradle?" 30. He said, "Truly I am a servant of God. He has given me the Book and made me a prophet. 31. And He has made me blessed wheresoever I may be, and has enjoined upon me prayer and almsgiving so long as I live, 32. And [has made me] dutiful toward my mother. And He has not made me domineering, wretched. 33. Peace be upon me the day I was born, the day I die, and the day I am raised alive!"

[22] God, the Truth ﷻ, says: *So she conceived him...* Gabriel ﷺ blew into the sleeve of her jubbah and that breath entered within her. It is also said that he lifted up her outer garment and blew into its pocket, or that he blew [in her direction] from a distance, that breath came to her like a breeze, and she conceived at that instant, or that the breath [of the angel] entered her mouth.

Some *tafsīrs* state that the length of her pregnancy was seven months and others, eight, adding that a fetus of eight months does not survive. Ibn ʿAṭiyya says, "There are numerous narrations which put the length of her pregnancy at eight months, adding that because a fetus of eight months does not survive, this too was a miracle for Jesus ﷺ alone." Others say the pregnancy was [the full] nine months, and others that it was only three hours: she conceived him in one hour, he was formed in one hour, and she bore him at sunset. Still others say that she became pregnant and bore him all in one hour. They have also said that her age at the time was thirteen, or according to some, ten, and that she had already had two menstrual cycles before that.

And she withdrew with him to a place far off. When she felt the birth was near, she withdrew with him to a place that was far from her family, behind the mountain, or some say to the furthest part of their house, *and the pangs of childbirth drove her to the trunk of the date palm,* either so she could hide herself or use it for support as she gave birth. The word *jizʿu* refers to the trunk of a date palm without its fronds or roots, and this may have been a dry trunk which had been brought to that place to be used in building a room, for this was winter. The definite article referring to *the* date palm is either to refer to a species by a single example of it or else because it was particular, and there were no others like it in the area. And it may have been that God Most High inspired her to go there in order to show her signs which would calm her fear as well as to nourish her with fresh, ripe dates, which are among the best foods for women who have just delivered.

[23] *She said, "Would that I had died before this..."* When the pangs of labor seized her, she said [these words] even though she knew that Gabriel عليه السلام had come to her and she had heard the noble promise made to her.[32] Still, she said these words perhaps out of the shame she would have to endure before people and her fear of their blame or simply in the manner of the saintly confronting distress, as when ʿUmar رضي الله عنه picked up a piece of straw from the ground and said, "Would that I were this piece of straw; would that I were nothing!"[33] and when Bilāl رضي الله عنه said, "Would that Bilāl's mother had never borne him!"[34] *Shay'an mansiyyan* means a thing of such little importance that it is forgotten and disregarded, and never occurs to people again.

[24] *So he called out to her from below her...* Most *tafsīrs* say that "*he*" refers to Gabriel عليه السلام who was in the place of a mid-wife, ready to receive the new-born. But it has also been said that the [feminine pronoun] *hā* [in the phrase *from below her*] refers to the date palm, and that the one who called to her was [the infant] Jesus عليه السلام himself... There is also a recitation in which the letters *mim* and *nūn* are read not as *min* ("from") but as *man* ("who"), meaning 'the one who was beneath her called to her, saying "*Grieve not!*"'[35]

Your Lord has made a stream to flow beneath you.... Ibn ʿAbbās رضي الله عنه wrote, "Gabriel عليه السلام struck the earth with his foot and there appeared a spring of fresh water which began to flow." It has also been said that it was [the baby] Jesus عليه السلام who struck the earth with his foot, or that there had already been a dry stream bed nearby which God Most High then caused to flow with water. [This would be a miracle] similar to what had happened with the palm tree,

32. That is, that God would make the child *a sign to people and a mercy* [19:22].

33. Recorded in Bayhaqī, *Shuʿab al-Īmān*, Ibn Abī Shayba, *al-Muṣannaf*, Ibn al-Mubārak, *al-Zuhd*, and others.

34. Recorded in al-Bazzār, *Musnad*, Ibn Abī Shayba, *al-Muṣannaf*, Bayhaqī, *al-Sunan*, and others.

35. It is useful to recall that the first copies of the Qur'ān were written without diacritical marks. This allowed for certain small variations which were eventually formalized by the science of recitation (*qira'āt*).

for it too had been dry, without a crown, and then God caused a crown, fronds, and fruit to emerge from it. Others have said that the flowing stream was already there, but the former explanation is the more likely because it is more in keeping with [all the other] miracles surrounding [this birth] which the verses of Noble Book mention.

It has also been said that [the word] *sarīyan* ("stream") may be understood to mean "a distinguished and high-ranking person," which would refer to Jesus himself ﷺ, in which case the nunation of the word would express honor and majesty. "Your Lord" (*Rabbuki*), in which the possessive refers to Mary ﷺ, again honors her and gives her solace.

[25-26] *And shake towards you the trunk of the date palm...* [Mary is told:] 'Pull the trunk in your direction,' for [the verb] *hazz* means a strong movement back and forth, ... and 'When you do so, *fresh, ripe dates shall fall upon you.*' *Ruṭaban* are the dates which have not yet dried but are ripe and ready to harvest, '[and they will continue to fall] as long as you continue to shake the tree. *So eat* of those dates *and drink* from that stream, *and cool your eye,*' that is, 'be gladdened and unburden yourself of all the cares that weigh upon you and make you sad. God Most High will exalt you above all blame, and your child's tongue will absolve you.' This may also be understood to mean, 'Rejoice in knowing that God will protect you and look after you no matter what you face.' *Qurratu'l-ʿayn* literally means "coolness of the eye," for while tears of sadness are warm, tears of happiness are cool. Thus do they say, "The coolness of the eye comes from seeing what is loveable, and heat of the eye comes from seeing what is abhorrent."

And if you see any human being... That is, 'If someone questions or blames you, [say to him] *'Verily I have vowed a fast to the All-Merciful,'* for their fasts were in silence and they would abstain from speech just as they would abstain from food. Ibn al-ʿArabī wrote in *al-Aḥwadhī*: "Our Prophet ﷺ chose for this community to allow speech while fasting—something which had been forbidden to those before us—but to prohibit it while offering the prayer."[36] *'So* after I have told you of my vow *I shall not speak this day to any man...* Rather, I shall speak with the angels and commune with my Lord.'

36. *ʿĀriḍatu'l-Aḥwādhī* is a commentary on the *ṣaḥīḥ ḥadīth* collection of al-Tirmidhī.

It has also been said that she was commanded to inform people of her vow by signs alone....[37] In fact, she was commanded to do this and made a vow to do so because to quarrel with the foolish is disliked, and the words of Jesus 🕮 would be enough to completely silence any who would revile her.

[27-29] *Then she came with him to her people, carrying him.* After she had performed the greater ablution that follows childbirth, she came to her people carrying the baby. According to al-Kalbī, "Joseph the carpenter, the son of her paternal uncle, took Mary and her son to a cave for forty days until the bleeding from childbirth ceased, and then he took them [to her people]. On the way, the baby 🕮 spoke, saying, "Rejoice, O mother! For I am a servant of God and His anointed one (*masīḥ*)." But when her people saw them, they wept with grief, for they were a righteous folk, and it was then that they said, *"O Mary! You have brought an amazing thing (shay'an fariyan)."* The adjective *farī* means anything extremely strange or incredible... and Abū ʿUbayda said, "Anything or any action that is extraordinary [may be] called *farīya*." Thus, the Prophet 🕮 said concerning ʿUmar 🕮, "I never saw a person so amazingly accomplished (*yafrī farīya*)," that is, skilled in what he was doing.[38]

By *"sister of Aaron,"* they meant Aaron, the brother of Moses 🕮, for Mary was descended from him through the lineage of siblings, though between them there was a thousand years. But this has also been said to mean 'O sister of Aaron in piety and devotion,' referring to a saintly man of the time named Aaron, about whom it was said that when he died, forty thousand followed his funeral procession and all of them had taken the name "Aaron of the Israelites." Yet others have said that the Aaron to whom they compared her was a man known to be among the vilest people of the Children of Israel and so this was a way of blaming her.

'Your father, 'Imrān, was not an evil man, nor was your mother unchaste, so how has this child come to you out of wedlock?' This may be either to stress how grave [they considered her sin to be] or else as a way of saying that for someone from such a pious lineage, to commit this kind of sin was worse [than it would have been in the case of another].

---

37. Ibn ʿAjība adds here that according to al-Farrā', the Arabs call anything which communicates meaning to people "speech" (*kalāman*).

38. A *ḥadīth* in Ṭabarānī, *al-Kabīr*, 12:232, the *Musnad* of Imām Aḥmad, 2:28, and elsewhere with slight differences in wording.

[29] *Then she pointed to him*...that is, towards Jesus ﷺ to indicate that they should speak with him, for she had vowed to remain silent. Her gesture towards the infant Jesus went back to the words that had been spoken to her, "*And cool your eye*," for her eye would only be cooled when the divine aid and sufficiency that she had been promised came to pass, and this would only happen by her turning to God alone and by her finding contentment in God alone. All this she showed by her gesture, which was thus [an expression] of her hand's obedience ...Here too is a reminder of the story of Jurayj.[39]

They said, not understanding her answer, "*How shall we speak to one who is yet a child in the cradle*, for it was something they had never encountered before ...

[30-31] *He said, "Truly I am a servant of God."* These were the words that God Most High enabled him to articulate, and they are both an affirmation of truth and an answer to those who ascribe to him divinity. It has been said that the one who spoke to Jesus was Zachariah (may peace be upone them both). According to al-Suddī, when Mary gestured towards the baby, the people were angered and said, "Her mocking us like this is even worse than [the sin] she has committed!" It has also been said that the baby Jesus ﷺ had been nursing and when he heard this [from the people], he stopped, turned in their direction, leaned a little towards the right, raised his index finger, and then spoke the words he spoke and did not speak again until he reached the age at which children [normally] speak.

39. The story of Jurayj is mentioned in a *ḥadīth* which appears in the collections of Muslim (2550), Aḥmad, *Shuʿab al-Īmān* of Bayhaqī, and others, and states: "None spoke in the cradle except three: (the first was) Jesus, (and the second was) a man from the Children of Israel called Jurayj. While he was offering his prayers, his mother came and called to him. He said (to himself), 'Shall I answer her or keep on praying?' (He went on praying) and did not answer her, and his mother said, "O God! Do not let him die until he sees the faces of prostitutes." Then, while he was in his hermitage, a woman (of ill repute) came and sought to seduce him, but he refused. So she went to a shepherd, offered herself to him, and later gave birth to a baby which she claimed was Jurayj's child. Upon hearing this the people came to him enraged, tore down his hermitage, drove him out of it, and began to hurl upon him abuse. Jurayj performed the ablution and offered the prayer, and then came to the baby and said, "O child! Who is your father?" and the baby replied, "The shepherd." Then the people said, "We shall rebuild your hermitage out of gold," but he said, "No. Use only clay."

"He has given me the Book..." That is, the Gospel (*al-injīl*) ... 'And along with that, God *has made me blessed wheresoever I may be,* blessed through service to people and through teaching them goodness wherever he was. God also enjoined on him the prayer (*ṣalāt*) as an affirmed commandment and almsgiving (*zakāt*) which may be understood either as the alms due on wealth and possessions, or else as purification from vice.[40]

[32] *And [God has made me] dutiful toward my mother...* All the verbs here are in the past tense either because he was speaking of something decreed before [his birth], or else to express the certainty of what was to happen.[41] *And He has not made me domineering,* or *wretched* before Him, but rather, humble, tender, blessed, and near. He would say to people, "Ask me, for truly my heart is tender, and in myself I am small," for God had granted him humility.[42]

[33] *"Peace be upon me the day I was born..."* These words are similar to what John 🕊 had said before him, and imply that for those who reject him, there would be the opposite of peace and security, similar to the words of God, *Peace be upon him who follows guidance!* [20:47] which mean 'and for the one who does not, punishment.'

This was the last thing Jesus 🕊 said [as a baby]. He was one of those who spoke in infancy, and we have mentioned the others in [the commentary on the chapter of] Joseph, both in rhyme and prose.[43] All of them are well-known except for the story of the handmaiden of Pharaoh's daughter, and since her story is not well-known, I shall mention it here as al-Thaʿlabī related it. On the authority of Ibn ʿAbbās the Messenger of God 🕊 said:

> "When the Prophet 🕊 was taken on the Night Journey, there passed over him a beautiful fragrance and he asked, 'O Gabriel, what is that fragrance?' He answered, 'That is

40. The words *zakāh*, charity, and *tazkīya*, purification, are from the same root.

41. *He gave me the Book... made me a prophet... made me blessed... enjoined on me prayer and almsgiving... and made me dutiful* ...See note 22, above.

42. This saying of Jesus 🕊 appears in the commentary of Ṭabarī. See note 38 above.

43. He is referring here to his commentary on verses 25 through 27 of the Chapter of Joseph, which recounts the incident between Joseph and the wife of the the high-ranking ruler, identified by some as Potiphar: "*And a witness from her own people testified, "If his shirt is torn from the front, then she has spoken the truth and he is among the liars. But if his shirt is torn from behind, then she has lied and he is among the truthful."* [Ibn ʿAjība states that according to some *tafsīrs*], the witness was a baby.

from the handmaiden of Pharaoh's daughter... One day as she was combing the daughter's hair, the comb fell from her hand, and as she picked it up she said, '*Bismi'Llāh*! (In the Name of God!)' [Hearing this], the daughter asked, '[Do you mean] my father?' The handmaiden answered, 'No. [I mean] my Lord, your Lord, and your father's Lord.' The daughter then asked, 'Shall I tell my father about this?' and she said, 'Yes.' So she told her father and he summoned [the handmaiden] and said, 'Who is your lord?' She said, 'My Lord and your Lord—[the Lord Who is] in the heavens.' So Pharaoh ordered that a huge brass caldron be brought and heated and then ordered that her children be brought [as well]. The handmaiden said to him, 'I have just one thing to ask of you.' He said, 'What is it?' She answered, 'I ask that my bones and my children's bones be gathered up and buried together.' He said, 'That is your right upon us.' Then he ordered that her children be cast therein, one by one, until they came to her last child, a suckling infant, and it was he who said, 'Dear mother, be patient.' Then they were cast therein, she and her baby."[44]

Spiritual Allusion

Several matters relating to Sufism can be found in these verses. One is that it is permissible to be secretive concerning things which can hurt one's reputation, and even to flee to a place where it can remain intact. [This is true] except for the one engaged in spiritual struggle [against the ego], in which case he should accept whatever helps him slay it. Another teaching is that it is permissible to seek refuge in what can lighten his pains and ease his hardships without this in any way contradicting the virtue of trust in God (*al-tawakkul*). Also, it is not sinful for someone to wish for death if he fears that he is losing either his religion or his reputation or that some tribulation is coming between him and his heart.[45] It may

44. This story is recounted in a *ḥadīth* found in Muslim, the *Musnad* of Imām Aḥmad, Ṭabarānī, *al-Kabīr,* and elsewhere.

45. This refers to the words of Mary ﷺ in verse 23, *Oh, would that I had died before this*. It should be added, however, that suicide is considered one of the gravest sins in Islam and is prohibited by verses 2:195 and 4:29, as well as numerous *ḥadīths*, principally, "Anyone who kills himself with something will be punished by that thing on the Day of Resurrection," or in some versions, "in the Afterlife."

be also understood from these verses that a heart may experience grief and shock at the first stroke of calamity and yet still be said to have the virtues of patience and acceptance. [Sadness and grief] are part of the human condition, and only if they are taken to an excess do they become contradictory to virtue.[46]

Also, the words of God Most High (to Mary) *And shake toward yourself the trunk of the date palm* teach that to pursue a lawful means [of earning a living] is not contradictory to having complete trust in God (*al-tawakkul*), as long as those means are light and do not prevent us from maintaining our *dīn*, and as long as our heart does not start to depend on them [rather than on God]. As for someone who has withdrawn from the workaday world (*al-mutajarrid*), however, he should not return to it until his certitude is complete and he has reached stability in his knowledge of God Most High, the Truth.

Thus, at the beginning of her path, provision would come to Mary ﷺ without secondary means, as mentioned in Sūrat *Āli ʿImrān*,[47] while at the end, God said to her, *And shake toward yourself the trunk of the date palm.* Concerning this, Shaykh Abū'l-ʿAbbās al-Mursī ﷺ said, "In the beginning [of her way], [God] was making Himself known to her through miraculous events without intermediary means. Then, when she had perfected her certitude, she was returned to those means, and this latter state is higher than the first. As for those who claim that at first her love was only for God, but that then, when she had given birth, her love became divided, we would say that such an explanation is unacceptable and unworthy of consideration. For Mary ﷺ was a *ṣiddīqa*—a person of complete veracity—and a *ṣiddīqa* only goes from one spiritual sta-

---

This *ḥadīth* appears in Muslim, the *musnad* of Imām Aḥmad, Tirmidhī, and many other collections.

46. "The first stroke of a calamity (*al-ṣadmatu'l-ūlā*)" is a term from a well-known *ḥadīth* reported in Bukhārī and Muslim which states that the Prophet ﷺ passed by a woman weeping beside a grave and told her to fear God and be patient. The woman, not recognizing him, replied (angrily), "Go away, for you have not been afflicted with a calamity like mine!" Later she was told that he was the Prophet ﷺ, and went to his house and found his door open without a lock. She went into where he was and said to him (in apology), "I did not know who you were," to which he replied: "Verily, patience is at the first stroke of a calamity." In Bukhārī, this is included in the chapter on funerals among *ḥadīths* which discourage excessive displays of mourning.

47. See note 12 above.

tion to another that is more perfect, not less."[48]

Another [notion of Sufism] to be taken from these verses is that there is nothing wrong for a person to take on some devotional practice in which he finds refuge from people or from his own self. This might be fasting, observing silence, or anything else that removes him from the generality of people and from the things which reinforce his ego.

[Finally], concerning the words [of Jesus], *And peace be upon me the day I was born*, al-Wartajibī said, "The peace invoked by John ﷺ was a particular blessing from Lordliness to servanthood, while the peace invoked by Jesus ﷺ arose from the manifestation of Lordliness in the core of servanthood.[49] More exalted than both these, however, was the [blessing of] peace invoked by God upon the master of those sent, Muḥammad ﷺ, directly connected to him and the unveiling of his beauty. .... Peace invoked by the tongue is by a created thing ... and so is not on the same level as a blessing that arises from God's eternal attributes."[50]

34. *That is Jesus son of Mary—a statement of the truth, about which they have doubts.* 35. *It is not for God to take a child. Glory be to Him! When He decrees a thing, He only says to it, "Be!" and it is.* 36. *"Truly God is my Lord and your Lord; so worship Him. This is a straight path."* 37. *Yet the parties differed among themselves, and woe unto those who disbelieve for the witnessing of a tremendous day!* 38. *How well they will hear and how well they will see on the Day they come unto Us. But the wrongdoers, today, are in manifest error.* 39. *And warn them of the Day of Regret, when the matter will have been decreed, for now they are in a state of heed-*

48. This is quoted from *Laṭā'if al-minan*, chapter 5, which is composed of Shaykh al-Mursī's comments on Quranic verses. See page 130 in the Arabic edition and page 196 in Nancy Robert's translation.

49. The invocation of peace upon a prophet brings God's invocation of peace to the servant, as the well-known *ḥadīth* states, "He who invokes God's blessings of peace upon me once, God blesses with peace ten-fold" (*Man ṣallā ʿalayya marra, ṣalla Allāhu ʿalayhi ʿashra*). This is analogous to asking God to bless John ﷺ. The invocation of Jesus ﷺ upon himself arises from his being described as the word of God and a spirit from Him in the verse: *Verily the Messiah, Jesus son of Mary, was only a messenger of God, and His Word, which He committed to Mary, and a Spirit from Him* [4:171].

50. He is referring to verse 33:56, *Verily God and His angels invoke blessings upon the Prophet. O you who believe, invoke blessings upon him and salutations of peace in abundance.*

lessness and believe not. 40. *Surely We shall inherit the earth and whatsoever is upon it, and unto Us shall they be returned.*

[34-36] God, the Truth ﷻ, says: *That is Jesus son of Mary....That* one, described by those majestic traits and virtues, *is Jesus the son of Mary,* and not as the Christians who claim he was divine describe him, attributing to him divinity. It is, in fact, an adamant denial of that claim, for what it says of him ﵇ is the opposite of what they say about him.[51] The demonstrative "that" (*dhālika*), which (normally) indicates something distant, conveys a sense of his high station and degree, how he is distinguished by these virtues from anyone else, and how his station was one that could be physically perceived.

A statement of the truth, about which they have doubts. What has been said is a statement from God, the Truth (*al-Ḥaqq*). In some *tafsīrs* these words are said to be a continuation of what Jesus ﵇ said: that without a doubt he was a servant of God and a messenger. And it is about this that *they have doubts* and dispute amongst themselves, the Jews calling him a deceptive sorcerer, and the Christians a god or son of God. But *it is not for God take a son*. That is, it is something inconceivable of God. *Glory be to Him* and exalted far above what they say, and above any other enormities they might utter concerning Him. For how can it be said of God that He takes a son when that implies a need for intermediaries and secondary causes? [In reality], His command is faster than the blink of an eye, for *When He decrees a thing, He only says to it, "Be!" and it is.*[52]

Then Jesus ﵇ said to them, *"Truly God is my Lord and your Lord; so worship Him."* This was all he uttered as a baby, but in these two utterances—'*Truly, I am God's servant*,' and '*Truly God is my Lord and your Lord, so worship Him* alone, associating no others with God in your worship'—is a direct disavowal of the errors concerning him. '*This* which I have mentioned to you of God's oneness *is a straight path*,' and anyone who follows it will not deviate nor lose his way.

[37] *Yet the parties differed among themselves....* Despite the clarity of [Jesus'] words...,the Jews and Christians disagreed about him, going to both extremes [in describing his nature].[53] Then the Chris-

51. In that he calls himself a servant, not a lord.

52. See note 29, above.

53. Literally, "by both falling short and going to excess," that is, by overestimating and underestimating [his true nature].

tians further divided into sects. The Nestorians said he was the son of God, the Jacobites that he was God who descended to earth and then ascended to heaven, and the Melkites that he was the third of a trinity. *And woe to those who disbelieve*, those who differ concerning him for whatever reason ... *for the witnessing* (*mash·had*) *of a tremendous day...* a fearful day of reckoning and recompense, which is the Day of Resurrection. *Mash·had* has also been said to mean 'the time of bearing witness,' 'the place of bearing witness,' or when the Day itself will bear witness against them, when the angels, the prophets ﷺ, and their own tongues, hands, and feet will all testisfy...[54]

[38] *How well they will hear and how well they will see.* These words express astonishment that after their having been deaf and blind in this world, *On the Day they come to Us*, their vision and hearing will be acute. They have also been said to mean that because [these faculties did not benefit them in the world], they will not avail them on that Day. Al-Kalbī said , "No one will hear or see better than they on the Day of Judgment when it will be asked of Jesus ﷺ, *Did you say to people, 'Take me and my mother as gods instead of God'?* [5:116].

There is also a recitation in which this verse is read in the imperative—"*Cause* them to hear and *cause* them to see the appointed meeting of that Day"—that they might be admonished concerning what will befall them ... *But the oppressors, today*, that is, in this world, *are in manifest error* because they have failed to see and hear. Referring to them by the word *ẓālimūn* (*oppressors*) instead of simply by the pronoun (*they*) is a reminder that when (human beings) cease to reflect, they become oppressors of their own souls.[55]

[39] *And warn them of the Day of Regret...* On that day, everyone will have regrets. The evil-doer will regret the evil he had done, and the doer of good will regret that it was so little. *When the matter will have been decreed*, that is, when the reckoning is complete, and the two groups have been sorted out, either for the garden or for the

---

54. Here, Ibn ʿAjība is referring to what is said in verses such as *How will it be when We bring forth a witness from every community, and We bring you as a witness against these?* [4:41] and also *On that Day We shall seal their mouths. Their hands will speak to Us, and their feet will bear witness to that which they used to earn* [36:66].

55. The word translated as 'oppressors'—*ẓālimūn*—comes from the same root as *ẓulma*, 'darkness,' and the causative form of the noun means, literally, that they are the ones who cast darkness upon others and upon themselves.

fire. It is related that the Prophet ﷺ was asked concerning this and said, "When death is brought forth in the form of a black ram with a white head and then sacrificed, and the two groups are looking on, they will be called to: 'O people of the garden! Eternal life without death! O people of the fire! Eternal life without death!' And for the people of the garden, it will add joy to their joy, while for the people of the fire, it will add woe to their woe." Then he recited ﷺ, *And warn them of a Day of Regret, when the matter shall have been decreed, for now they are in a state of heedlessness*, and he indicated with his hand the world."[56] Al-Muqātil said, "If God had not decreed that they would enter the Garden and dwell there eternally, they would die of sorrow and regret once they see it." *For now they are in a state of heedlessness* concerning what is meant for them in the Next World *and they do not believe* in it because they have been deluded by this world and its splendors. Yet its splendors must fade, its buttresses must crumble, and all that is upon it must pass away.

[40] *Surely We shall inherit the earth and whatsoever is upon it.* 'No one except Us will have possession of both it and you;' or, 'We shall cause the earth and all who are upon it to pass away through extinction and destruction so that the True Heir might receive His inheritance, *and to Us shall they be returned* to be recompensed, *to Us* and to no one else, either solely or in partnership.

Spiritual Allusion

The servant who cares about of the state of his own soul should guard his beliefs with decisive evidence and clear proofs and in accordance with the people of the *sunna*, and then seek the company of the gnostics, the people of direct experience [of the divine] and ecstasy, that he might be raised to the station of excellence, the station of witnessing and vision.

If he falls short in this, remorse and a sense of loss will overtake him on a day when it shall be to no avail. Anyone who turns back from seeking the station of direct experience and ecstasy wrongs his own soul by denying its true worth and because of this, will experience some sense of loss, and there will remain within him some portion of error and remoteness. This will be because he missed [the chance] to follow the way of the Sufis. *But the wrongdo-*

56. This *ḥadīth* is found Bukhārī and Muslim as well as many of other principal collections.

ers, today, are in manifest error.

And warn them of the Day of Regret, a day when the ones who have been brought near [to God] will be raised up and the pretenders will fall.

For the people of direct experience and ecstasy, the meeting with their Lord begins in this world and continues in eternity. And thus it is related that one day as he was sitting in the presence of his master, Shaykh Abū'l-Ḥasan al-Shādhilī ۞ said, "O God, forgive me on the day I meet You!" And his master, the Pole, Ibn Mashīsh ۞, said to him, "He is nearer to you than your night and day. But the wrongs that people commit lead them astray, and by an eternal decree, their intimacy and union with God is lost, so for the wrongdoers there has to be a day about which there is neither deception nor doubt, even while the foremost will have already arrived: *How well they will hear and how well they will see on the Day they come to Us. But the wrongdoers, today are in manifest error.*"[57]

> 41. *And remember Abraham in the Book—verily he was truthful, a prophet—42. When he said unto his father, "O dear father! Why do you worship that which neither hears nor sees, nor can avail you in any way? 43. O dear father! Verily knowledge has come unto me that has not come unto you. So follow me, and I shall guide you upon a sound path. 44. O dear father! Worship not Satan; surely Satan rebelled against the All-Merciful. 45. O dear father! Truly I fear that a punishment from the All-Merciful will touch you, such that you will become a friend of Satan."*

[41] God, the Truth ۞, says: *And remember Abraham in the Book...* That is, recite to those around you from the Qur'ān, or from this *sūrah*, the story of Abraham ۞ because they trace their ancestry to him and perhaps hearing it might uproot them from idolatry and sin. *Verily he was a person of truth (ṣiddīq),* someone who was truthful in his dealings and in everything he took or promised. A *ṣiddīq* can also mean a person of affirmation (*taṣdīq*), someone who affirms with fervor the truth of God's unseen matters, as well as His signs, His books, and His messengers, or a person who believes in and affirms the Oneness of God, His prophets, and His commandments, and acts in accordance with that affirmation. This is why Abū Bakr ۞ is referred by this name. As for what the Sufis mean by this term, that will be explained in the spiritual allusion of these verses

---

57. See al-Amrānī, *Taqyīd*, page 29.

below, God willing...

[*And he was*] *a prophet...* Abraham ﷺ combined within him the state of being a *ṣiddīq* with that of being a *nabī*, and while every prophet is a *ṣiddīq*, the opposite is not true. The verse, therefore, does not say 'he was a prophet and truthful,' because the latter could not exist without the former.

[42] *When he said to his father...* Azar[58] with kindness and hope, addressing him with with *O dear father* (*abati*) instead of 'O my father' (*yā abī*),[59] '*Why do you worship that which neither hears* your praises when you worship it, nor brings you closer when you call to it, nor sees you when you humble yourself before it and revere it. These words may also be taken in a general sense: [why worship] something that does not hear or see anything [at all], for it is self-evident [that if it does not hear you, it does not hear anything]. *Nor can [it] avail you in any way,* for it has no power to benefit you in what you seek nor protect you from harm.

Consider how Abraham ﷺ appealed to his father in the most beautiful and upright way and carefully reasoned with him with civility and care. But because his father had already lived his whole life in obstinance and intransigence, he rejected completely what his son tried to say to him: that it would be impossible for anyone with discernment to have the least faith in something [that neither hears nor sees nor can bring any benefit], let alone show it the highest form of veneration, which is worship. In reality, the only one worthy of such veneration is the One endowed with absolute independence and all-inclusive grace, the Creator and Provider, the Giver of life and death, of reward and chastisement. In fact, anyone of sound mind would be repulsed by the notion of worshipping even a created being who could hear, and see, bring benefit or cause harm, let alone by the notion of worshipping a statue made of wood or stone which lacks not only life itself but even the least traces of life.

---

58. The name 'Azar' is mentioned in 6:74. Baghwī (d. 510/1116), in his commentary on that verse, says that 'Azar' was a nickname for Abraham's father, whose actual name was Tārikh ('Terah' in Genesis 11:26-27). Baghwī also quotes earlier sources saying that the meaning of *āzara* in the Assyrian language of their time was "bent or crooked."

59. The form Abraham ﷺ uses is a much kinder and sweeter way to address one's father.

[43] *O dear father! Verily knowledge has come to me...* With the same kindness and compassion, he invites his father to follow him on the straight path... He makes no mention of his father's ignorance, which was extreme, nor does he seek to attribute to himself ultimate knowledge, even though he possessed its highest form. Rather, he addressed him with compassion, aware of the conditions which had taken his father along the path he had come, and sought to convince him through kindness, saying, '*So follow me, and I shall guide you upon a sound* and straight *path* which will lead you to the highest goal and deliver you from perdition.'

[44] *"O dear father! Worship not Satan...."* Trying to dissuade him from idolatry, he implores his father not to worship Satan, saying in effect 'When you worship idols, you are actually worshipping the devil who made them alluring to you and deluded you...' Then, as further explanation, he said: '*Surely Satan rebelled against the All-Merciful.* That is, 'The reason not to worship him is that he rebelled against your Lord,[60] against the One Who gives you all manner of blessings, the One Whose vengeance will come to pass ...'

[In this verse], repeating the noun *Satan* instead of using the pronoun "he" intensifies the tone of gravity in this pronouncement. And if only Satan's sin of not prostrating [to Adam ﷺ] is referred to here, among all the other crimes of which he is guilty, that is because it is the gravest of them all, or because it was the result of his hatred for Adam ﷺ and his progeny to come. To remind his father of this was a way of cautioning him against taking [the devil] as a protecting friend and obeying him, and to specify [that this sin] is against *the All-Merciful* emphasizes its gravity.

[45] *O dear father! Truly I fear that a punishment from the All-Merciful will touch you...* (Abraham's) warning was that the ultimate punishment which comes from worshipping Satan is to be joined to him in shame and disgrace, and to say that this punishment comes from the *All-Merciful* is a reminder that God's All-Mercifulness (*al-Raḥmāniya*) will not prevent it. It is thus similar in meaning to His words (elsewhere), *What has beguiled you away from your Lord, the Most Generous?* [82:6]. So the words, *Such that you will become a friend of Satan,* mean 'such that you will be joined to him and cursed, as

60. That is, when God bade him to prostrate before Adam, first mentioned in 2:34: *And when We said to the angels, "Prostrate unto Adam," they prostrated, save Iblīs. He refused and waxed arrogant, and was among the disbelievers.*

he is, for eternity.'

In al-Khalīl's admonition to his father[61] there is civility and respect expressed in five ways. The first is that he addresses his father not as "O Azar," or even "O my father," but rather, "*O dear father!*" The second is that he asks "[Why do you worship] what does not hear [or see]?" rather than saying, "Why do you worship pieces of wood and stone?" The third is that he says, "There has come to me knowledge that did not come to you," rather than saying, "You are ignorant and wrong!" The fourth is that he says, "I fear for you," speaking of how he feared for his father rather than threatening him with punishment. The fifth is that he says, "[I fear that punishment] will *touch* you," using the verb *touch* (*mass*) and not "strike you" or "befall you." And God Most High knows better.

Spiritual Allusion

God, the Truth, blessed and exalted be He, combined in the person of Abraham, His friend, the station of utter veracity and the station of prophecy, giving him both His message and His intimate friendship (*al-khulla*). In God's words, *Verily he was truthful, a prophet*, utter veracity (*al-ṣiddīqiya*) is mentioned before prophethood because, in an ascending order, it comes first and prophethood comes after it, as we have already mentioned in *Sūrat al-Nisā'*.[62]

---

61. *Khalīl Allāh*, "God's intimate friend," is the name of honor by which the Prophet ﷺ referred to Abraham in many *ḥadīths*.

62. In his spiritual allusion on *Sūrat al-Nisā'*, verse 100—*Whosoever migrates in the way of God will find upon the earth many a refuge and abundance, and whosoever forsakes his home, emigrating to God and His Messenger, and death overtakes him, his reward will fall upon God, and God is Forgiving, All-Merciful*—he writes: "Whoever migrates from the land of his ego for the sake of reaching the presence of his Guardian Lord will find in the earth of his own soul expanses of knowledge, keys to the treasuries of understanding, and a breadth of vision so vast that all existence will be subsumed in the eye of his inner vision, and he will be granted stability in his consciousness of the Necessary Being. And if someone forsakes the home of his own ego and the prison of his own form for the sake of reaching God and His Messenger and is overtaken by death before having been granted stability [in this knowledge], his recompense will be for God to complete and God will bring him to what he had been seeking and hoping for in the company of the utterly veracious and the people of deep-rootedness and stability, the station just preceding prophethood. Similarly, anyone who dies while seeking formal knowledge that he does not find during his lifetime will be gathered on the Day of Judgment with the learned, for the Prophet ﷺ said: 'If someone seeking knowledge is overtaken by death, there will be nothing between him and the station of prophethood except a single de-

For the Sufis, a *ṣiddīq* is someone of the greatest sincerity and affirmation. He affirms the existen ce of God and God's promise so much, without hesitation or pause, and without recourse to scripture or other formal proof, as if it were something ever before his eyes, and he gives freely of his life and wealth for the pleasure of his Guardian Lord. This is what al-Khalīl did when he presented his body to the fire, offered food to his two guests, and offered his own son as sacrifice,[63] and what [Abū Bakr] al-Ṣiddīq did when he offered solace and support to the Prophet ﷺ in the cave[64] and gave all he possessed five times. This is also similar to what al-Ghazālī did upon finding his shaykh in the Way, when he let his worldly life fall to ruin and left behind all he possessed in order to seek his Guardian Lord. This is why Abū'l-Ḥasan al-Shādhilī ؓ said [of al-Ghazālī]: "In him we witness the greatest station of veracity (*al-ṣiddīqiyya al-ʿuẓmā*),"[65] and someone in whom al-Shādhilī witnessed the greatest station of veracity is example enough.

Among the traits of the utterly veracious is that a miraculous event which manifests the eternal power of God does not surprise them, nor do they find it something too great or too strange (to accept). Thus, God Most High describes Mary as *ṣiddīqa* but not Sarah, who was incredulous [when the angel brought her news of a child] and said, *I am to bear a child when I am an old woman, and this my husband is an old man? That is truly something strange!* [11:72] As for Mary, her only response was to ask how it would take place, whether by natural means or not. And God Most High knows best.

Also in these verses is an example of using kindness when exhorting or reminding someone, especially someone held in high esteem such a parent or a person of rank. If you appeal to such a

---

gree, and that single degree is the station of the utterly veracious (*al-ṣiddīqīn*)...' And in another version, 'If someone seeking knowledge by which Islam may be revived is overtaken by death, there will be only one degree between him and the prophets in paradise.'" This *ḥadīth* is included in *Kashf al-khafā'*, *Kanz al-ʿummāl*, *Iḥyā' ʿulūm al-dīn* (I:1:2), in Suyūṭī's *Jāmiʿ al-aḥādīth*, and other sources.

63. These incidents in the life of Abraham ؑ are mentioned elsewhere in the Qur'ān. The first is mentioned in 21:68-69; the two guests in 51:24-26; and the story of his son in 37:101-102.

64. This refers to the famous incident during the flight from Mecca to Madina when the Prophet ﷺ and Abū Bakr ؓ were forced to hide in a cave, referred to in 9:40: *Remember when those who disbelieved expelled him, the second of the two. Yea, the two were in the cave, when he said to his companion, "Grieve not; truly God is with us."*

65. Mentioned in *Laṭā'if al-minan*, p. 97.

one, you should use kindness and tact. You need to take into account the station in which God Most High has placed him, address him in a manner appropriate to that station, and then try to attract him to one that is even better. But if you completely ignore his station in life, he will flee from your presence and never listen to you, as experience clearly shows. And in God is all accord.

> 46. *He said, "Are you rejecting my gods, O Abraham? If you cease not, I shall surely stone you. Take leave of me for a long while!"* 47. *He said, "Peace be upon you! I shall seek forgiveness for you from my Lord. Verily He has been gracious to me.* 48. *And I withdraw myself from you and that which you call upon apart from God. And I shall call upon my Lord; it may be that in calling upon my Lord, I will not be wretched."*

[46] God, the Truth ﷻ, says [recounting Azar's answer]: *"Do you reject my gods, O Abraham?* ... Are you turning away from them in favor of others?' This is said in amazement, as if it were it were impossible to believe that a sane person would not only reject his gods but be desirous of another in their place. Then he adds a warning: *If you cease not* your exhortations, *I shall surely stone you.* That is, 'By God, if you do not stop criticizing my worship of idols, I shall cast stones at you,' though some have understood the word *arjumannaka* to mean 'I shall verbally curse you.' *Depart from me,* that is, leave me, *for a long while* (*maliyyan*), though this word can also mean "forever," for [the Arabs] referred to night and day as *malwān*....

[47] Abraham says to his father both as a farewell and a truce, answering evil with good: *"Peace be upon you!* 'I will not answer you with hatred, nor respond to you with insult or hurt, but rather *I shall seek forgiveness for you from my Lord...*' And this is what he did, as his words quoted in *Sūrat al-Shuʿarāʾ* show: *And forgive my father -- truly he was among those astray* [26:86].

[Abraham's words] may also be understood to mean 'I will ask God to accord you the chance to repent and guide you to faith.' If it is said with this meaning to a non-believer before it is clear that he will die in disbelief, then there is no question about its permissibility. What is sanctioned, however, is to pray for forgiveness for someone who the revelation has made clear is among the damned, while to ask forgiveness for someone who died in disbelief is something the mind cannot accept.[66] This is why the Prophet ﷺ said to his uncle Abū Ṭālib, "I will continue to ask forgiveness for you as long as I am not prohibited from doing so," and then he was prohibited, as has already been mentioned in our commentary of *Sūrat al-Tawba*.[67] As Abraham's words *I shall surely ask forgiveness for you* [60:4], *And forgive my father -- truly he was among those astray* [26:86], these were said when there was still hope that he might believe... *But when it became clear to him that he was an enemy of God, he repudiated him* [9:114].

Verily He has been gracious to me... [When he describes God as] *ḥafīyan*, it means, 'He is so abounding in goodness, kindness, and mercy to me in all things that He has made me accustomed to my prayers being answered,' or 'He knows me and answers me when I pray to Him.' It can also mean 'God knows best [my needs] and answers me when I call on Him.' In the dictionary, [the verb] *ḥafīya* is similar to *raḍīya*, and *iḥtifan* means "to go to extremes in showing someone generosity and honor, to express joy and happiness with him, and to ask concerning him is many times," and the one who does this is called *ḥāfin* or *ḥafīyin*.

[48] *And I shall withdraw myself from you...* That is, 'Because my counsel has no effect, I shall go far away from you and your people, *and from those whom you call upon apart from God*, and become an emigrant for my faith. *And I shall call upon my Lord*, that is, 'I shall worship Him alone,' or 'I shall pray to Him for forgiveness upon you...,' this being before he was forbidden from doing so. It has also been said to mean 'I shall pray to God for a son,' as his words elsewhere affirm, *My Lord, give to me a son from among the righteous* [37:100].

It may be that in calling upon my Lord, I will not be wretched, 'I will not be grieved and miserable in my worship of God,' or by way of implication, 'I will not be made miserable by supplicating Him as you are by supplicating idols.' Using the word *ʿasā* ("it may be") expresses humility and propriety before God and also reminds us that if God answers our prayers, it is not because He has to, but rather it is by His generosity and grace, that the real test is to reach the end our lives among those who are delivered, and that in all

66. For example, it was not allowed for the Prophet ﷺ to ask forgiveness for Abū Lahab and his wife after the revelation of *sūrah* 111.

67. Specifically, in the verse which states *It is not for the Prophet and those who believe to seek forgiveness for the idolaters, even if they be kin, after it has become clear to them that they shall be the inhabitants of Hellfire* [9:113].

of this there are surely hidden matters chosen by the One Who is Infinitely Knowing and Informed (*al-ʿAlīm al-Khabīr*).

Spiritual Allusion

Consider how Azar rejected anyone who reviled his gods, even the person who was closest to him. So how is it, O believer, that you do not reject the one who rejects your God, who worships something else besides Him, and turns away from [the way of] God's Prophet and Messenger ﷺ.[68] In fact, you must reject everything that takes you away from Him out of jealousy for your Beloved. If you look with the eye of the Inner Truth, you will find nothing to be jealous of except [your love] of God the Truth, for there is nothing in existence except the Truth, and all else besides Him is assuredly false.

The one who withdraws from everything besides God, and makes his Guardian Lord his sole direction, will never be grieved in his search and his efforts. Rather, God will raise him up to the mysteries of His Essence and the lights of His Attributes until he ceases to see in existence anything other than the One, Alone, the Unique and Eternally Besought. And in God is all success.

> 49. *So when he had withdrawn from them and that which they called upon apart from God, We bestowed upon him Isaac and Jacob, and each We made a prophet.* 50. *And We bestowed of Our Mercy on them, and We granted them lofty honor on the tongue of truth.*

[49] God, the Truth ﷻ, says: *When* Abraham ﷺ *had withdrawn from them and that which they called upon apart from God*, and had left Kūthā in the land of Iraq and migrated to Shām[69] where he dwelt for a time, *We bestowed upon him Isaac...*, his son, *and Jacob*, his grandson. This was after he had fathered Ishmael with Hajar, a slave girl who had been given to Abraham's wife Sarah, and who in turn, gave her to Abraham. When Hajar became pregnant with Ishmael, Sarah grew jealous of her, so [Abraham] went forth with her and her baby and took them to [the valley of] Mecca, and that

68. Here he is referring to avoiding too much contact with worldly people.

69. Kūtha is now an archaeological site known as Tell Ibrahīm, located in the Babil province of central Iraq, near the ruins of the ancient city of Babylon. Shām currently refers to the entire Levant (Syria, Iran, some of Iraq, Lebanon, some of Turkey, Palestine, and Israel). In its use above, it is roughly equivalent to Syria, Lebanon, and Palestine.

is how it first came to be settled. Later, Sarah became pregnant with Isaac, and it was to him that Jacob would be born. They are mentioned in particular because both of them had been with him in his land, and Isaac had worked by his side, so God's grace to him through them both was great.

And it may be that he was blessed with Isaac and Jacob after he had separated himself [from the idolators] as a way of showing the greatness of God's grace to him compared to [the trial] of leaving kith and kin behind. Moreover, both his sons were a tree of the prophets, both had children and grandchildren, both had a great role to play, and both were granted many descendants.

And each We made a prophet. These words may be understood to mean either that both (Isaac and Jacob) were themselves prophets or else that 'from each of them, God made a prophet and a messenger.'

[50] *And We bestowed of Our Mercy on them... Our Mercy* (raḥmatunā) here means prophethood, and to say this after having said *and each We made a prophet* is a reminder that all the prophets 🌷 were brought by way of God's mercy and grace. Some *tafsīrs* state that mercy may also mean wealth, children, and ease of provision, and others state that it means scripture. In general, however, it refers to all manner of good: the goodness of faith and goodness of this world. *And (We) ordained for them* lofty honor, exalted by the people of (three) faiths who mention their names with praise and honor. This, in fact, was in answer to Abraham's prayer: *And make for me faithful renown among later generations* [26:84].

As for the words *the tongue of truth* (lisān al-ṣidq), for the Arabs, "tongue" means speech, and so in this context it means that they were worthy of the praise given them, praise that has not disappeared in all the years between their time and ours, and through all the changing dynasties, peoples and beliefs. And God Most High knows best.

Spiritual Allusion

Anyone who withdraws from people (al-khalq) to be alone with the True Sovereign (al-malik al-ḥaqq), seeking a vision of the Truth, will surely be flooded with sacred gifts, God-given mysteries, and knowledge which comes from the Divine Presence (al-ʿulūm al-la-

duniyya), such being the fruits of meditation with a clear heart.[70] In the Ḥikam [12], it is written, "Nothing benefits the heart more than a spiritual retreat wherein it enters the domain of meditation." Junayd ؓ said, "The noblest and most sublime of assemblies (*majālis*) is to sit in meditation in the domain of Oneness." And Shaykh Abū'l-Ḥasan ؓ said, "The fruits of a spiritual retreat are four gifts: the lifting of the veil, the descent of Divine Mercy, the realization of love, and a truthful tongue, as God Most High says, *So when he had withdrawn from them and that which they called upon apart from God, We bestowed upon him Isaac and Jacob, and each We made a prophet. And We bestowed of Our Mercy on them, and We granted them lofty honour on the tongue of truth.*"[71] One of the sages said, "When you mix with people, you want to ingratiate yourself with them, and when you ingratiate yourself with them, you will be inclined towards affectation before them, and if you incline towards affectation before them, you will fall into what they have fallen and perish as they have perished."[72]

A certain Sufi said, "I asked one of the great saints[73] who had withdrawn from the world to worship God, 'What is the way to realization?' He said, 'Do not look at people, for looking at them is darkness.' I answered, 'But I have to!' He said, 'Then do not listen to their talk, for listening to their talk hardens the heart.' I said, 'But I have to!' He said, 'Then do not have dealings with them, because dealings with them will bring you loss and estrangement.' I said, 'I live among them, so I have to deal with them.' He said, 'Then do not try to find your peace amongst them, for to do so is ruin.' I said, 'If only that were possible!' To which he replied, 'O man! You look at those who are lost in play, listen to the talk of the ignorant, deal with artifice and vanity, and try to find peace among the perished? And yet you want to find sweetness in obedience to God and you want your heart to be with God? What illusion! That will never happen!' And so saying, he disappeared from my sight."[74]

---

70. The adjective *ṣāfiya*, clear, and its nominal form, *al-ṣafā'*, clarity, along with its opposite, *al-kadar*, turbidity or murkiness, was possibly first used to speak of water or any liquid through which light may pass. The notion being expressed is that a heart which withdraws from the mundane world and its distractions is more easily infused with God's light.

71. Ibn Sabbāgh, *Durrat al-asrār*, p. 26.

72. This saying appears in *Iḥyā' 'ulūm al-dīn*, II:6, p. 274, and elsewhere.

73. Literally, "one of the substitutes" (*al-abdāl*).

74. Quoted in Abū Ṭālib al-Makkī, *Qūt al-qulūb*, v. 1, p.181.

Al-Qushayrī said "When the people of spiritual effort wish to safe-guard their hearts from base thoughts, they stop looking upon those who are pleased with the world. This is one of the greatest principles in their spiritual efforts ..." And [Abū Ṭālib al-Makkī] said in *Qūt*, "An aspirant is not sincere until he finds a sweetness, joy, and strength in seclusion that he does not find in public, until his most intimate moments are in solitude, his rest is in spiritual retreat, and his best actions are those which he conceals."[75]

To withdraw from people and to flee their company is a condition for an aspirant at the beginning [of the path], but when he has been granted stability in his consciousness of God, and his heart has found intimacy with the Beloved Sovereign, and he has tasted the sweetness of the spirit, then he should mix with people and strengthen his contemplation, for at the point, they will increase his gnosis and he will be broadened by them. He will see them as lights of God's Self-revelations and flowers he is tending, from whom he gathers the sweetness of perceptions. This is what the shaykh of our shaykhs, Sīdī [ʿAbd al-Raḥmān] al-Majdhūb, meant when he sang:

> People are blossoms and I gather from among them.
> They are the greatest veil and the entrance is through them.

And in the lines of al-Shushtarī,

> The road to Our presence is through the middle of the crowd.[76]

And in God is all success.

Then God mentions the story of Moses ﷺ.

> 51. *And remember Moses in the Book. Verily he was pure, and he was a messenger, a prophet.* 52. *We called out to him from the right side of the Mount, and brought him near in intimate discourse.* 53. *And We bestowed upon him, from Our Mercy, his brother, Aaron, a prophet.*

[51] God, the Truth ﷻ, says: *And remember Moses in the Book. Verily he was pure.* 'Pure' (*mukhliṣan*)[77] in this context means he was a

75. Al-Makkī, op. cit. v. 1, p. 178.

76. That is, 'If you want to find the saintly, look for them in the throng of humanity.'

77. *Mukhliṣ* is sometimes translated as "a sincere person" and *sūrah* 112, *Sūrat al-Ikhlāṣ*, is often called in English "Sincerity." The root KhLṢ means to be clear,

monotheist whose worship was pure of associating others with God and also pure of ostentation before people. He *surrendered his face to God* [2:112, 4:124] and purified his soul from all others besides God. [In some recitations], *mukhliṣ* is read *mukhlaṣ*, meaning someone whom God Most High has made pure. Al-Qushayrī said, "He was wholly for God, had no other direction, and nothing turned him away from God."

And he was a messenger, a prophet... God Most High sent him to humanity and then he prophesized to them concerning Him, and this is why the verse mentions him first as being a messenger (*rasūl*), even though it is higher and more particular being a prophet (*nabīy*).[78]

[52] *We called out to him from the right side of the mountain...* The word *Ṭūr* refers to a mountain between Egypt and the land of Midian.[79] *From the right side* means from the direction that was on his right عليه السلام and also that the tree was on the side of the mountain to Moses' right عليه السلام. But the word *ayman* (right) may also mean "blessed" (*maymūn*), and so the verse could also be understood to say, "from the side of the mountain that was blessed."[80] *We called out to him* means he heard the words of God from that direction.

And [We] brought him near in intimate discourse ...That is, 'We spoke to him without an intermediary' for to be brought near means in nobility and honor, like someone a king brings near and chooses to speak to personally.[81] The word *najīyan* ("*intimate discourse*") is derived from *al-najwat*, "an elevated or raised place," and so some *tafsīr*s state that the verse means, "We raised him up from heaven to heaven until he heard the scratching of the Pen writing in the tablets of destiny."

[53] *And We bestowed upon him, from Our Mercy* (*min raḥmatinā*), *his*

---

pure, unadulterated, to be free of impurity, and can also mean to pay a debt (and be clear or finished of it).

78. Ibn ʿAjība is referring to the fact that *rasūl* can also be understood as "one who was sent."

79. *Ṭūr* is an ancient name for mountain. It occurs in ten places in the Qur'ān, including as the name of the fifty-second *sūrah*.

80. See footnote 1 concerning the linguistic connection between "right" and "blessed."

81. Both this comment and the explanation of *from the right side* are an attempt to clarify how God, Who is beyond place and time, can nonetheless be described with language that seems to speak of physical location.

brother Aaron. That is, 'for the sake of Our mercy and kindness to him,' or 'as a portion of Our mercy,' he was granted his brother Aaron as a helper and supporter. This was also in answer to his prayer, *And give me a helper from my people, Aaron, my brother* [20:29-30]... For Aaron was older than he, and also a prophet and messenger who would share the task of delivering the message. And God Most High knows better.

Spiritual Allusion

Just as God described His intimate friend (*khalīlahu*) as having utter veracity, here He describes the one to whom He spoke (*kalīmahu*) as having complete purity of intention (*ikhlāṣ*). Both these [qualities] are conditions for reaching the state of the elect (*al-khuṣūṣiyya*), whether it pertains to prophethood or to sainthood. Without sincerity, there is no journey, and without a pure intention, there is no arrival.

The essential meaning of *ikhlāṣ* is that we purify our interactions with the Creator from [wanting anything in return from] creation, and this may be at three levels: the lowest, the middle, and the highest. At the lowest level, we accomplish worship for the sake of God alone, but still hope to receive in return some sort of benefit in this world, such as ample provision, or the protection of our bodies and wealth. Such is what *ikhlāṣ* means for the generality of the faithful, and it is still a form of *ikhlāṣ* because deeds are not done for the eyes of people. The middle level is that we worship God with totality in hopes of being given some sort of recompense in the Next World such as the maidens [of Paradise] and [its] palatial abodes. The highest level, however, is that we accomplish worship because it is part of our being God's servants and it is right conduct before the grandeur of the Divine. We do it without regard for either Paradise or Hell, this world or the Next, and if we nonetheless cherish the gift of Paradise, it is because there we will be granted the [supreme] vision. As Ibn al-Fāriḍ ﵁ said:

> My yearning is not for the bliss of Heaven
> except that I shall see You there.

If we realize the station of complete *ikhlāṣ*, we become among those who are brought near in the place of intimate discourse, witnessing, and communion. And in God is all success.

54. *And remember Ishmael in the Book. Verily he was true to the promise, and he was a messenger, a prophet. 55. He used to bid his people to prayer and almsgiving, and he was pleasing to his Lord.*

[54] God, the Truth 🙵, says: *And remember Ishmael in the Book.* The fact that God speaks of him separately from his father and his brother shows a special attention to his story, and the words, *Verily he was true to the promise*, explain why. It is related that Ishmael 🙵 once promised to meet a man at a certain place, and he came to that place and waited for a day and a night—some *tafsīrs* say three days—and when the man finally got there on the last day, Ishmael said to him, "I have been here since yesterday." Al-Kalbī said, "He waited an entire year," but this seems very unlikely. Ibn ʿAṭiyya said, "According to al-Naqqāsh, our Prophet 🙵 did something similar to this before his prophetic mission began." This is also related by al-Tirmidhī and others, who say that it was when he was involved in trade and commerce.[82]

Al-Qushayrī said, "[Ishamel] had promised his father to be patient, even with prospect of being offered in sacrifice, and he remained so until the moment the ransom appeared.[83] Keeping a promise is evidence of keeping the covenant." Ibn ʿAṭāʾ said, "He promised his father that he would be patient, saying *You will find me, God willing, among those who are patient* [37:102], and he kept that promise." This was about his being made a sacrifice, a question which will be examined later, God willing.

*And he was a messenger, a prophet...*Ishmael was a messenger to the Jurhum and those whom they ruled, and brought them prophecy of the unseen.[84] His descendants continued to follow the law he brought until it was altered by ʿAmr b. Luḥayy al-Khuzāʿī, the

---

82. Before he was called to prophecy, the Prophet Muḥammad 🙵 spent several years conducting trade through the caravans belonging to his wife Khadīja 🙵.

83. That is, the ram. According to Muslim tradition, the son whom Abraham was commanded to sacrifice was Ishmael 🙵. The Quranic account of this event also differs from the Biblical version (Genesis 22) in that Abraham tells his son in advance what he has dreamed: *When he had become old enough to partake of his father's endeavors, Abraham said, "O my son! I see while dreaming that I am to sacrifice you. So consider, what do you see?"* And Ishmael 🙵 responds with the words quoted in the text.

84. The Banu Jurhum were the Arab tribe, originally from Yemen, who had been the guardians of the Kaʿba before the Quraysh and among whom Ishmael grew up.

person who brought idols to Mecca[85] which continued to be worshipped until our Prophet, Muḥammad ﷺ, destroyed them and brought his purified law.

[55] *(Ishmael) used to bid his people to prayer and almsgiving...* He began with his own family, concentrating on those who, after his own soul, were closest to him and most important. Thus does God Most High say, *and admonish your nearest relations* [26:214], ... *Enjoin upon your family the Prayer* [20:132], and *deliver yourselves and your families from the fire* [66:6]. By beginning with his family, he intended the good of all, for his family was a model who supported him in his calling. It is also said that the word *ahlihi* ("his family") may be understood to mean "his community," for the prophets ﷺ are fathers to their people. *And he was one with whom his Lord was well pleased* because of the virtues God mentions. And God Most High knows best.

Spiritual Allusion

God ﷻ describes His Prophet Ishmael ﷺ with virtues that made him pleasing to his Lord and if we are able to realize these same virtues, we too will be pleasing to our Lord. The first is to keep our promises; the second is to be honest in our speech, which is includes keeping promises, and the third is to encourage people towards goodness. Keeping promises is one of the traits of the virtuous, and God Most High praises and encourages people to do so in His words, *And those who keep their pledges when they pledge.* [2:177], and also, *And fulfill the covenant of God when you have made a covenant* [16:91]. Conversely, breaking promises is a trait of the hypocrite, as the words of the Prophet ﷺ attest: "The signs of the hypocrite are three: when he speaks, he lies; when he makes a promise, he breaks it; when he is given a trust, he betrays it."[86] Breaking a promise is malicious if that was the intention at the moment it was made, or if it was made intending to fall short in fulfilling it. But if someone makes a promise intending to keep it, and then is prevented from doing so by circumstances, he is not at fault. This is especially true concerning the people of effacement for they themselves are

85. In *Kitāb al-aṣnām*, this man is identified as the chieftain of the Khuzāʿī tribe and a soothsayer-priest (*kāhin*). It is recorded in that same source that he had an oracle among the jinn who ordered him to dig into the sands of Juddah where he would find stone idols buried and then to take these to Mecca. See p. 54, ff.

86. *Ḥadīth* found in Bukhārī and Muslim as well as numerous other sources.

not in control of whether they are bound to something or not. They are acted upon: the reins of their camels are in the hands of Another and they look at every moment towards what God is doing with them. People such as these are not held to account for being bound or unbound to anything. In the sight of God, they are like children being watched over in what they do, which is why they say, "The Sufis are children being brought up by God." So beware of condemning God's friends for something you might see them do. Rather, search for the best interpretation, which is what I have just mentioned to you. This will come by experience and taste, and God Most High knows better.

Then God mentions His prophet Idrīs.

56. *And remember Idrīs in the Book. Verily he was a person of truth, a prophet.*

57. *And We raised him to a sublime station.*

[56] God, the Truth, says: *And remember Idrīs in the Book. Verily he was a person of truth, a prophet.* Idrīs was the grandson of Seth and great grandfather of Noah, for Noah was the son of Lamech (*Lāmaka*), son of Methuselah (*Mattūshalakh*), son of Enoch (*Akhnūkh*), who is [also known as] Idrīs. His name comes from the same root as the word *dars* (a lesson or study), because of how much he studied what had been revealed to him and also because of his abundant remembrance of God Most High.

It has been related that Idrīs was a tailor and that he would not begin or end a stitch without invoking God. According to the commentary of al-Sanūsī, the Devil once came to him as he was sewing to test him by means of a pistachio nut and said, "Is your Lord able to put the entire world into this nut?" Idrīs answered, "God is able to place the entire world into the eye of this needle," and then pricked the Devil's eye with it. Ibn Wahb said, "He called his people to *Lā ilāha illā Allāh* [before Noah] but they rejected him and were destroyed, and in the *ḥadīth* related by Abū Dharr, he is called a messenger." He reconciles this with what is said to Noah in the *ḥadīth* of Intercession[87]—"You were the first of the Messengers"—by explaining that the scripture [revealed to Idrīs] was only for his

87. The *ḥadīth* of intercession (*ḥadīth al-shafāʿa*) is found in various versions in Bukhārī, Muslim, and most of the other principal collections. It describes people going from prophet to prophet on the Day of Judgment looking for the one who can intercede on their behalf before God. When they come of Noah, they say,

own people, as was the case for Hūd and Ṣāliḥ, as well as for Adam and Seth. (Adam) was sent to his folk that he might teach them laws and faith and that they not be disbelievers, and Seth followed him in this." According to al-Fāsī's *Ḥāshiya*, "Concerning Noah ﷺ, what is most apparent to me is that he was the first messenger, not in an absolute sense, but rather the first of the people of resolve."[88] And Ibn ʿAṭiyya says, "What is generally agreed is that Idrīs ﷺ was not sent as a messenger, but rather as a prophet only. This was also the view adopted by Ibn Baṭāl in order to avoid dispute and is supported by what we have already mentioned."[89]

In short, the consensus is that Idrīs was a messenger to his own people. It is said that God revealed to him thirty pages of scripture, that he was the first to write with a pen, that he knew the science of the stars and of calculation, and also how to sew clothes. It has also been said that he was the first prophet sent to the people of the earth.

Describing him, God Most High says: *He was a person of truth; a prophet....*

[57] *And We raised him to a sublime station...* That is, to the nobility of prophethood and proximity to God Most High. It has also been said that this refers to a high degree by the goodness with which he is mentioned in the world, similar to God's words concerning our Prophet ﷺ, *And did We not elevate your mention?* [94:4]. Some *tafsīrs* say that *a sublime station* means paradise, and some that it means the fourth heaven, and this latter is correct.

The circumstances of Idrīs' ascension were related by Kaʿb who said that one day Idrīs was walking down the road to fulfill some need, and as the glaring heat of the sun got harder and harder for him to bear, he said, 'O Lord. I have been walking [beneath this sun] for one day, but what of the one who bears it on a journey of five hundred years in a single day? Dear God, lighten for him its burden and remove from him some of its heat!' and when the

---

"O Noah, you were the first of the messengers to the earth, and God called you a grateful servant...."

88. "The people of resolve" (*ahlu 'l-ʿazmi*), or more commonly "those endowed with resolve" (*ūla 'l-ʿazmi*), is an expression mentioned in Q. 46:35, and is generally understood to refer to the prophets who brought major revelations to humanity: Noah, Abraham, Moses, Jesus, and Muḥammad (AHMS).

89. The passage beginning, "according to Ibn Wahb..." is also a quote from al-Fāsī's *al-Ḥāshiya* on the *tafsīr* Jilālayn, v. 1, p. 477.

angel [charged with bearing the sun] began the next day, he found it lighter and its heat lessened and did not know why.[90] He said, 'O Lord, You have charged me with bearing the sun, but what have You decreed concerning it?' And God answered him, 'Truly My servant Idrīs asked Me to lighten for you its burden and its heat, and I answered his prayer.' The angel then said, 'O Lord, let us come to know one another.' So God allowed this, such that Idrīs came to him and said, 'I have been told that you are considered the noblest of the angels by the angel of death, so intercede for me that my term might be delayed and I might add to my gratitude and worship.' The angel answered him, 'God will not grant any soul reprieve when its term has come.' Idrīs answered, 'I know that, but it would delight my soul.' The angel then said, 'Yes,' and bore him upon his wings and it has been related that it was there that he died and then his spirit was returned to him after some time and so that he is alive in the fourth heaven.[91] This is a story, and God knows best its truth, and with God is all accord.

Spiritual Allusion

Your rank and standing with God are in proportion to the purity of your heart and the extent to which you turn towards the Most Generous Giver... Thus, in accordance with your direction and turning is your union and standing.

> The greater the effort, the higher the station.
> Who would reach to the heights keeps vigils at night.
> Do you wish for honor and then sleep the whole night?
> Let those who seek pearls dive into the sea.

One of the Sufis also said, "He who serves God on the carpet of nearness will surely be raised to the Sacred Presence." And in God is all accord.

90. A *ḥadīth* found in Ṭabarānī, *al-Kabīr* [8:7705] states that there are nine angels charged with bearing the sun and in a version of this *ḥadīth* found in al-Suyūṭī's treatise on angels, *al-Ḥabā'ik fi'l-Malā'ik* (*ḥadīth* 432), the number is seven. It is also reported that Maʿrūf al-Karkhī said to some people who were delaying the prayer, "The angel bearing the sun runs and does not stop, so when do you want to stand and offer the prayer?" See *Majālis wa jawāhir al-ʿilm*, Abū Bakr al-Dīnūrī (d. 333/944).

91. In the long *ḥadīth* in Bukhari and Muslim which recounts the Prophet's ﷺ *miʿrāj*, when he is taken to the fourth heaven, he finds there Idrīs ﵇ whom he greets and who returns his greeting.

Then God praises them all.

58. *They are those whom God has blessed among the prophets of the progeny of Adam, and of those whom We carried with Noah, and of the progeny of Abraham and Israel, and of those whom We guided and chose. When the signs of the All-Merciful were recited to them, they would fall down, prostrate and weeping.*

[58] God, the Truth ﷻ, says: *They are those*, mentioned in this noble *sūrah, whom God has blessed* with myriad blessings, both worldly and religious. *The prophets of the progeny of Adam* were Idrīs and Noah (may peace be upon them both). Those *We carried with Noah*, meaning his posterity, was Abraham, descended from Shām, son of Noah. *The progeny of Abraham* were Ishmael, Isaac, and Jacob. And [the progeny of] *Israel*, that is, of Jacob, were Moses, Aaron, John, and Jesus. [In the mention of Jesus ﷺ] is scriptural evidence that lineage can be traced through the mother [as well as the father]. *And those* means all others *whom We guided* to the truth *and chose* for prophecy.

When the signs of the All-Merciful were recited to them, they would fall down, prostrate and weeping. This describes their profound humility before God Most High even while they had been granted the highest human station and state, the noblest lineage, perfect character, and closest proximity to God ﷻ. *When the signs of the All-Merciful were recited to them* may mean either at the moment the verses were revealed to them or when they heard them recited by someone else, as when the Prophet ﷺ said, "I love to hear (the Qur'ān) recited by another,"[92] and wept when he heard the verse, *How will it be when We bring forth a witness from every community, and We bring you as a witness against these?* [4:41]. All the prophets ﷺ were like him: when the verses of the All-Merciful were recited to them, they would fall down prostrate and weeping. He said ﷺ, "Recite the Qur'ān and weep, and if you cannot weep, then try to weep," and it is related that ʿUmar ؓ once recited *sūrah Mary*, prostrated (at this verse), and then said, "Here is the prostration, but where are the tears?"[93]

One of [the learned] said, "When you make the prostration associated with a verse, ask God [in that prostration] for something

92. In Muslim and Bukhārī.

93. Related by Bayhaqī in *Shuʿab al-Īmān*, in *Kanz al-ʿummāl*, and in *al-Bukā'* by Ibn Abī al-Dunyā.

that accords with that verse." For this verse, for example, it might be, 'Dear God, make me among the servants You have blessed and guided, those who prostrate to You and who weep as they recite Your signs," while for the verse of prostration in *Sūrat al-Isrā'*,[94] it might be, "Dear God, make me among those who are humble before You, who glorify and praise You. I seek refuge from being one of the haughty who are too proud to follow Your commandments..." and so forth.[95] And it is conveyed in a *ḥadīth* that [the Prophet ﷺ would] say, "My face is prostrate before the One who created it, and formed it, and brought forth its hearing and sight by His power and strength... Dear God, write for me [by this prostration] reward, and remove from me sin. Make it a treasure for me in Your presence, and accept it of me as You accepted it from Your servant David ﷺ"[96] And God Most High knows better.

Spiritual Allusion

God Most High praises those blessed people because when they heard the speech of the Beloved, they were humbled and their hearts were touched. This is the first stage of love. Above it is the joy of hearing the Beloved's speech from a place that is near, and above that is the joy of witnessing the One who speaks. Here, all

---

94. Q. 17:109.

95. The verses of prostration, which number 14 according to some schools of jurisprudence, or 15 according to others, are those in which the act of prostration is either mentioned with praise or enjoined. It may be that the Shaykh is recalling here the words of Abū Ṭālib al-Makkī in *Qūt al-qulūb:* "When the servant prostrates at a verse of prostration, he should ask his Lord for whatever goodness is referred to by the verse and seek refuge from whatever evil is mentioned in the verse. Such is the way of the learned who are beloved to God [when they recite] the Qur'ān ..." He then gives examples of what such supplications would be similar to those quoted above. [I:16:94]

96. The first of these two is the well-known supplication recorded in the *sunnan* collections of Tirmidhī and Abū Dawūd, the *musnad* of Imām Aḥmad, and many other sources. The second is related in a *ḥadīth* recorded by al-Ṭabarānī in *al-Awsaṭ* and elsewhere in the words of Abū Saʿīd al-Khudrī: "I saw in a dream that I was beneath a tree and it was as if the tree were reciting *Ṣād* [Q. 38] and when it came to the verse of prostration, it prostrated and said [the supplication quoted above]. When I awoke, I went to the Prophet ﷺ and related to him my dream. He asked, 'And did you prostrate, O Abū Saʿīd?' I said no. He said, 'You had more reason to prostrate than the tree.' Then he recited *Sūra Ṣād*, and when he came to the verse of prostration, he made the supplication that the tree had made in its prostration."

weeping ends, for the worshipper has entered the Heaven of gnosis, and in heaven there is no weeping.

Also, it is common at the beginning of the way for the heart to be tender and easily moved by sudden influxes of spiritual inspirations and states. Over time, however, it gets strengthened and solidifies to the extent that these no longer affect it. This is what Abū Bakr 🕮 was referring to when he saw people weeping as they listened to the Qur'ān and said, "Thus did we use to be, then our hearts grew hard."[97] Calling stability "hardness" was out of humility and in order to conceal the matter. God praises those noble people for their weeping because it is a ladder that leads to something higher. And God Most High knows better.

Then God speaks of the opposite of those blessed people:

59. *Then they were succeeded by a generation who neglected prayer and followed base desires. So they shall meet [the reward of] error, 60. Save for those who repent and believe and work righteousness. It is they who shall enter the Garden, and they shall not be wronged in the least: 61. Gardens of Eden, those which the All-Merciful promised His servants in the Unseen. Verily His Promise shall come to pass. 62. They shall hear no idle talk therein and therein they shall have their provision, morning and evening. 63. That is the Garden which We shall bequeath to those among Our servants who were reverent.*

[59] God, the Truth 🕮, says: *Then they were succeeded...* Those noble people *were succeeded by a* wicked *generation (khalfun)*. If this noun is pronounced *khalfun*, it carries a negative connotation, while if it is pronounced *khalafun*, it carries a positive one. The posterity they left were bad people who *neglected prayer*, either by not offering it all together or by delaying it past its time, and *who followed base desires*. These included drinking wine, making lawful marriage to [two sisters] of the same father, and a variety of other sinful practices. 'Alī 🕮 is reported to have said, "They were a people given to decadence, who rode on plush saddles, and dressed ostentatiously." The word *manḍūd* [used to describe their saddles] literally means "inlaid with jewels and gold." But al-Mujāhid said, "This refers to a people who will come when the Hour is near and when the good and righteous of Muḥammad's 🕮 community

---

97. See also our translation of Ibn 'Ajība's commentary on verse 16, *Sūrat al-Ḥadīd* (Iron), 57:16 in *The Immense Ocean*.

are gone. They will copulate with one another in the streets and alleyways."

So they shall meet [the reward of] error (ghayyan). Ghayy denotes any form of evil, just as *rashād* denotes any form of goodness.[98] Ibn ʿAbbās ﷺ said, "*Al-Ghayy* is a river in hell. All the other rivers of hell seek refuge from its heat. It is prepared for the habitual fornicator, the alcoholic, the usurer, [the one who] brings misery to parents,[99] the one who bears false witness, and the woman who tells her husband she is pregnant with his child when it is really the child of another."

[60] Save *for those who repent and believe and work righteousness...* These words show that the previous verse refers to the disbelievers. If they repent, have faith, and accomplish the good, they *shall enter the Garden* by [God's absolute] promise...[100] *They shall not be wronged in the least*: the recompense for whatever good they did will not be diminished in the least, which means that once they have rectified their relationship with God, the state of denial and disbelief they had been in before will not harm them or diminish their reward.

[61] *Gardens of Eden...* The word *ʿadnin* (Eden) literally means "a dwelling place" because those who enter them will dwell therein forever. [Such are the gardens] *which the All-Merciful has promised to His servants in the unseen*, 'unseen' because [God's servants] are now veiled from [these gardens]. They have never seen them but have believed in them purely from what has been conveyed [by revelation]. *Bi'l-ghayb* (*in the unseen*) may also be understood to mean that the gardens are absent from them, not present.[101] Connecting this to God's Name *the All-Merciful* is a reminder that both His promise and recompense are purely by way of His infinite mercy. *Verily His promise shall come to pass*, it will surely be fulfilled for whomsoever

---

98. *Ghayy* literally means "error," the opposite of which is *rashād*, "guidance" or "direction."

99. *Al-ʿuqūq*. Ibn al-Farrā mentions that when asked to define goodness towards parents (*birr al-wālidayn*), Ḥasan, the son of ʿAlī (may God be pleased with them both), said, "It is to spend generously upon them from your wealth and to obey them in what they tell you to do unless it entails disobedience (to God)." Then he was asked, "And what does causing them misery (*al-ʿuqūq*) mean?" He answered, "It is to abandon them and deprive them of support."

100. Ibn ʿAjība notes here that there is a second recitation of this verse in which the verb is pronounced *yudkhalūna*: "They will be brought into the Garden."

101. *Al-ghayb*, often translated as "the unseen," also means "absent."

it was promised. It has also been said that the grammatical form of the word *ma'tiyya* ("something that is coming to pass") means that it is coming without doubt, or that it has already been fulfilled.

[62] *They shall hear no idle talk therein.* That is, they shall hear no worthless chatter. This is a way of saying that the people of Heaven do not engage in chatter and also reminds us that a servant of God should also avoid it in this world as much as possible and follow the Prophet's words, "One of the best ways a person can practice Islam is to avoid what does not concern him,"[102] which includes speech. *But only "Peace,"* that is, they will not hear empty talk, but rather the salutations of peace bade them by the angels, or the salutations of peace they bid one another.

*Therein they shall have their provision, morning and evening...*That is, in proportion to what morning and evening mean in this world, for in heaven there is neither day nor night, but rather an eternal brilliance and light. Al-Qurṭubī said, "Their night is the lowering of the veils and closing of the gates; their day is the lifting of the veils and opening of the gates."[103] And al-Qushayrī said, "This verse strikes a comparison to those who are granted ease in this world and is a way of saying that [the people of Paradise] are without need and are at ease at all times..."

[63] *That is the Garden...* This simple nominative sentence expresses the grandeur of the Garden and the distinction of those who dwell in it. The demonstrative "that," which normally denotes distance, here expresses sublimity and loftiness. The verse thus means, 'that Garden described by those majestic qualities is the one *We shall bequeath to those among Our servants* who were reverent for the sake of God by obeying Him and avoiding transgressions ...We give them this Garden to enjoy eternally by way of their reverence,' like wealth that has been bequeathed to its inheritors for their benefit. Inheritance is the strongest form of ownership since it is a gift that cannot be undone, returned, or invalidated. It has also been said that the reverent will inherit the abodes [that would have been oc-

102. Recorded in Muslim and many other principle sources with the exception of Bukhārī.

103. In his *tafsīr* of this verse [19:62], al-Qurṭurbī says, "The learned say that there is neither night nor day in heaven. Rather, they are in eternal light, but know the length of the night by the lowering of the veils and closing of the gates and know the length of the day by the raising of the veils and the opening of the gates."

cupied by] the people of hell had they believed and obeyed... And God Most High knows better.

Spiritual Allusion

Then they were succeeded by a generation... until the end of the verse, relates to someone whose forefathers were among the righteous but who deviated from their way, lost his religion, waxed proud towards the poor and weak among the Muslims, followed the designs of his ego and its desires, and thus acquired the traits of the arrogant. If he adds to those faults pride of ancestry, rank, or wealth, then he is truly someone drowned in delusion and error, someone of whom the poet's lines ring true:

> If they promise you goodness or make a vow,
> They break it after swearing to its truth,
> And yet about their ancestry they wax proud.
> How excellent were those ancestors of old,
> But how wicked the descendants who followed.

Those who repent are those who return to the way of their forefathers, the way of beneficial knowledge, good works, and humility before both the saintly and the sinful. Then they shall be in the company of their forefathers in the Garden of adornment or of gnosis which the All-Merciful has promised to His chosen servants *in the unseen* which then became for them visible and perceived. *Verily His promise shall come to pass. They shall hear no idle talk therein*, for the Divine Presence is sanctified from idle talk. *But only "Peace!"* because of the peace which fills their hearts, *And therein they shall have their provision* of knowledge, mysteries, and inner gifts at every moment and time. None shall inherit this garden except those who stay clear of what is other than God and devote themselves totally to their Lord and Protector. And in God is all success.

[It has been related that] when the revelation stopped coming to the Prophet ﷺ for a period of time, he said, "O Gabriel! What has kept you from visiting us more often?"[104] and then the verses which follow were revealed:

> 64. *We descend not, save by the Command of your Lord. To Him belongs that which is before us and that which is behind us, and whatsoever lies between that, and your Lord is not forgetful,* 65.

---

104. This is recorded in Bukhārī, *K. al-Tawḥīd*.

> *The Lord of the heavens and the earth and whatsoever is between them. So worship Him and be steadfast in His worship. Do you know any who can be named alongside Him?*

The context of these verses is that God, the Truth ﷻ, has related the stories of the prophets and what came to pass after them, and [the angel] Gabriel ﵇ was the bearer of revelation to them. Here it is explained that [Gabriel's] descent was not by his choice.

[64] God, the Truth ﷻ, says, relating the words of Gabriel ﵇: "*We descend not...*" This is generally understood to be the speech of Gabriel ﵇ to the Prophet ﷺ and refers to the lapse in the revelation when the Prophet ﷺ was asked concerning the companions of the Cave, Dhū'l-Qarnayn, and the Spirit (*al-Rūḥ*), and did not know how to respond. He had hoped that the answer to those questions would come to him by way of revelation, but it ceased for forty days, according to ʿIkrima (or for twelve or fifteen nights according to al-Mujāhid). This distressed the Prophet ﷺ greatly, until he finally said, "O Gabriel! I long to see you!" and Gabriel responded, "And I long to see you even more, but I am only a servant subject to God's command. When I am brought forth, revelation is sent down, and when it ceases, I am kept away." Then God revealed this verse and also the totality of *Sūrat al-Ḍuḥā*."[105]

The word *al-tanazzul*, besides meaning "descent" in a general sense, can also mean "a gradual descent." So the exact sense of the verse is 'We do not descend time after time except by God's command and according to His wisdom.'

It has also been said that these are the words of the blessed to one another in their exuberance and joy upon entering Paradise, and that they mean, 'We have not come to dwell (*natanazzal*) in these gardens except by the command and kindness of God Most High. To Him belong all matters—their past, present, and future. All that we have found and all that we will find is by way of His infinite kindness and grace.' Understood in this sense, its relation to the verses which precede it (about Paradise) is clear.

To Him belongs whatsoever is in front of us and whatsoever is behind

105. This incident is mentioned in many of the oldest books of *tafsīr*. It was also the circumstance in which two verses of *Sūrat al-Kahf* were revealed—*And say not of anything, "Surely, I shall do it tomorrow," save that God wills...* [18:23-24], which is the scriptural origin of why the expression, "*In shā' Allāh*" (If God so wills), is so much a part of the language Muslims use when speaking of the future.

us, and whatsoever lies between that. To God belongs every time and place, and so 'we do not move from one place to another, nor descend at one particular time rather than another, except by God's command and will.' According to al-Muqātil, *whatsoever is in front of us* are the matters of this world, *whatsoever is behind us* are the matters of the Next World, *and whatsoever lies between that* refers to the time between the two Trumpet Blasts, which has been said to be forty years.[106] It has also been said that *whatsoever is in front of us* means 'after death,' *whatsoever is behind us* means 'before God created us,' and *whatsoever lies between that* means the days of our lives on earth. The knowledge of all that belongs to God.

And your Lord is not forgetful. [Addressed to the Prophet ﷺ], this verse means 'God has not abandoned you. He is not unaware of your situation, nor has He forgotten to send the revelation to you, for such a thing is impossible to believe of God. Gabriel ﵇ brought no revelation only because there was no commandment from God, according to His perfect wisdom, and is neither neglect nor abandonment as the disbelievers claim.' To join God's Name *Rabb* (Lord) to the possessive particle *ka* ("your") referring to the Prophet ﷺ, both honors him and indicates this order's sublime source.

[65] The words of God Most High, (He is) *the Lord of the heavens and the earth and whatsoever is between them,* explain why forgetfulness or neglect is impossible to believe concerning the One in Whose Hand is the dominions of the heavens and earth and all that is between them.

So worship Him and be steadfast in His worship. The particle *fā* ("so") which begins this phrase denotes a causal relation between what comes before it and what follows it: '[Worship Him] *because* He is Lord of the Heavens and earth and what is between them' or 'because He would never abandon you' or 'because He never forgets the deeds of those who do good.' The first of these, however, expresses the meaning (of the other two). That is, 'Since you know God Most High by what has been mentioned concerning His perfect Divinity, worship Him,' or 'Since you know God does not forget you;' or 'Since you know God does not forget the good deeds of those who do them,' turn to Him in worship and bear patiently any

106. As recounted in Q. 39:68: *And the trumpet will be blown, whereupon whosoever is in the heavens and on the earth will swoon, save those whom God wills. Then it will be blown again, and, behold, they will be standing, beholding.* The period of forty years is mentioned in a *ḥadīth* recorded in Muslim, Bukhārī, and many other collections.

hardships that come with it. Let neither this lapse in the revelation nor the taunts of those without faith sadden you, for God is surely watching over you and will show you His kindness in this life and the Next.'

Do you know any who can be named alongside Him? Is there anyone who resembles God or is His equal or anyone who can be called by this name other than God Most High? Naming creates a correspondance between two things which resemble one another, but there is nothing like Him either existing or conceivable, and even the polytheists, in all their pride, never gave one of their idols the name of majesty, *Allāh*. None would risk naming any other by this Name, and were someone to dare, he would be destroyed. About this, al-Qushayrī relates in *al-Taḥbīr* that there was a tyrant who intended to give his son this name and both he and the land over which he ruled were swallowed up by the earth. And God Most High knows better.

Spiritual Allusion

Gabriel's words—that he does not descend except by the command of his Lord—do not only apply to [the descent of an angel]. No creature moves or is still except by God's will. No speech nor action nor movement nor rest originates from any of His servants except that the manner in which [it will happen] is already in God's knowledge and decree. There is no movement from one place to another and no descent except by what has been destined... "Not a breath do you expire but a Decree of Destiny makes it go forth."[107] And the poet has said,

> We walk the steps that were written for us to take.
> He whose steps have been written will walk them,
> And he whose death has been decreed in a certain place
> Will end his days in no other land.

So it is in being the child of the moment that we find out rest. If at every moment, we can behold what God is doing with us, we will be delivered from weariness and be granted right action. And in God is all accord.

66. *Man says, "When I am dead, shall I be brought forth alive?"*
67. *Does man not remember that We created him before, when*

107. *Ḥikam*, 22.

he was naught? 68. *And by your Lord, We shall surely gather them and the satans, and We shall surely bring them around Hell on their knees.* 69. *Then indeed We shall pluck out from every group whosoever among them was most extreme in insolence toward the All-Merciful.* 70. *Then We shall surely know those who most deserve to burn therein.* 71. *And there is not one of you, but that he will come to it. It is, with your Lord, a decree determined.* 72. *Then We shall save those who are reverent and leave the wrongdoers therein, on their knees....*

[66]... "Man" (al-insān) usually refers to human beings in general, but here refers (more particularly) to the unbelievers... According to some tafsīrs, the one who said this was Ubayy ibn Khalaf , who once picked up a piece of dry bone from the ground, crumbled it in his hand, and said, "Muḥammad claims that we will be resurrected after we die and have become like this!"[108] Then this verse was revealed: that a human being, in denial and incredulity, might say: "When I am dead, shall I be brought forth alive?" ...

[67] *Does man not remember...?* Here, *remember* (*yadhkuru*) means 'reflect upon,' and in some recitations the verb is pronounced with a doubled *dhāl* and *kāf.*[109] Repeating the noun "man" (*al-insān*) instead of using a pronoun is a reminder that it is part of our human state to reflect upon the question of our creation, and that without this reflection, we are but animals. So why does he not reflect upon his origin: *that We created him before* this present state, meaning his earthly life, *when he was naught?* That is, 'He was originally nothing and then We brought him into creation from that state. So for Us to bring him forth whole again from his state of dissolution is easier,' for to repeat something is easier than to do it for the first time starting from nothingness.

[68] *And by your Lord, We shall surely gather them...* After they have been brought forth from the earth, they will be gathered to the Concourse.[110] God's oath by His own Lordliness connected to the

108. Other *tafsīrs* say that Ubayy, one of the most extreme opponents of the Prophet ﷺ, spoke these words directly to him ﷺ, and that he is also the one referred to in the verses *[God] created man from a drop, and behold, he is a manifest adversary* [16:04], and *[The human being] has set forth for Us a parable and forgotten his own creation, saying, "Who revives these bones, decayed as they are?"* [36:78].

109. That is, *yadhdhakkaru*, which expresses more specifically the act of reflection.

110. See *The Remembrance of Death and the Afterlife*, p. 177.

pronoun referring to the Prophet ﷺ [*your*] stresses the certitude of the Gathering (*al-Ḥashr*), honors the Prophet ﷺ, and exalts his station. It affirms the Resurrection by the clearest and most certain proof, as if it were so evident that it needed no explanation other than to mention the calamities which follow it. The Resurrection itself is not explained, only affirmed by the oath *and by your Lord, We shall surely gather them... and the satans* who seduced them... It is said that the disbelievers will be brought [to the Gathering], along with the devils who were their companions and seducers, in chains, *and We shall surely bring them around Hell on their knees,* when they are driven down from the terror of the Vantage Point.[111]

The verse, as you see, is an explanation of the [state of] the disbelievers. They are the ones who will be herded from the place of standing to the edge of hell on their knees in humiliation or because they will be too frightened to stand. God's words elsewhere, *And you shall see every community on its knees* [45:28], refer to the state of all people in the place of standing before God, before the reward or punishment. People of this station will be kneeling as they were used to do when they practiced divination. It may also be that this is speaking only to those who dispute their reckonings. As for the others, they will acknowledge their sins and then be enveloped by a shade-giving cloud, as the *ḥadīth* states.[112]

[69-70] *Then indeed We shall pluck out from every group...* From every religious community, *whosoever among them was the most extreme in insolence towards the All-Merciful,* that is, the most rebellious and intransigent, will be cast into hell-fire. According to Ibn ʿAbbās, *a·shaddu* (the most extreme) refers to the most audacious of them,

111. *Al-maṭlaʿ* (or *muṭṭalaʿa*) is an elevated place from which someone looks down upon what is below. In this context, it refers to a place from which people will see the terrifying sights of the Concourse, the vast plain where the gathering of the Day of Judgment takes place. See also Ibn ʿAjība's introduction to this *tafsīr*, p. 3 ff above..

112. The *ḥadīth* he is referring to begins, "The believer will be brought near his Lord on the Day of Judgement until he is covered by God's protection. Then he will be asked 'Do you acknowledge [committing this sin]?' And he will say, 'My Lord, I acknowledge it..." and this is repeated in some versions of the *ḥadīth* many times. Then [God will say to him], 'I concealed it for you in the world and I forgive you for it today.' Then he is brought the scroll of his good deeds." This *ḥadīth* appears in the *Ṣaḥīḥ* collection of Ibn Ḥibban, in Abū Nuʿaym's *Ḥilyat al-awliyā'* in the chapter on Ṣafwān b. Muḥriz, in the *Sunnan al-Kubrā* of al-Nasā'ī, and numerous other collections.

according to al-Mujāhid, the most degenerate and lying of them, according to Muqātil, the most haughty and extreme in their rejection, and according to al-Kalbī, the rulers and leaders. That is, the first to face punishment will be the most powerful, and their punishment will be most severe, and then those who followed them in their crimes. 'The most extreme' also implies that God Most High will pardon some of those whose transgressions were other than disbelief. This is if we take these words as speaking of all human beings, but if we take them to be speaking only of the disbelievers, then they mean that [those of them who were most extreme in their insolence] will [enter the Fire] first.

God Most High says: *Then We shall surely know those who most deserve to burn therein, ...* The punishment of those who are "plucked out," either the worst of the sinful or else the leaders, shall be doubled, for not only had they themselves gone astray but they had led others astray as well.

[71] *And there is not one of you, but that he will come to it ...*[113] These words may be understood to be addressed to all people and to say, 'O mankind... there is not one of you *but that he will come to it*,' that is, he will reach [the fire of hell] and come into its presence. The faithful, however, will pass it when it is quiescent, while for others it will be raging. This is what is recorded in a *ḥadīth* transmitted by Jābir which states that someone asked the Prophet ﷺ about this verse, and he replied, "When the people of Paradise enter Paradise, some will ask others, 'Did our Lord not promise us that we would come to [Hellfire]?' And it will be said to them, 'You did, but you came to it when it was quiescent.'"[114] Thus, God's words, ...*They shall be kept far from it* [21:101], mean 'far from its torment.' It is also said that 'coming to it' (*wurūduhā*) means they will pass over it when they cross the Span (*al-ṣirāt*), while according to Ibn Masʿūd, the pronoun "it" refers [not to hell but] to the Resurrection. Understood in this latter sense, there is no disagreement between this verse and the words *Not the slightest sound* (of Hell) *will they hear* [21:102], nor with what has been conveyed concerning those who will enter Paradise without a reckoning, nor with [the explanation that it means] passing over the Span.... The difference arises

113. Ibn ʿAjība notes that there is a variant recitation in which the first words of this verse are read *there is not one of them*.

114. In *al-Awsaṭ* of Ṭabarānī, Bayhaqī's, *Shuʿab al-Īmān*, Abū Nuʿaym's *Ḥilyat al-awliyā'*, Tirmidhī's *Nawādir al-uṣūl*, and other collections.

in how *al-wurūd* is understood. It has also been said, however, that *wurūd* means [that all people will enter hell], but for the believer it will be *coolness and peace.*[115]

It has been said that *wurūd* means 'passing over it,' as we mentioned before, or 'coming to its brink and looking down into it.' Al-Qushayrī said, "Everyone will approach the Fire (*yaridu al-nār*), but no one will be harmed by it or even feel it except to the degree of the wrongs and sins he committed. Those who were most immersed in them will be most immersed in the fire, in its blazing and burning, while for those whose slate is clean, without the slightest trace of sin, it will be as a tradition states: "When they pass over it, the fire will become solid, like bricks of baked clay, so they will enter it but not feel it. And when they have crossed over, they will say, 'But it was promised that we would pass through hell,' and it will be said to them, 'You did, but you did not feel it.'[116]

[71-73] *It is, with your Lord, a decree determined...* That all shall come to hell is a decree which God has imposed upon Himself and so must come to pass. It has also been said that this is also the oath referred to in [the words of the *ḥadīth*] "...except in fulfillment of (God's) oath."[117] *Then We shall save those who are reverent* and who avoided disbelief and sins by making the fire coolness and peace for them. This is if we understand *wurūd* to mean 'entering,' and Jābir said, "I heard the Prophet ﷺ say, '*Al-wurūd* means entering it. There will be not one of the pious or the sinful who does not enter it, but for the faithful the fire will be coolness and peace as it was for Abraham and hell will bellow at their coldness.'"[118] But if we take *al-wurūd* to mean 'passing by,' then [the verse means] they will safely pass over it and be saved from falling into it.

And [We] *leave the wrongdoers therein ....* kneeling. Ibn Zayd said, "Kneeling is the worst way to sit. A man does kneel except when some hardship has befallen him."

---

115. This is a phrase from Q. 21:69 taken from the story of when Abraham ﷺ is thrown into a fire and God says to it *Be coolness and peace for Abraham.*

116. See also, Winters, *op. cit.*, p. 59, note A.

117. He means the *ḥadīth* in the collections of Bukhārī and Muslim that says, "Any Muslim who has lost three children to death will not enter hell except for what is sworn in [God's] oath," at which Abū Muḥammad (a narrator of the *ḥadīth*) added, "*And there is not one of you, but that he will come to it.*"

118. This *ḥadīth* was recorded by Aḥmad in *al-Musnad*, al-Ḥakim in *al-Mustadrak*, Bayhaqī, in *Shuʿab al-Īmān*, Tirmidhī, in *Nawādir al-uṣūl*, and others.

Spiritual Allusion

Anyone who wishes for honor in the Next World should nurture his certainty about it until it becomes ever before him; then will he surely come to God with honor. And anyone who wants safety from the calamities [of the Next World] should lessen his portion of this world and his involvement in it, and maintain his obedience to God and to following the Messenger ﷺ. And anyone who wants to pass quickly over the Bridge (*al-ṣirāt*) should be constant today in following the Straight Path (*al-ṣirāt al-mustaqīm*),[119] for the more he keeps to the Straight Path [in this life] the firmer his footing will be when he crosses the Bridge, and the more he slips from it [in this life] the more his feet will slip from it then.

In speaking of making sure that the measures and scales we use [in our worldly dealings] are just, (al-Ghazālī) said in *al-Iḥyā'*, "Every responsible person is endowed with scales [with which] to weigh his actions, words, and thoughts. So woe be to the one who strays from what is just and veers away from what is straight. But if this were not something extremely difficult or even impossible to avoid, then the words of God Most High, *And there is not one of you, but that he will come to it*, would not have been conveyed [to us]. No one is entirely safe from veering away from rectitude, but the degrees to which people do this vary greatly, and it is according to those degrees that their time in the fire, before deliverance, will differ. For some, the stay will only be long enough to fulfill [God's] oath,[120] and for others it will be thousands of years. We ask God Most High to keep us ever near to uprightness and justice! To cross the Bridge—which is thinner than a hair and sharper than a sword—upright and without swaying, is unimaginable and were it not for the justice [we observe in life], no one on that Bridge, which is thinner than a hair and sharper than a sword, would get across. The more we keep to the straight path [in this life], the easier the crossing will be on the Day of Resurrection.[121]

Al-Tirmidhī al-Ḥakīm said, "The saints and veracious ones will

119. Asking for guidance to *al-ṣirāṭ al-mustaqīm*, the straight path, is in the sixth verse of *Sūrat al-Fātiḥa*, repeated in the *ṣalāt* and in other forms of invocation numerous times a day. *Al-ṣirāt* is also the name of the bridge that spans hell mentioned in the many *ḥadīths* which describe the Day of Resurrection. See Winters, *Op. cit.* p. 205.

120. See note 118 above.

121. *Iḥyā' 'ulūm al-dīn*, II:13, Dar al-Minhāj, vol. III:303.

pass [over the Bridge] without even feeling the fire, as God Most High has said, *Surely those for whom what is most beautiful has already gone forth from Us; they shall be kept far from it* [21:101]. They will be far from the fire because they will be borne by light and enveloped in light until they leave it. Then some of them will ask others, 'Were we not promised the fire?' And then [al-Tirmidhī] mentions what we have already quoted...[122] He continues: "And as for the bellowing of the fire, that will be because of the coolness [which the saintly will bring to it]. For God's Mercy is cool and extinguishes His wrath and it was by His mercy that they attained their light, which then dawned in their hearts and breasts. So on that day, God's Light will be in their breasts, His mercy will shade them, and the fire will die down from the coolness they bring when they enter it. Then will it bellow because it was created for vengeance, and it will fear that their coolness will weaken its vengefulness. Thus, there is a *ḥadīth* that states that the Fire will say, 'Pass through, O faithful one, for your light has extinguished my flames.'[123]

And al-Wartajibī said, "If the beauty of God, the Truth, is with them, no harm will come to them even in the flames, and in those flames are people of paradise."[124]

When Salma comes to camp in the dry river bed,
its waters begin to flow and its bitter herbs turn to roses.

Jaʿfar al-Ṣādiq said, "Were it not for the soul's attachment to the ego, no one would enter the fire. But since they are attached to one another, they will be brought to hell together. Then, those who strove hardest to oppose the malice of their egos will be delivered from the fire in the shortest time, even as the words of God Most High attest: *Then We shall deliver those who were God-fearing*."

And as we have already mentioned, there will be those who have no reckoning—they are the *ones brought nigh* (*al-muqarrabūn*)—who will pass over the Bridge without even noticing it, pass over it like birds or like lightning. May God make us among them by His

122. This passage which the shaykh quotes from *Nawādir al-uṣūl* is closer to a paraphrasing of the passage we found in the printed edition of that book. See *Nawādir al-uṣūl*, I:127.

123. This *ḥadīth* is recorded in Ṭabarānī, *al-Kabīr*, Tirmidhī al-Ḥakīm's *Nawādir al-uṣūl*, and Ibn Rajab's *Jāmiʿ al-ʿulūm wa'l-ḥikam*.

124. In another rendering of these lines, the wording is "if the beauty of the Eternal is with them..."

generosity and grace and by the honor of the best of creation, our protector Muḥammad, His Prophet and beloved friend. Amen!

> 73. *And when Our signs are recited to them as clear proofs, those who disbelieve say to those who believe, "Which of the two groups is better in station or more handsome an assembly?"* 74. *How many a generation We destroyed before them who were fairer in furnishings and in appearance.*

[73] God, the Truth ﷻ, says: *And when Our signs are recited to them... Our signs* (*āyātunā*) are those verses of the Qur'ān which remind the disbelievers of their precarious state and of the tragic end towards which they are heading, as well as those verses which describe the beautiful destination of the faithful. They are called *clear proofs* (*bayyināt*) because they themselves are clear, or because they are clearly miraculous, or because their meanings are clear.

Those who disbelieve...Here, the verbal phrase (*al-ladhīna kafarū*) in place of the pronoun (they) emphasizes the fact that those who said what they said were disbelievers in what had been recited to them and were responding to it. This may also be understood to refer to those who are [most] extreme in their rejection and intransigence, such al-Naḍr bin al-Ḥārīth and his followers, who *say to those who believe ... "Which of the two groups,* we or you, *is better in station.*" In some recitations, the word *maqāman* ("station") is read *muqāman* ("a place of residence"). "*Or* [which is the] *more handsome an assembly?"* or, 'which of us has a better station in life? Which has the more beautiful houses? Which group looks better?' In respect to this latter, it has been related that [the disbelievers of the time] would apply pomade to their hair and comb it into waves, adorn themselves in finery, and then say these words to the poor and needy among the faithful. They thought that appearance was proof of their superiority and that God had honored and preferred them, while the state of the faithful in their neediness and rags showed a lowly standing with God. Such an empty and demented view came only from their ignorance. *They know nothing except some outward aspect of the life of this world* [30:07] ... *That is the extent of their knowledge* [53:30]. Thus God says to them:

[74] *How many a generation We destroyed before them who were fairer in [their] furnishings and appearance. Athāthan* may mean both wealth and household furnishings while *ri'yan* means 'to see.' So the verse

says, 'There were many past generations who had been given more favor than they and who took even more pride in their worldly lot, peoples such at the ʿĀd and Thamūd, who were then brought to destruction through various afflictions. If what We had given them had truly been a sign that We preferred them, why did We deal with them as We did?'...[125]

Spiritual Allusion

Worth and standing [before God] is not in anything outward such as fine food and dress, nor handsome forms. Rather, it is in the certitude of our hearts, and our ascent to the secrets of the unseen, even as we maintain the practices fitting our essential servanthood out of reverence for the majesty of the Lord, and in forgetting and ignoring our selfish goals as we strive to stay in the Sacred Presence. People of the heart pay no heed to the outer aspect of physical forms,[126] but concentrate instead on the life of the soul.

> Perfect of your true nature what you have not yet perfected
> And leave your body down below.

They find the nourishment of their hearts in ecstatic movement[127] and invocation and the life of their souls in knowledge and mysteries. And thus, they chant:

> The body lives by food,
> The heart and soul, by God's remembrance.
> It is their sustenance, their being, their true life;
> It is their rest and their wine.

Those in extreme ignorance and the densest veil look only at outward splendors and vanities, worldly rank, and numbers of followers. Such was the way of the *jāhiliya*—the age of ignorance—when

---

125. Ibn ʿAjība adds here that while "*ri'yā*" is generally understood to be related to "*ru'ya*", something that you can see, another possible derivation is from *al-rayy*, "to irrigate or give water to something," which would mean that they were "saturated or soaked" with worldly favor. In the recitation of Ibn ʿAbbās, this word is read not with the letter *rā'* but rather the letter *zāy*, which would make the word *ziyyā*, meaning "in form or appearance."

126. Literally, "to phantoms" (*al-ashbāḥ*).

127. *Al-tawājud*, literally, "seeking ecstasy (*wajd*)" through outward movements such as rocking back and forth, standing, or participating in the sacred dance which combines movement with invocation. See our translation of Ibn ʿAjība's lexicon, *The Book of Ascension to the Essential Realities of Sufism*, item 60.

people heard admonitions and reminders recited to them but said in response, "*Which of the two groups is better in station or more handsome an assembly? .... They know the outward aspect of the life of this world, but of the Hereafter they are heedless* [30:7]." And in God is all success.

Then God speaks of the ultimate ends for both groups.

> 75. *Say, "Whosoever is in error, the All-Merciful will extend his term till, when they see that which they have been promised, be it the punishment or the Hour, they will know whose position is worse, and whose host is weaker."* 76. *God increases in guidance those who are rightly guided. And that which endures—righteous deeds—are better in reward with your Lord, and better in return.*

[75] God, the Truth ﷻ, says: *Say*, O Muḥammad, "*Whosoever* is entrenched *in error*, immersed in ignorance, heedless of his final end, and engrossed in ephemeral desires—the *All-Merciful will extend his term*, that is, lengthen his life and make his portion of this world easier. This could be either as a way of leading him further astray (*istidrāj*), as in the words of God Most High, *We only grant them respite that they may increase in sin* [3:178], or as a way of taking away from him any excuses, as in the words of God Most High, *Did We not give you long life, enough for whosoever would reflect to reflect therein?* [35:37].[128] It may also be a sign that he has been abandoned to error, disbelief, and rebellion, as in the words of God Most High, *And We shall leave them to wander confused in their rebellion* [6:110]. That this is attributed to *the All-Merciful* shows that their actions are by way of divine mercy even while they may deserve their deaths to come sooner.

It is as if God ﷻ, after having recounted how certain communities of the past came to ruin despite the many fleeting pleasures they enjoyed, then commands His Messenger ﷺ to answer those who are arrogant and proud of their worldly situation to now consider the ultimate ends of both groups: either to be led further astray and then be seized [by death] or to be increased in guidance and then be honored. (Referring to the former situation), God Most High says: *...Till, when they see that which they have been promised*, which means, 'when they are brought to the utter limit.'

128. The *tafsīr* of al-Thaʿlabī states, "The exegetes have differed about how long this span of life is. Qatāda and al-Kalbī said eighteen years, al-Ḥasan said forty, and Ibn ʿAbbās, sixty."

In other words, 'We will lengthen [their time] in this world and [increase] them in all manner of sensual pleasure, until what they have been promised descends upon them—*Be it the punishment* in this world of being slain, captured, or defeated in battle against the faithful—*or the Hour*, that is, the Day of Judgment, and the disgrace and debasement it will bring them...[129]

They will know at that moment which of the two groups' *position is worse*, for they will see that the reality of the situation is the opposite of what they had thought. Then they will know that they are in a worse, not better, place, and they will know *whose host is weaker*, that is, [they will know that they] are actually the ones with fewer allies and not the *more handsome assembly*, as they had claimed. The intended meaning here is not that they will have a force that will be overpowered on the Day of Judgment, as in God's words *Then he had no host to help him against God, nor was he of those who can save themselves* [28:81]. Rather, it is to state that their claim of having so many supporters and allies of whose numbers and strength they wax proud is pure pretense.

[76] ... *God increases in guidance those who are rightly guided...* Just as those in error are increased in their error, those who are guided are increased in their guidance as recompense for their obedience to God, for each is recompensed according to his state. Guidance continues to increase in their hearts until there come to them miraculous gifts. In this world, these are the lifting of the veils and parting of the clouds so that they come to witness the Lord of lords and what they had worshipped in the unseen becomes seen, and in the Next World, it is the bliss of Houris and palaces and the vision of God, the Infinitely Clement and Forgiving.

Thus, God Most High speaks of the state of those who are guided after having spoken of the state of those who are lost, and makes clear to us that if the disbeliever is left to enjoy worldly riches, it is not [a sign of] God's favor, and if the believer is kept from them, it is not [a sign of] its absence. Rather, there are some to whom good things come sooner in this ephemeral world and others for whom they are stored up in eternity.

And that which endures—righteous deeds—are better in re-

129. Ibn ʿAjība notes here that the particle *immā* (translated above as "either") is used in the sense of eliminating any other possibility but not of eliminating the possibility of both occurring.

ward with your Lord, and better in return. They are better because the benefits and return they bring are eternal...[130] The words with your Lord" honor the Prophet ﷺ and the words better in return mean that they are ultimately more valuable than the ephemeral bounties of which the unbelievers wax proud. The final result [of those riches] will be perpetual loss and painful chastisement, while the final result of righteous deeds will be on-going bliss in the Eternal Abode. All this is expressed in the phrase better in return, that is, 'in their yield and their result.' Finally, repetition of the word better (khayrun) stresses their goodness and affirms that they are truly God's grace. And God Most High knows better.

Spiritual Allusion

Know that God ﷻ provides for the servant according to his intention and aspiration. If someone's aspiration is towards worldly goals and passing desires, then God will give him those things, and he will enjoy them for as long as God wills and to the

130. The term *al-bāqiyātu al-ṣāliḥātu*, translated above as "*that which endures—righteous deeds...*," occurs twice in the Qur'ān, once in this *sūrah* and once in the *sūrah* which precedes it (*al-Kahf*, 18:46). In his explanation of the latter, Ibn ʿAjība writes: "*Wealth and children are the adornment of the life of this world,* meaning the things which are sown by the winds of destiny and which will eventually pass away leaving behind bare earth. They include worldly rank and the objects of every eogistic desire, all of which is ephemeral. Then God mentions... *that which endures—righteous deeds.* This has been said to mean good works in general, the five Prayers in particular, or [the words], 'Glory be to God, praise be to God, there is no divinity but God, and God is greater,' to which some versions add, 'There is no strength nor power but through God, the Mighty and Sublime.' Of these words, the Prophet ﷺ said, 'They are among the treasures of Paradise, the most beloved words to God, the *righteous deeds which endure*, and they will come to the Day of Judgment in front of [the faithful] and behind them.' The expression has also been said to mean 'high aspirations and pure intentions,' since it is by them that deeds are accepted, or to mean 'everything which is done for the sake of God,' called 'enduring' (*bāqiya*) because their reward endures after every other object of egoistic desire and every other worldly adornment has passed away.

[Imam al-Ghazālī] said in the *Iḥyā'*, [III:28] "The *adornments of the world* are everything that is carried away by the winds of death," such as wealth, rank, and anything else that takes people away from God. And the *righteous deeds which endure* are all that is not cut off by death, such as knowledge and freedom from lusts, because they endure in their perfection, and are means to nearness with God Most High ... Freedom from being a prisoner of desires releases the servant from what is other than God and true knowledge brings him into solitude with God and union."

extent of the portion of this world [he has been destined], but his final end will one of regret and loss. And if someone's aspiration is towards the Next Life, then God will grant him the practices, such as prayer, fasting, charity, and the teaching of knowledge, that will lead to its delights. He will taste such sweetness from them that any bitterness he had ever tasted will seem paltry and his final outcome will be the eternal bliss of heavenly palaces, Houris, and *whatever souls desire and eyes find pleasing* [43:71].

And if someone's aspiration is towards God, which is to say, towards reaching His Presence and nothing else, then God will provide him with practices which will take him to it: the practices of the heart such as ridding the soul of vices and adorning it with virtues, and reaching the stations of the way through various kinds of spiritual effort, the first of which is to find a complete master who combines within himself the inner Truth (*al-ḥaqīqa*) and the Law (*al-sharīʿa*), who is both ecstatic and methodic, and who himself has travelled the Way with a complete master. If he finds such a one, and is shown the secret of that master's special gift, then let him rejoice, for he will reach the goal. And in God is all accord.

> 77. *Have you not considered the one who disbelieves Our signs, and says, "I shall be given wealth and children."* 78. *Has he ascended to the Unseen, or made a covenant with the All-Merciful?* 79. *By no means! We shall record that which he says, and We shall add and add the punishment.* 80. *And We shall inherit from him that which he claims, and he will come to Us alone.*

[77] God, the Truth ﷻ, says: *Have you not considered the one who disbelieves Our signs....* [These verses are said to have been revealed concerning] al-ʿĀṣ ibn Wāʾil and *Our signs* are what the Qurʾān says concerning the Resurrection and reckoning. Khabbāb bin al-Aratt said, "I went to al-ʿĀṣ ibn Wāʾil to collect a debt he owed me and he refused to pay me, saying, "By God, I will not pay it until you renounce Muḥammad." I answered, "By God, I will not renounce Muḥammad until you die and are brought back to life." To this, al-ʿĀṣ replied in mockery, "When I die and am brought back to life, come to me. I will have wealth and children and be able to pay you, because you claim there is gold and silver in heaven!" In the version of this narrative in Bukhārī, Khabbāb is reported to have also said, "I was a smith in the *jāhiliyya* times and had fashioned a sword for al-ʿĀṣ. When I went to him to collect my fee for it, he

said..." and the rest is as quoted above.

The letter *hamza* (*a*) in this context expresses amazement at the strangeness and ugliness of such a person's state...[131] Literally, the verse is saying, 'Look, and you will see someone who rejects Our luminous signs, which merit the belief of any who witness them, and says in mockery and jest..., swearing by God a false oath, *I shall certainly be given wealth and children* in the Next World ....'

[78] *Has he ascended (aṭṭalaʿa) to the Unseen?*[132] 'Has he reached such greatness that he can ascend to the knowledge of the unseen, which belongs solely to God, and claim—even swear—that in the Next World he will be given wealth and children? *Or has he made a covenant with the All-Merciful* concerning this. For those are the only two ways he could have such knowledge. Thus, this verse expresses amazement [at the audacity of the claim] while at the same time repudiating it and showing its falseness ...

To refer this covenant to All-Mercifulness (*al-raḥmāniya*) reminds us that any kind of giving is an aspect of God's mercy, while the covenant (*al-ʿahd*) has been said to be the words of the Testimony [of faith], or the accomplishment of righteous deeds, for the promise of God Most High to reward (either of these) is like a covenant.

Al-Qushayrī said, "*Has he ascended to the Unseen* so that he speaks from direct knowledge of God, *or* [has he] *made a covenant with the All-Merciful?* Neither of these is the case..." Then he says, "But in this verse is evidence that if a believer who does have such a covenant aspires towards something goodly from God, He will bring it to pass for him, for *God does not fail the tryst* [3:9]."

[79] ... *We shall record that which he says*, that is, 'We shall show what We have written against him...;' or: 'We shall preserve what he says and recompense him according to it in the Next World;' or, 'We shall requite the one who says this now and punish him for it in the end.' For there is no delay in the recording [of deeds], as shown by the words of God Most High, *No word does he utter without a ready watcher beside him.* [50:18]. Of this, Ibn Juzayy said, "[The verb] is

131. Similar in English to an exclamation such as "What a day!" or "How strange!"

132. The verb *aṭṭalaʿa* literally means "to climb to a high place which allows someone to look down on something." By extension it means "to look into something" and "to peruse a book."

in the future because reward and punishment will appear in the future." And the *Ḥāshiya* notes, "Stating it in the future affirms that it is not subject to abrogation."[133]

And We shall add and add the punishment...Instead of his being given more wealth and children as he claims, 'We will prolong for him the punishment and increase its severity because of his disbelief, the abominations he utters against God ﷻ, and his mockery of God's mighty signs.' The emphatic structure in this verse expresses the extremity of divine wrath.[134]

[80] *And We shall inherit (from him) that which he claims* .... That is, 'We shall take back from him all that We have given him' *and he will come to Us* on the Day of Resurrection without even the wealth or children he had had in the world, let alone anything more. Of this, al-Qushayrī said: "[It means he will come] alone, devoid of the least evidence for his words and his oath "*I shall certainly be given wealth and children,*" which were only mockery and sheer disbelief." And God Most High knows better.

Spiritual Allusion

It may be understood from these verses that if a person believes in God's signs and accomplishes what God enjoins upon him, he has a covenant with God, such that if he wishes for something, or someone else wishes something from him, God will not disappoint him. People differ in this covenant according to how they differ in their worship and knowledge of God. This will be explained more with the verse below: *They have no power of intercession, save the one who has made a covenant with the All-Merciful.* And God Most High knows better.

Then God answers the misguided who claim to derive benefit from idols.

> 81. *And they have taken gods besides God, that they should be for them power and honor.* 82. *By no means! They shall soon deny their worshipping them, and they shall be the opposite.* 83. *Do you not see that We have sent satans against the unbelievers, in-*

133. *Al-Ḥāshiya*, I:481.

134. The Arabic here reads *wa namudda lahu ...madda*, in which *madda* is an adverbial intensifying the verb: literally, "and We will prolong ...with a prolonging." Another well-known example can be found in *Sūrat al-Fajr* [89:21]*: idhā dukkati'l-arḍu dakkan dakkā*, "When the earth is pounded with a pounding."

citing them by incitement? 84.*Therefore be not in haste against them. We only number out to them a number (of days).*

[81] God, the Truth ﷻ, says *And they have taken gods besides God, that they should be for them power and honor...* That is, the polytheists have taken idols which they worship besides God, [hoping] that they will bring them power and honor, and be intermediaries who will intercede for them on the Day of Judgment. [The word] *Kallā (by no means!)* both responds to their false beliefs and denies that what they hope for will happen. *They shall soon deny their worshipping them.* That is... on the day when God Most High gives them speech, their gods will say, 'You did not worship us.' This has also been said to mean that when the disbelievers see before them the evil outcome of their idolatry, they will deny ever having done it, as God's words elsewhere declare: *By God, our Lord, we were not polytheists* [6:23]

And they shall be the opposite. That is, the idols whom they had hoped would be their power and honor will be their weakness and abasement. This is because they had sought strength and honor from what is created at the expense of incurring the wrath of the Creator, and as the Prophet ﷺ said, "He who seeks to please creatures by disobeying the Creator will see the praise he gets from people turned into blame."[135] So the idols will turn against them and become the very instruments of their punishment, used to kindle the fire and fuel hell. These words have also been said to mean that the disbelief of the idolaters will become its opposite, that they themselves will turn against their idols and reject them after having loved them as they should have loved God, and worshipped them instead of God...[136]

And the reason for their idolatry is that the devil made it attractive to them, as he vowed he would when he said: *I shall surely make* [it] *attractive to them on earth* [15:39] ... That is, God gave devils

135. This appears to be a version of the well-known *ḥadīth* found in Ṭabarānī, *al-Awsaṭ*, the *Muwaṭṭa'* of Imām Mālik, the *Musnad* of Imām Aḥmad, and several other sources, including the wording, "[Let there be] no obedience to creatures that entails disobeying the Creator."

136. The last phrase in this verse states, literally, "they shall be *an opposite*" (*ḍiddan*). Ibn ʿAjība notes that this noun is singular even though it is referring to a plurality (either 'the unbelievers' or 'their idols') because they will be united in their opposition, as if they were a single thing, similar to the words of a *ḥadīth* that says, "They are *a hand* against any who oppose them."

power over humankind and the ability to incite them on towards evil when He said [to Iblīs]: *So incite whomsoever you can* [17: 64].[137]

[83] Do you not see that We have sent satans against the unbelievers...? [These words] express amazement to the Prophet ﷺ at the extent of their iniquities in word and deed, the extremity of their folly, their immersion in error, the absolute inflexibility of their disbelief, and how they join forces against the truth even after it has been made clear to them. [It] also expresses amazement at all that arises from their having been seduced and led astray by the devils... [Thus, it is as if God were asking His Prophet ﷺ], 'Have you not seen what the devils have done with the disbelievers so that such iniquities and enormities arise from them?' The amazement being expressed to him ﷺ is not at the simple fact that devils are sent to them, as someone of limited understanding might imagine, but rather at all that arises from them because of that incitement, as the [the last] words of the verse -- inciting them by incitement—announce. That is, 'They are incited to the worst transgressions by demonic whisperings and insinuations.' Here there is a relationship between the words *azz* and *istifzāz*[138] in the sense that both mean 'to make someone extremely nervous, anxious, and dissatisfied ...' So it is as if these words were in answer to [the unstated question]: 'What are the devils doing to the disbelievers? They are inciting them by incitement.'

[84] *Therefore be not in haste against them*, hoping that they might perish because of the offenses they have committed and the earth might be cleansed of their corruption. *We only number out to them a number (of days).* That is, ... in reality all they have left are a few days, a few breaths, which We have extended to them and then We shall seize them completely. And God Most High knows better.

Spiritual Allusion

Anyone who seeks power and honor from something other than

137. The complete verse, which begins quoting God's words to Iblīs, reads: "*So incite whomsoever you can among them with your voice, and bear down upon them with your cavalry and your infantry, and become a partner in their wealth and children, and make them promises." Satan promises them nothing but delusion.*

138. *Azz*, the gerund that appears in this verse, literally means "to make a whistling or buzzing sound," while *istifzāz*, mentioned in 17:64 means more literally "inciting or arousing."

God and the obedience due Him will see it turned to weakness and humiliation. This is why they say, "The honor of someone who seeks it from creatures is dead." So, "If you wish for power and honor that does not perish, do not seek it through what is perishing,"[139] meaning wealth, status, or any other ephemeral thing. This will be explained more in connection to God's words *Whoever desires honor—to God belongs all honor* [35:10] and His words, *Yet to God belongs power and honor, and to the Messenger and to the believers* [63:8].

In addition, even as God sends devils to the disbelievers who incite them towards sin, so does He send angels and divine inspirations to the faithful to inspire them towards obedience and encourage them in the journey towards knowing God. The angels move the servant to acts of obedience, and inspirations encourage him towards the Presence of God, even as the *Ḥikam* states, "Inspiration comes from the Presence of the Omnipotent. As a result, nothing opposes it without being smashed to bits. *Nay, but We hurl the Truth against falsehood, and It prevails against it, and lo! Falsehood vanishes* [21:18]," and also, "When divine inspirations come upon you, they demolish your habits. '*Verily, kings, when they enter a town, bring it to ruin* [27:34].'"

Concerning God's words, *Inciting them by incitement*, al-Qushayrī said, "[It means that] they fill them with anxiety. An inspiration from the Devil comes with anxiety and darkness, while an inspiration from God comes with relief and tranquility. This is one of the ways to distinguish between them." Others are that an inspiration from God only commands towards what is good with coolness, open-heartedness, and slowness, even as the *ḥadīth* states, "Haste is from the devil, and slowness is from the All-Merciful."[140] By contrast, an inspiration from the Devil always incites towards evil, but it may be by way of what is good if the one who receives it can then be taken in that way towards what is evil. The signs of this [kind of inspiration] are that it contains shadows, ambiguities,[141] haste, and a feeling of having been seized. This has been abundantly explained in *al-Naṣīḥa al-Kāfiya*.[142] And in God is all success.

Then God speaks of the faithful and of the lost:

139. This paraphrases *Ḥikam*, 79.

140. Al-Tirmidhī, *K. al-Adab*.

141. *Al-dukhān*, literally, 'smoke,' but meaning in this context 'a mixture of light and darkness.'

142. See bibliography, al-Zarrūq.

85. *On the Day We shall gather the reverent to the All-Merciful as an honored delegation.* 86. *And We shall drive the guilty into Hell as a thirsty herd.* 87. *They have no power of intercession, save the one who has made a covenant with the All-Merciful.*

[85] God, the Truth ﷻ says: *On the Day We shall gather the reverent to the All-Merciful* ... That is, the reverent will be gathered to their Lord Who will envelop them in His all-encompassing Mercy like *an honored delegation* being taken before a king, expecting His generosity and favor. Of this verse, ʿAlī (may God ennoble his countenance) said, "When it was revealed, I said, 'O Messenger of God, I have seen kings and their delegations, and the delegations are always mounted. So what about God's delegation?' He said, 'O ʿAlī, when the time draws near to leave [the standing] before God, the angels will meet the faithful with white she-camels, each with a saddle and reins of gold, and a robe more costly than all the wealth in the world. The faithful will don their robes and mount their camels which will carry them to the Garden and there the angels will greet them with the words: *Peace be upon you; you have done well; so enter and abide* [*therein*] *forever*.'" [39:73][143]

[86-87] *And We shall drive the guilty into Hell*... like thirsty cattle drawn to water. 'The Day We gather the two groups, We shall do what We shall do: affliction [on one hand], honor and generosity [on the other], and both beyond what words can express. This verse may also be read as an exhortation and warning [which says:] 'Call to mind the Day when We shall gather to Us the two groups.'

They have no power of intercession, save the one who has made a covenant with the All-Merciful. These words continue the description of the terrifying events [of that Day]. The plural form (*they have*) may be understood as referring to all humanity, or else only to the reverent, or only to the guilty.... [No one] will have the power to intercede for another except those who had prepared [for that moment] by having been beautified with piety and faith. So these words are an encouragement to strive towards attaining [those virtues] which will bring them to that high station. They may also be understood to mean that the reverent will only be able to intercede on behalf of someone who has entered into the covenant of

143. A narration similar to this is quoted by Ibn Abī al-Dunyā in *Ṣifat al-Janna*, as well as in al-Muttaqī, Kanz *al-ʿummāl*, *Tafsīr*, and al-Suyūṭī, *Jāmiʿ al-aḥādīth*, *Musnad ʿAlī b. Abī Ṭālib*.

Islām and accomplished righteous deeds; or that the wicked will only benefit from the intercession of someone among them who is a Muslim. Any of these three understandings [of the verse] is possible, but the first, being the most inclusive, is best.

Ibn Masʿūd ﷺ said, "I heard the Prophet ﷺ say, 'Let none of you fail to make a covenant with God every morning and every evening by saying at those times: 'O God! Fashioner of the heavens and the earth, Knower of the unseen and the seen, truly I pledge to You in this world that I bear witness that there is no god except You, one, without partner, and that Muḥammad is Your servant and messenger. So do not leave me to the power of my ego, for if You leave me under to power, You place me closer to evil and farther from good. I depend only on Your mercy, so please make for me a covenant with You that will grant me Your accord on the Day of Resurrection—*Verily, You never break Your promise* [3:194]' If he supplicates God with these words, they are stamped with a seal and placed beneath the Divine Throne. Then, on the Day of Resurrection, a caller will call out, 'Where are those who have made a covenant with God?' and they will be brought into Paradise."[144]

Spiritual Allusion

People will be brought to God on the Day of Resurrection according to how they come to Him today in this world, and the generosity and honor granted to them in the Next Life will be in proportion to the degree that they turn to Him in this life. Those who come to God Most High through the door of outward devotions will be borne by the forms of those devotions to the Next Life; those who come to Him through the door of the heart's devotions will be borne by lights to the highest of the paradisiacal gardens, and those who come through the door of devotions of the innermost soul, devotions such as meditation and reflection in the station of direct perception, will be borne by God, the Truth, into the Holy Presence, *upon a seat of truth before an Omnipotent King* [54:55].

The master of our masters, Sīdī (al-Fāsī) al-ʿĀrif, said concerning the word *delegation*, "They will be brought mounted on the best of their devotions, and these will vary. Some will be borne on the form of physical devotions, some on the form of sublime aspira-

144. This *ḥadīth* appears in Ṭabarānī, *al-Kabīr*, Aḥmad, *al-Musnad*, Abū Nuʿaym's *Ḥilyat al-awliyā'*, and several other sources.

tion, some on the form of lights, and some will be borne by God the Truth to their destinations, just as He bears them today in this world, and to be borne by God is unlike being borne by any created thing."[145]

In respect to God's words *They have no power of intercession....[save the one who has made a covenant with the All-Merciful*], know that the covenant with God which allows intercession on the Day of Resurrection is [physical] devotions, the cultivation of certitude, and gnosis. Intercession will be granted to the people of physical devotions in proportion to their obedience and sincerity; it will be granted to the people of certitude, who are greater than the first, in proportion to their certitude, and it will be granted to the people of gnosis, who are greater that the first two groups, in proportion to their gnosis, and among these latter, there will be those who are able to intercede for all the people of their age. I have heard from our shaykh, the scholar Sīdī al-Tāwūdī ibn Sūda that one of the saints said at the time of his death, "O Lord, grant me intercession for the people of my time." And he heard a voice say to him, "Your rank does not reach that far." So the saint said, "O Lord! If [my rank] is by way of my deeds and efforts, then it is surely not enough, but if it is due to Your generosity and magnanimity, then by Your glory and might, it is greater than that level." And it was said to him, "You are granted intercession for the people of your time."

The meaning here is that anyone who returns to God's generosity and excellence and enters by that door will find the answer closer to him than anything else. And in God is all accord....

> 88. *And they say, "The All-Merciful has begotten a son."* 89. *You have indeed asserted a terrible thing.* 90. *The heavens are well-nigh rent thereby, and the earth split asunder, and the mountains made to fall down in ruins,* 91. *That they should claim for the All-Merciful a son.* 92. *It is not fitting for the All-Merciful to take a son.* 93. *There is none in the heavens and on the earth, but that it comes to the All-Merciful as a servant.* 94. *He has taken account of them, and numbered them exactly.* 95. *And each of them is coming to Him on the Day of Resurrection, alone.*

[88-89] God, the Truth ﷻ, says: *And they say, "The All-Merciful has begotten a son."* This was a saying that came from Jews, Christians,

145. *Al-Ḥāshiya*, I:482.

and those of the Arabs who claimed that angels were the daughters of God, (...may He be glorified high above all that they claim). God mentions their transgression after having mentioned the transgression of the idolaters, melding [the two] stories into one, inasmuch as they shared a common error. Of them, God Most High says *You have indeed asserted a terrible thing,* that is, 'You have committed an offense of immeasurable gravity.'[146] This is both a response to their false assertion and an expression of extreme divine wrath that inscribes against them the utmost insolence and ignorance.

[90] Then, explaining the gravity of what they say, God says: *The heavens are well-nigh rent thereby...* The verb *yatafaṭṭarna* ("rent") literally means 'to be split again and again by the enormity of [their claim].' *And the earth is split asunder*, that is, it almost splits apart and vanishes, *and the mountains* [are] *made to fall* and crumble into dust leaving behind them not a trace. Such is the enormity of this claim that if it could take a physical form, these mighty creations—the heavens, the earth, and the mountains—would not be strong enough to bear it and would crumble to pieces. It may also be understood to mean that the extent to which it brings forth God's wrath is such that were it not for His clemency, the world would collapse and its foundations fall apart. Muḥammad ibn Kaʿb said, "The adversaries of God well nigh bring the Hour upon us," because what is mentioned [in this verse] also describes the Final Hour.

[91] This is that *they should claim for the All-Merciful a son.* Because of this claim, the sky is almost rent asunder, the earth split, and the mountains are turned to dust. *It is not fitting for the All-Merciful to take a son....* The repetition of God's Name *al-Raḥmān* (*the All-Merciful*), instead a pronoun, is a reminder of the sublimity of this pronouncement: that everything else besides God is blessed by His Mercy or an effect of that Mercy in creation. So how is it conceivable that the One Who is the source of benefaction and possesses both its root and branches can be compared to a created thing that begets off-spring? This is further explained in the words of God Most High which follow:

---

146. The verse literally says, "You have come (*ji'tum*) with something extreme." Ibn ʿAjība notes that the verb "come" sometimes means "do" in the sense of "commit" and that the noun *idda*, translated as "something extreme," relates to the noun *al-addu*, meaning "the most severe catastrophe."

[93-95] *There is none in the heavens and on the earth*, neither the angels nor the "two heavy ones,"[147] *but that it comes to the All-Merciful as a servant*, belonging to God now and forever. *He has taken account of them, and numbered them exactly.* [The verb *aḥṣā*] in this context means 'delimited and surrounded' them so that no one of them is beyond His all-encompassing knowledge and the reach of His power. Not one of them exists, nor will exist, nor is able to exist, apart from God's knowledge, decree, destiny, and planning .... This is an image of God's Lordhood over all things, and Knowledge of all things, both in general and in particular.

And each of them is coming to Him on the Day of Resurrection, alone, without possessions, allies, or followers, but solely with his deeds. If such is God's role and such is theirs, then how can it be imagined that He take any of them as a son?[148]

In a *ḥadīth qudsī* found in Bukhārī, God Most High says, "My servant has lied about Me, and he should not have done so. And My servant has blasphemed against Me, and he should not have done so. As for his lie, it is that he says, 'Who will bring us back as we were in the beginning?' And as for his blasphemy, it is that he says, 'God has taken a son,' while I am the One, the Eternally Existing. I do not beget nor was I begotten and there is none like unto Me."[149] And God Most High knows best.

Spiritual Allusion

Since you know, O person of faith, that God ﷻ is angered by those who ascribe to Him a partner or believe concerning Him something that is unworthy of His transcendence and perfection, you yourself should purify the drink of your *tawḥīd* from both manifest and hidden polytheism, be it in knowledge, doctrine, state, or taste, until there remains in your heart love, fear, attachment, and dependence only for your Guardian Lord, exclusive of any created thing. Then will your drink of *tawḥīd* be pure, and then will you be a complete servant of God, free from all else. But to the extent that you still love the objects of your desires, your *tawḥīd* will remain incomplete, and as long as you continue to crave those things, you will not reach union with God. As al-Shushtārī ؓ said:

147. This is a Quranic expression from 55:31 signifying 'human beings and jinn.'

148. Ibn ʿAjība notes here that the participial form of the verb, *ātī* ('is coming'), conveys a greater sense of certainty than the simple present ('comes') would.

149. This *ḥadīth* is found in Aḥmad, Ibn Ḥibbān, and several other collections.

If you desire to reach Us, then your death is a condition.
No one arrives if his ego remains.[150]

Be truly God's servant—one of those about whom God says: *There is none in the heavens and on the earth but that it comes to the All-Merciful as a servant*—and at that moment you will be free of all else besides God and be given dominion over all existence such that it will come under your command and prohibition. Or as someone has said,

They called me to their realm (mulkihim),
 and when I answered them,
They said, "We called you to sovereignty,
 not to some possession (milk)."

When both the eye of Divine Power and Divine Wisdom are opened, you see everything in its rightful place. With the eye of Power, you range the inner gardens of the Divine Dominions and the Oceans of the Divine Omnipotence, and with the eye of Wisdom you range the splendors of the Kingdom and the mysteries of Divine Wisdom. The eye of Divine Power says, 'Everything in the heavens and earth is a light from the lights of the All-Merciful and a secret from the secrets of His Essence;' and the Eye of Divine Wisdom says: 'Everything in the heavens and earth is a servant possessed [by God] and subordinate to His overwhelming power.' If you come to know both these opposites, [Wisdom and Power], and situate each in its place, you are a gnostic, but if you wish to know Him by only one of them, you will remain ignorant of God. Divine Wisdom affirms the form of servanthood to protect the treasure of God's Lordhood, while Divine Power effaces you from that form in a vision of the mysteries of His Divinity. As the *Ḥikam* [109] puts it: "Praise be to Him Who has hidden the inner reality of holiness by manifesting the quality of human nature, and who has appeared in the sublimity of Lordhood by manifesting the attribute of servanthood." Servanthood is a quality that is innate to the servant, and to be absent from it is necessary from the perspective of the Lord. So the affirmation of servanthood by Divine Wisdom is separation, while to be pass away from it in a vision of the lights of Lordhood is union. The

150. Although the Shaykh attributes this line to Shushtarī, it is actually found in the Diwān of ʿAbd al-Hādī al-Suwīdī, known as al-Yamanī (d. 932/1525), in a *qaṣīda* which begins "He clothed me in the garments of infirmity and lowliness" (*qad kasānī libās saqamin wa dhullihi*).

gnostic is united in his separation, and separated in his union.[151]

After speaking of the ugliness of disbelief, God speaks of the beauty of faith.

96. *Surely those who believe and perform righteous deeds, for them shall the All-Merciful ordain love.*

... God will place love and affection in people's hearts for the faithful such that anyone who hears of them will love them. God will love them and make them beloved to His creatures in the heavens and on earth and He will bring about this love not through any special means other than their faith and good works. The love mentioned here may also be understood to be what exists between them. They will love one another and befriend one another and God will love them as well.

Al-Qushayrī said, "There will be placed in their hearts love for the sake of God arising from the sincerity of their deeds, even as the *ḥadīth* states, "My servant will not cease to draw near to Me by supererogatory worship until he loves Me and I love him."[152] That this is ordained by *the All-Merciful* reminds us that this love is promised to them through God's mercy and is itself a mercy to them and to those who love them. The Prophet 🕮 said to ʿAlī 🕮, "Say: 'O God, make for me a covenant with You, and place love for me in the breasts of the faithful,' and then this verse was revealed.[153] And in a *ḥadīth* in the collection of Bukhārī and others, [the Prophet 🕮 is reported to have said] "When God loves a servant, He says to Gabriel, 'Truly I love this servant, so love him as well,' and Gabriel

---

151. That is, it is an innate quality of being human to see oneself as a servant, limited, imperfect, and separate from God, and this is what Ibn ʿAjība and other Sufis before him have designated by the term Ḥikma (Wisdom). But it is also essential to the realization of God's supreme reality to pass away from the individual perspective of the servant and from all separation, which is what is contained in the term Qudra (Power).

Thus, Ḥikma is everything by which God is mercifully veiled from creation and Qudra is everything by which God is revealed in creation. For more concerning these terms, see his commentary on the Ṣalāt al-Mashīshiyya in *Two Sufi Commentaries*, pp. 182-183.

152. This is a variation of the well-known *ḥadīth qudsī* in Bukhārī and numerous other sources with the wording, "My servant does not cease to draw near to Me by supererogatory worship until I love him, and when I love him, I am his hearing by which he hears...."

153. This *ḥadīth* is mentioned in the commentary of al-Thaʿlabī on this verse and is attributed to Barāʾ b. ʿĀzib 🕮.

loves him and calls out to all the dwellers of the heavens, 'Verily, God loves this servant, so love him as well,' and they do, and then love for him is placed on earth."

Concerning the words, *The All-Merciful will make for him love*, Qatāda said "By God, this means love in the hearts of the faithful. Harama ibn Ḥayyān used to say, 'No servant turns with his heart towards God except that God turns the hearts of the faithful towards him and nourishes him with their love and mercy.'" And a *ḥadīth* in *al-Targhīb* which speaks of this says, "No servant turns with his heart towards God ﷻ except that God causes the hearts of the faithful to turn towards him with love and mercy and hastens to him every goodness."[154] Another *ḥadīth* states, "The believer engenders love in the breasts of the pious and fear in the breasts of the dissolute."[155]

So people's love for a servant is evidence of acceptance from his Lord: "You are God's witnesses upon His earth."[156] And in a certain narration, "The righteous servant does not die before his ears are filled by what he loves, and the wicked man does not die until his ears are filled by what he hates," or words similar to this.[157]

God ﷻ revealed this verse in the future tense (*sa yajʿalu*) because this *sūrah* is Meccan and came at a time when the faithful where despised by the unbelievers. This was a promise for the future which God made true when Islam came, the faithful were given strength and support, and hearts on every side turned towards them with love, as their historians have described. It has also been said that this is a promise relating to the Day of Resurrection when the righteous deeds of the faithful will appear like radiant suns above the heads of all those who are present. That this love promised is expressed as singular (*waddan*) among all the many sublime gifts bestowed upon them contrasts it with the division, anger, and opposition that will befall the disbelievers

154. This *ḥadīth* is found in Ṭabarānī, *al-Awsaṭ*, Abū Nuʿaym's *Ḥilyat al-awliyā'*, Ibn Shāhīn, *al-Targhīb fī faḍā'il al-aʿmāl wa thawābu dhālik*, and other sources.

155. We were unable to find the source of this saying.

156. This *ḥadīth* is found in Bukhārī, Muslim, Nasā'ī, Tirmidhī, and others, with the wording, "You are God's witnesses upon earth," meaning that if a person is considered good or bad by those who know him and have dealings with him, that is evidence before God.

157. This *ḥadīth* is found in Bazzār, *al-Musnad*, Bayhaqī, in *Shuʿab al-Īmān*, al-Ḥakīm al-Tirmidhī in *Nawādir al-uṣūl*, al-Suyūṭī's *Jāmiʿ* and others, with the wording, "The believer is someone who will not die until...."

that day. And God Most High knows best.

Spiritual Allusion

It is God's way with His saints, at the beginning of their journeys, to make them subject to people, anonymous, and lowly among His creatures, until even those close to them might come to despise them. This is actually a form of God's mercy and care for their hearts so that they do not find peace anywhere except in God. Thus, Shaykh Abū'l-Ḥasan al-Shādhilī says [in *al-Ḥizb al-Kabīr*], "O God, there are people for whom You have decreed lowliness in order that they might be honored..." Then, when they are purified from what remains of their lower natures, have been perfected by virtues, and are stable in their knowledge of God, He honors them and places love for them in people's hearts. Such is usually God's way, but it may be that He decrees for some to live in anonymity until the day they meet Him without this being in any way a deficiency or lack, but rather a part of their perfection. They are the witnesses (*al-shuhadā'*)[158] of the heavenly domains, and take nothing of their [worldly] recompense. And God Most High knows better.

In completing this noble *sūrah*, God commands His Prophet ﷺ to convey it.

> 97. *So We have made this easy upon your tongue that you may give glad tidings to the reverent thereby, and that thereby you may warn a contentious people.*
>
> 98. *How many a generation before them have We destroyed? Do you perceive even one of them, or hear from them a murmur?*

[97] God, the Truth ﷻ, says: '*We have made this* Qur'ān *easy for you*, for We have revealed it in your own language...' And some say that the ease referred to means the revelation itself. That is, 'We have made this Qur'ān easy in itself and We have revealed it in your language.' [This is so] *you may give glad tiding to the reverent*, those who are journeying towards piety by following the commandments and prohibitions that it contains, and so that you *may warn... a contentious people* who out of obstinacy and hostility do not believe in it ...

[98] *How many a generation before them have We destroyed?* 'That is,

158. This phrase could also be understood to say 'they are martyrs,' meaning that they have sacrificed their lives to God by living in anonymity.

there have been generations of peoples in the past whom We destroyed before these obstinate ones.' These words are thus a promise to the Messenger ﷺ of victory over the unbelievers, an encouragement to warn them, and a threat to them of their ruin. [They mean:] 'Continue to warn them that they will meet their ruin just as We brought to ruin generations before them.'

Do you perceive even one of those past peoples? Do you see anything that remains of them *or hear from them a murmur?*[159] Not in the least. Their traces are erased, their voices silenced, and their palaces and houses lie in ruins. 'And such is what We may bring to pass for others as well. We destroyed them so completely and uprooted them so totally that not a single one of them is visible, nor can a sound, either faint or deafening, be heard from them... And God Most High knows better.

Spiritual Allusion

God revealed the Qur'ān and made it easy for His servants [to recite] only so that they might receive admonition and reminder. He commanded His Messenger ﷺ during his life to give glad tidings and warnings by way of it, and that commandment remained for the caliphs who followed him. It is thus incumbent upon the learned and the righteous to do the same and not simply teach the outward formalities of religious law. Preaching is meant to inspire fear and convey glad tidings. This is what the words of God Most High mean: *That you may give glad tidings to the reverent thereby, and that thereby you may warn a contentious people.*

But none should approach this task except someone who has been given a light by which to walk among men,[160] so that the light of his heart will go before him into the hearts of those who are listening and his words will reach them. It is said in the *Ḥikam* [182], "The lights of sages precede their words, so that, wherever illumination occurs, there the expression arrives." This light is the light of gnosis, which itself is the station of self-effacement (*maqām al-fanā'*).

---

159. Ibn ʿAjība notes that the word which ends this verse (and the *sūrah*), *rikza* (translated as "murmur") is related to the noun, *al-rikāz*, which literally means "buried treasure." Hence, the literal meaning here is "a hidden sound."

160. He is echoing [6:122]: *Is he who was dead, and to whom We give life, making for him a light by which to walk among mankind, like one who is in darkness from which he does not emerge?*

Another condition for anyone who preaches is to have permission to do so from a complete spiritual master or by way of true spiritual inspiration, for in that case his words will reach people's hearing. Again, in the *Ḥikam* [184] we find: "Whoever has been given permission to speak out will find that his expression is understood by his listeners and that his symbolic allusion is clear to them," and also [185], "Sometimes the lights of inner realities will appear eclipsed when you have not been given permission to express them."

Concerning those who are given the task of preaching and reminding, there has come to us this *ḥadīth qudsī*: "The most beloved to Me of those whom I love are those who make Me beloved to My servants, make My servants beloved to Me, and who walk the earth with good counsel."[161]

May God, by His grace and generosity, make us among His elect, and may He shower blessings and salutations of peace upon our beloved master, Muḥammad, and upon his family and companions.

161. This is narrated as a *ḥadīth qudsī* with similar wording by Ibn Abī al-Dunyā, in *al-Awliyā'*, Ibn Rajab, *Jāmiʿ al-ʿulūm wa'l-ḥikam*, al-Ḥakīm al-Tirmidhī in *Nawādir al-uṣūl*, and by Suyūṭī in *al-Jāmiʿ al-ṣaghīr*.

The Chapter of *Ṭā Hā*
(*Sūrah Ṭā Hā*)

This *sūrah* was revealed in Mecca and comprises one hundred and thirty-five verses. It is connected to the one which precedes it by God's words, *We have made this easy upon your tongue* [19:97], and the words, *We have not revealed this Qur'ān to you to cause you misery*, as if God were telling him ﷺ, 'We have made this Qur'ān easy for you so that you might find rest in it and not weariness,' and then He opens the *sūrah* with symbols that are between Him and His beloved friend ﷺ.

> 1. *Ṭā Hā.* 2. *We have not revealed this Qur'ān to you to cause you misery,* 3. *But only as a reminder to anyone with reverent fear,* 4. *A revelation from the One Who created the earth and the heavens sublime:* 5. *The All-Merciful established upon the Throne.* 6. *To Him belong what is in the heavens and what is in the earth, and what is between them, and what is beneath the soil.* 7. *And if you speak aloud, He knows what is secret and what is more hidden.* 8. *Allāh! There is no god except Him. His are the most beautiful Names.*

[1] According to Ibn ʿAbbās, *Ṭā Hā* is one of the Names of God Most High. But some have said the letters mean 'Blessed be the one who is guided' (*Ṭūbā liman hudiya*); and some have said they mean 'O you who are pure! O you who guides!' (*Yā Ṭāhir, Yā Hādi*) with the *ṭā'* referring to the Prophet's own purity ﷺ and to his having purified (others) from the stains of the sensual world, and the *hā'* to his having been guided himself and having guided others to the Sacred Presence. It has also been related that he said ﷺ, 'I have ten names,' and among them he mentioned *Ṭā Hā* and *Yā sīn.*[1]

Some have also said that (these letters) mean 'Place (*ṭi'*) your

1. The full wording of this *ḥadīth*, quoted in the commentary of al-Qurṭubī, is: "Verily, I have ten names with my Lord, be He glorified: Muḥammad, Aḥmad, Abū'l-Qāsim, *al-Fātiḥ*, *al-Khātim*, *al-Māḥī*, *al-ʿĀqib*, *al-Ḥāshir*, Ṭā Hā, and Yā Sīn." This

foot down upon the earth,' for while offering lengthy night prayers, (the Prophet) would sometimes raise one foot up to rest it... The letter *hā'* would then be understood as (a pronoun) referring to the earth...And some, including Ibn ʿAbbās, Ḥasan, Mujāhid and others, who considered these letters to be Nabatean or Syriac, have said that they mean 'O man!' (In respect to recitation), those who understand *Ṭā Hā* to mean 'O man' or to be a name of the Prophet, or an oath by one of the Names of God, do not pause between it and the verse that follows, while those who consider it to be simply the opening of the *sūrah*, similar to *Alif Lām Mīm* at the beginning of *al-Baqara*, pause after it.

What is most agreed upon, given (both) the circumstances of the revelation and the words which follow, is that *Ṭā Hā* may be understood either as an oath or as a form of address. As the former, it is one of God's names and as the latter, it is God's calling (to human beings), 'O man!' or (to His Prophet) by one of his names ﷺ...

[2] God, the Truth ﷻ, says to His Prophet ﷺ to console him or to give him rest from his exertions: 'O Muḥammad, *We have not revealed to you this Qur'ān* so that you should weary yourself in physically taxing devotions.' For it is narrated that the Prophet ﷺ would stand so long in night prayers that his feet would swell up, until Gabriel came to him and said, 'Ease up on your soul, for verily it has a right upon you.' (So these words mean) 'We have not revealed this Qur'ān for you to exhaust yourself with practices that are physically taxing and hard to bear. You "were not sent except with what is *pure and lenient*."'[2] This verse may also be understood to mean, 'We have not revealed it to you so that you wear yourself out trying to convey it to people who are intransigent and staunchly opposed, so that you become grieved and saddened because they do not believe'—as God's words elsewhere declare, *And it may be that you grieve your soul that they are not among the faithful* [26:3]. [We have sent it] only that you might convey it, and this you have done...'

Some *tafsīrs* have also said that these words were God's answer to (the taunts of) Abū Jahl and al-Nadr bin al-Ḥārith who had said to the Prophet, "You are miserable since you left the religion of

ḥadīth, with slightly different wording, is mentioned by al-Iṣfahāni in *Dalā'il al-Nubūwa*, and in *Iḥyā ʿulūm al-dīn*, II:20.

2. This refers to a *ḥadīth* in the *Musnad* of Imām Aḥmad and elsewhere: "Verily have I been sent with what is pure and lenient (*al-ḥanīfiya al-musammaḥa*)..."

your forefathers! This Qur'ān was only sent to you to cause you misery." But the first (explanation) is the most widely accepted, and the more general meaning is better for it negates, in his respect, misery in this world or the Next.[3]

[3] *But only as a reminder to anyone with reverent fear.* That is, 'We have not revealed the Qur'ān to weary you, but rather as a reminder and exhortation to anyone with reverent fear of God, whose heart is sensitive enough and whose nature supple enough to be affected by it...' And if only this kind of person is mentioned, even though the Reminder and its communication is meant for all, it is because they are the ones who will truly benefit from it.

[4] *A revelation* (*tanzīlan*),[4] that is, it is a revelation sent down, *from the one who created the earth and the heavens sublime...*To say that it *is from the one* after having said "We," expresses the majesty of God in His Essence after having expressed the majesty of His Attributes and Actions,[5] and if only *the earth and the heavens* are mentioned here, it is because in their opposite natures [they encompass all other created forms], with mention of the earth preceding that of the heavens because it is physically closer to human beings. Lastly, the exaltedness of the heavens expressed in the plural form—*ʿulā*—indicates both their multiplicity and sublimity.[6] All this, up to the words *His are the most beautiful Names*, affirms the greatness of the One who sends down the revelation as well as the one who to whom it was sent, and invokes a sense of awe that should bring the haughty down from the heights of their arrogance and encourage them towards reverence, remembrance, and faith.

[5] Then God Most High says: *The All-Merciful* (*al-Raḥmān*). After having described Himself as the Creator [of the earth and heavens], He describes Himself as *the All-Merciful*, meaning that He is Lord and nurturer of all things not by necessity but by His mercy. Here, too, is a reminder that the revelation of the Qur'ān is also by His mercy, as His words elsewhere declare: *The All-Merciful, Who taught the Qur'ān* [55:1,2]. This Name may be understood to refer to what precedes it [in the *sūrah*] or as the subject of the phrase which

3. The adjective *shaqī* (miserable) is also used to refer to the denizens of hell.

4. Literally, "a sending down."

5. The sovereign "We" relates more strongly to God in His Attributes and Actions,

6. *ʿŪlā* is the feminine plural form of *ʿalī*, 'high, elevated, sublime.'

follows it: *established upon the Throne*. To all this God gives the title *mercy*, indicating that it is something clear, self-evident, and needing no other explanation for any one being addressed.

Established upon the Throne is a figurative expression of dominion and authority. We may say that someone "assumed the seat of power" even if he is not physically sitting. Here it means that the Divine power (*qudra*) and overwhelming strength (*qahhariyya*) are expressed throughout all existence through God's direction and control.[7]

When Aḥmad ibn Ḥanbal was asked about (these words) he said, "(They refer to) the One Who overwhelms and subdues all, not to (any action) that human beings could ever imagine." And when Imām Mālik and al-Shāfiʿī were asked, they said: "*Being seated* (*al-istiwā'*) is understood. Its manner is unknown. To believe in it is obligatory, and to ask about it is reprehensible innovation and error. Believe (in it) without making comparisons, affirm it without mental images, and totally avoid vain discussions concerning it." Junayd said, "God created the Throne above the seven heavens and made it a *qibla* for the supplications of all creatures. Then He placed it facing the heart of His believing servant, so that this heart might be a place of epiphany, revelation, and intimate discourse..."

[6] *To Him belongs what is in the heavens and what is in the earth...*, each and every individual thing they contain and both of them taken in their totality. *What is between them* means the creations always found there, such as clouds and wind, or often found there, such as birds. To Him alone does all this belong and to no other, neither as a partner or independently. All that is mentioned is His to possess and act upon, in its life and in its death, in its existence and its non-being. (To Him, as well, belongs) *what is beneath the soil*, meaning beneath the (layer of the) earth that is in contact with the atmosphere. For Muḥammad bin Kʿab, however, this means what is beneath the seven earths, and according to al-Suddī, the word 'soil' (*al-tharā'*) refers to the stone upon which they rest.

[7] *And if you speak aloud ...*, that is, if you invoke or supplicate God

7. Echoing the words of the Qur'ān in 10:4, 10:31, 13:2, 32:5: *He directs all things* (*yudabbiru'l-amr*). An example of what Ibn ʿAjība means here may be found in what are called "the immutable laws of nature." It is by divine direction and planning (*al-tadbīr*) that the sun, at least from our perspective, rises in the east, and it is by divine constraint (*al-qahhariya*) that it cannot do otherwise.

out loud, know that He does not need your invocation or supplication to be in a loud voice for *He knows what is secret and what is more hidden.* He knows what you confide to someone else, and what is even more hidden than that: what you conceive of in your mind but do not utter, and what you conceal inside yourself now and in the future.

These words may also be understood as prohibition against loudness in invocation, as in the verse *And remember your Lord in yourself* [7:205], or taken as an instruction to God's servants that if they invoke (Him) aloud, it is not so that He may hear them, but rather for other reasons. It may be to help the soul grow fond of invocation and thus make it easier to establish as a practice, or it may be to help it avoid distractions, or to cut it off from whisperings, or to humble it in neediness and fervent prayer. This verse, then, is an expression of God's All-Encompassing Knowledge, just as (the previous verse) was an expression of His All-Inclusive Sovereignty and Power.

[8] Then, to explain Who is described by all these perfections, He says: *Allāh! There is no god except Him.* That is, He is the only one truly worshipped and none other is worthy of worship. This is a statement of the exclusive divinity of God, for to be the Creator of all that exists, the possessor of infinite Mercy, the omnipotent, and omniscient requires that divinity and Lordhood be exclusively God's. Thus, the words of God Most High which follow—*His are the most beautiful Names*—explain that all that has been mentioned so far about His being Creator, Merciful, Omnipotent, and Omniscient are qualities among His Names and Attributes, without any plurality in His Essence. Though the Names and Attributes are many, there is but One Whom they describe... And God Most High knows best.

Spiritual Allusion

Anyone who reflects deeply upon the Qur'ān and what the Prophet ﷺ brought will find that all of it directs us towards what will give us rest and relief, not weariness and distress, and to supreme happiness, not misery. But no one achieves this rest except after exertion, and no servant will reach supreme happiness except by seeking it. If he makes efforts to seek his Lord, God will put him in the care of a spiritual master who will then guide him from physical practices to practices of the heart, and when practice reaches the heart, the limbs of the body rest and the seeker is brought to *repose and tranquility and a garden*[8] and the Divine Pleasure, by which I mean the garden of gnosis. Even thus did Shaykh Abū'l-Ḥasan (al-Shādhilī) say: 'Your shaykh is not the one who leads you to weariness. Your shaykh is the one who relieves you of weariness.'[9]

And when the master of our masters, the *quṭb*, Ibn Mashīsh, was asked about the words of the Prophet ﷺ: "Make it easy for them; do not make it difficult,' he replied: 'He means direct them to God and do not direct them to anything else. For whoever directs you to the world cheats you, and whoever directs you to deeds wearies you, but whoever directs you to God gives you true counsel."[10] This is because when he directs you to God, he helps you to lose yourself in the consciousness of your Lord, and this is the supreme happiness....If you take as a master someone who does not convey you out of the station of physical weariness, and does not convey you from station to station, then know that he is not really fit to teach others in the path.

And as for His words, *Except as a reminder to one who has reverent fear*, the master of our masters, Sīdī ʿAbdurraḥmān, the gnostic, wrote: "God revealed the Qur'ān as a reminder of our pre-temporal state. For when the soul enters the body, it acquires a sense of fear, estrangement, and separation from their Source. So God revealed the Qur'ān as a way to restore to us our intimacy (with Him), for a lover finds intimacy both in the writing and the speech of his Beloved. Jāfar [al-Sādiq] said, 'God sent down the Qur'ān as admonition to those who fear, mercy to those who believe, and intimacy to those who love...The Qur'ān, which reminds us of the Majesty of God, instills reverent fear, and this removes heedlessness ... In the consciousness (of God) which comes through the Reminder, weariness is lifted from our shoulders, and we find rest in our devotions because they are borne (by God). Thus did He say, *And establish prayer for My Remembrance,* that is, in order that you might

8. *Rawḥūn wa rayḥānun wa jannatun* is a reference to 56:88-89: *And if he be among those brought nigh, then repose and tranquility and a Garden of delight.*

9. Mentioned in *Laṭā'if al-Minan,* Chapter 1, page 88.

10. The *ḥadīth* "Make it easy for them; do not make it difficult (and give them glad tidings and do not repel them)" can be found in the collections of Muslim, Bukhārī, and many others. This saying is also quoted in *Laṭā'if al-Minan,* Chapter 6, page 140.

be conscious of Me when you offer it, for in this (consciousness) you will find such rest, relief, and intimacy, that your state will come to resemble that of Moses ﷺ communing (with his Lord). This is why he is mentioned here in this *sūrah*. And God Most High knows better.'"[11]

And as for His words: *The All-Merciful, established upon the Throne*, its explanation is in what Ibn ʿAṭā'illāh meant in the *Ḥikam* [34]: "O You who are upon the Throne in Your All-Mercifulness so that the Throne is hidden in Your All-Mercifulness just as the universe is hidden in Your Throne. You have effaced created beings by created beings and effaced alterities (*al-āthār*) by all-encompassing spheres of Light."[12]

And you, (O aspirant), know well that All-Mercifulness (*al-Raḥmāniyya*) is an attribute of the Essence and that an attribute cannot be separated from the One Described. So if All-Mercifulness has settled upon the Throne and subsumed it, then the very Mysteries of the Essence have settled there and subsumed it, these being the spheres of Light which encompass the Throne, created beings, and everything else, effacing all until there remains but the One Who is like no other, the One with Whom there is nothing else, *and He is the Hearer and the Seer.* There is no more resemblance between those physical creatures and the spheres of Divine Mysteries settled upon the Throne than there is between motes of dust and the air in which they float.[13] And God Most High knows better and is greater.

Then, as comfort to the Messenger ﷺ, God mentions the story of Moses ﷺ.

> *9. Have you heard tell of Moses, 10. When he saw a fire and said to his family, "Wait here. Verily I see a fire. Perhaps I shall bring you a brand therefrom, or find guidance at the fire"? 11. Then when he came to it, he was called, "O Moses! 12. Verily I am your Lord. Take off your sandals. Truly you are in the holy valley of Ṭuwā. 13. I have chosen you, so listen to what is revealed. 14. Truly I, even I, am God. There is no god except Me. So worship Me, and perform the prayer for My remembrance. 15. Surely the Hour is*

11. *Al-Ḥāshiya*, I:484.

12. *Ḥikam, al-Munājāt* (Intimate Conversations), 34.

13. Referring to the saying of al-Shādhilī: "We do not see creation, but if we must, we see it like motes of dust floating in the air. If you look closely, you find nothing."

> *coming. I would keep it hidden, that every soul might be recompensed for its endeavors. 16. So do not be turned away from it by the one who does not believe and who follows his caprices, or you will perish.*

Al-Qushayrī says, "It is God's way in His Book that in most of the places in which He speaks directly to our Prophet ﷺ, He then mentions (some of) the story of Moses ﵇. This is an indication of (Moses') great importance, for just as it is an honor to the one mentioned to be chosen for mention, to then repeat that mention in different places increases that excellence. Rhetorically, when something is repeated, it is more complete, especially when each mention expresses another virtue."

Another aspect of why [the two are mentioned together] may be in the fact that they had similar roles to play and shared qualities in respect to how they guided and dealt with their [religious] communities. The community of the Moses ﵇ spread through the earth in a way that would never happen for any other prophet except for our Prophet, may the most excellent and purest blessings be upon him, whose community spread to every land in the orbits of the sun and moon. This is shown in a *ḥadīth* found in the Bukhārī collection [which states] that when the religious communities were shown to the Prophet ﷺ, he first sees the multitude of followers of Moses ﵇ and then sees his own community completely filling the horizons.[14]

Abū al-Saʿūd said, "This is in the context of the affirmation of God's oneness which end God's words to Moses ﵇—*Truly, I, even I, am God. There is no god except Me. So worship Me* [20:14]—and with which Moses ﵇ ends his address [to Pharaoh]: *Your only god is Allāh, besides whom there is no other god* [20:98]. Then the discourse returns to consoling the Prophet ﷺ, since in the context of the

14. The text in al-Bukhārī states that God's Messenger ﷺ said [speaking of his ascension] , 'Communities were displayed before me. In some cases, one or two prophets would pass by along with a few followers and there would be prophets who passed by with no one. Then a multitude was brought before me and I asked, 'What is this? Is this my community?' And it was said to me, 'No. This is Moses and his people.' Then it was said to me, 'Look at the horizon.' And behold! There was a multitude who filled the horizon. Then it was said to me, 'And look there into the heavens,' and behold, there was a multitude filling the heavens.' Then it was said to me, 'This is your community, of whom seventy thousand shall enter Paradise without reckoning.' Bukhārī, *Kitāb al-Ṭib*, h. 5705.

Noble verses, all this is to relieve him ﷺ of grief...

[9] *Have you heard tell of Moses...* that is, the story of Moses' dealings with Pharaoh. 'We shall mention it to you as consolation and confirmation of (God's) Oneness.' *When he saw a fire* burning in the distant valley. This (occurred) when he had asked permission of Shuʿayb ﷺ to go and visit his mother and brother and had gone forth with his family on a road not used by the kings of Shām. And when they reached the valley of Ṭuwā, which is on the west side of the mountain, in the middle of a dark and freezing Friday night, his wife bore him a son. Also, he had lost his way, his flock had scattered, he was out of water, and had tried to kindle a fire, but his flint would not give spark.

In the midst of all this, he saw a (distant) fire on the side of the mountain *and said to his family, "Wait here..."* commanding them thusly so that they would not follow him, as is a habit of women. These words he said either to his wife, maid-servant, and baby son, or to his wife alone, in which case he used the plural (*umkuthū*) out of respect. *Verily I see a fire.* It is said that the verb *anasa* is more particular than *abṣara* and denotes 'seeing something familiar.'[15] *Perhaps I shall bring you a brand therefrom* by lighting a torch from the larger fire, referred to in *Sūrat al-Qaṣaṣ* by the word *jadhwā*, 'a burning ember,' [28:29] and (in *Sūrat al-Naml*) as *shihābin qabasin* [27:7], 'a burning branch from which to kindle another fire.' *Or* (I may) *find guidance at the fire*, that is, 'someone who will direct me to the right road...' but the word "or" (*aw*) in this context also means "both," for it is possible that he would be able both to kindle a branch from the fire and also find someone to guide him...[16]

[11-13] *Then when he came to it*, according to Ibn ʿAbbās ﷺ, he saw a green tree, said by some to have been a boxthorn or an acacia, engulfed from top to bottom in a white fire, glowing with the brightest light there is. And as he stood there, gazing upon it, amazed by its intensity, *he was called, "O Moses! Verily I am your Lord..."* The emphatic form (*innīya Ana*) adds affirmation and identification, and

---

15. Both these verbs may be translated by the word "see", but *anasa* means to see something familiar and welcoming (*mā yu'nasu bihi*). From this same root is derived the word *uns*, intimacy, and *insān*, a human being.

16. Here he also explains that the phrase *ʿalā al-nār*, translated above as *at the fire*, literally means 'over the fire' or 'upon the fire,' because that is the way people sit around a fire warming their hands.

removes any doubt (who the speaker is). About this, it has been related that when Moses first heard his name called, he said ﷺ, "Who is speaking to me?' and God answered, "I am your Lord (*Ana Rabbuka*)," but the thought occurred to him that perhaps he was hearing the speech of the Devil." And Moses said: "But when He said, *Verily I am* (*innanīya Ana*), I knew it was the speech of God, be He glorified." And according to some *tafsīrs*, he heard this voice from all directions and with all the limbs of his body.[17]

Then God said to him, *Take off your sandals*, for that is correct comportment (*ḥusni'l-adab*) at such a moment. From this have the Sufis (may God be pleased with them) taken (their habit of) removing their sandals in the presence of spiritual masters and leaders, and from this, too, comes (the practice of) removing them—even if they be pure—upon entering a mosque as a sign of reverence. Some commentators have said that (he had to remove) his sandals because they were made from untanned donkey leather (and so were impure), and some say (that it was) so that his bare feet might touch the earth of the holy valley of Ṭuwā. Others have said that the sandals (signify) the two realms of existence (this world and the Next), and that if you wish to enter the Divine Presence, you must first empty your heart of both. *Truly, you are in the holy valley of Ṭuwā* states the reason why he was commanded to remove (his sandals), and it has been related (that as soon as he heard this), he took them off and cast them out of the valley...[18]

'*I have chosen you* to receive prophecy and scripture... *So lis-*

17. This narrative is recounted in the commentary of Rāzī in more detail: "When Moses ﷺ beheld the fire rising up from the tree into the sky and heard the glorifications of the angels, he covered his eyes with his hands. Then he was called to, 'O Moses!' and answered, 'I am at your service! (*Labayka*). I hear Your voice but do not see You. Where are You?' And God answered, 'I am with you and before you and behind you and surrounding you, and I am nearer to you than you are to yourself.' Then Iblīs cast doubt into the mind of Moses, saying, 'How do you know you are hearing the words of God?' And Moses answered, 'Because I hear these words from above me and below me and behind me and on my right and on my left, even as I hear them from in front of me. And so I know that this is not the speech of a created being. And it comes from all directions, so that I might hear Him with every part of me, with every limb, as if my whole body had become a single ear.'"

18. The word *wādi*, here translated as 'valley,' may also mean 'a dry river bed.' In respect to the word *Ṭūwā*, Ibn ʿAjība notes here that if this word is recited with nunation (*Ṭūwan*), it refers to a specific place, and if without nunation, it refers to a piece of ground.

ten to what is revealed to you by inspiration, listen to Our revelation to you: *Truly, I, even I, am God. There is no god except Me* (*innanīya Ana'Llāhu, lā ilāha illā Ana*)*... So worship Me,* and submit to Me alone.' The conjunction "then" (*fa*) marks a causal order between what is before it and what is after it, meaning that since Divinity is uniquely His, worship must be uniquely His.

And perform the prayer for My remembrance that you may remember (and invoke) Me, for the prayer is comprised of remembrance and invocation. And if only the prayer is mentioned as the embodiment of worship (*'ibāda*), this is because it involves both the heart and the tongue with remembrance of the One worshipped, making it superior to all other devotional practices. Indeed, it is only within a devotional practice (such as the prayer) that remembrance is fully realized.

For My remembrance, may also be understood to mean 'Totally for the sake of My remembrance, seeking My Face, and not for the purpose of being seen by another;' or 'Because I have mentioned the prayer and commanded it in (all the sacred) scriptures;' or 'So that I might remember you in the prayer with praise;' or 'At the times established for My remembrance,' these being the times of prayer.[19] Others have said that these words mean, 'Upon remembering the prayer due to Me if you forget it,' based on the saying of the Prophet ﷺ, 'If one of you sleeps through the prayer (time) or forgets to offer it, then offer it when you remember it, for God Most High says: *And perform the prayer* at *My remembrance*.'[20]

And one of them has said: 'The principles of practice are three: speech, actions, and state. The best of speech is *lā ilāha illā Allāh;* the best of actions is the prayer for God or by God, and the best of states is the tranquility that comes from your witnessing God.'

[15] *Surely the Hour is coming...* It exists and is inevitable, and this is a reason that worship and the establishment of the prayer are obligatory. The participial form, 'coming' (*ātiya*), affirms its imminence.... *I would keep it hidden,* that is, 'I have not made it known, but only say, 'it is coming,' for it does not come *except unexpect-*

19. Referring to 17:78, *And establish the prayer at* (li) *the going down of the sun until the dark of night, and (recite) the Qur'ān at dawn. Truly (the recital of) the Qur'ān at dawn is witnessed.*

20. This *ḥadīth* is found in both Muslim and Bukhārī. The variations in meaning arise from the ways the particle *li* may be understood in this context: 'for the sake of...,' 'for the purpose of...,' 'because of,' and 'at the moment of...'

edly [7:187]...'[21] Al-Thalʿabī, quoting Ibn ʿAbbās and the majority of commentators, said (these words mean) 'I have almost hidden it from Myself so what about from others?' Thus does it appear in the copy (of the Qur'ān) made by Ubayy, while in the copy made by ʿAbdallāh (Ibn Masʿūd) are the words 'How can a created being know it?' and in some readings, 'How can I reveal it to you?'[22] Concerning this, Quṭrub said, 'And if it be asked, 'How could God hide something from Himself when He has created all things?' We would say, 'God Most High spoke to the Arabs in a manner they could understand.'... Even the appearance of the signs (of the Hour) do not make it less hidden. Ibn ʿArafa says in his commentary, "If it appeared the moment all its signs had been fulfilled, this would not make it any less hidden. Indeed, by mentioning its signs,[23] God has made it something midway between concealed and revealed, equally close to either."

The words of God Most High, *so that every soul might be recompensed for its endeavors* ... (may be understood to refer) either to the Hour's coming or to its being hidden... *So that every soul might be recompensed* by its deeds according to what it strove for, be it goodness or malice.

[16] So *do not be turned away from it ...* That is, *do not be turned away from* remembering the Hour and preparing for it *by someone who does not believe in it* lest you become lazy in making provision for it. This prohibition, *do not be turned away from it*, which in the context is directed to Moses ﷺ concerning his impending encounter with Pharaoh, is actually a warning to (the Prophet) ﷺ to avoid the means which might lead someone astray, similar to God's words elsewhere: *Let not the schism with me cause you to sin* [11:89].[24] Thus, the verse is saying, 'Do not follow anyone who denies the Hour, nor be turned away from it as he has been, and become one *who follows his own desires*, meaning the desires of his ego for ephemeral pleasures, *lest you be destroyed* ... For to remain heedless of (the Hour) and of how to be delivered from its calami-

21. Here Ibn ʿAjība explains that some in *tafsīrs*, the verb *ukhfī* ('I would keep it hidden') is explained to mean its opposite, but he rejects this possibility on linguistic grounds.

22. Certain among the Companions made copies of the Qur'ān for their own use, some of which contained notations on meaning or variant recitations.

23. The signs of the Hour are mentioned both in the Qur'ān and *ḥadīth*.

24. These are the words of the Prophet Hūd ﷺ to his people.

ties is surely self-destructive. And with God is all accord.

Spiritual Allusion

Have you heard tell, O gnostic, of how Moses journeyed to the Light of the Beloved and to intimate discourse with the One Who is Near? *When he saw a fire* in the eye's vision, and it was the Light of the Beloved revealing Himself with nothing between them. *And he said to his family* and those attached to him, *Wait here,* remain in this station of seeking, and *be patient, and vie in patience* [3:200] and strengthen each other's hearts in reaching what is Sought. *Verily, I see a fire*, which is the Light of the Beloved's Face perceived in a vision of His theophany, and this is the Station of Effacement (*al-fanā'*). *Perhaps I shall bring you a brand therefrom* that you might kindle from it lights for your hearts and your innermost souls. *Or (I might) find there guidance* that will direct me to the Station of Subsistence (*al-baqā'*) and stability. *Then when he came to it*, and was granted stability in his vision of it, *he was called, "O Moses! Verily I am your Lord.* Here there is no fire, there is nothing created, only the Face of the Beloved unveiled in world of effects. *Take off your sandals* and leave behind both realms of existence if you wish to witness the Presence of the One Who brings all into being:

> Take off your sandals if you have come
> To that precinct where Our holiness resides;
> Cast off both the realms of creation,
> And be rid of all that is between us.

Truly you are in the holy valley of Ṭuwā, that is, in the Ocean of the Divine Presence and the Abode of Intimacy. Existence has been folded up (*ṭuwīyat*) such that you see with the light of witnessing and vision. *I have chosen you* to be in My Presence and selected you for intimate discourse, *so listen to what is revealed* to you from Me: *Truly I, even I, am God. There is no god except Me.* Then, when you have been granted stability in your consciousness of Me, go down in gratitude to the Station of Servanthood and *perform the prayer for My remembrance. Surely the Hour is coming* without doubt, and I have honored you, exalted you, and elevated you to be among those brought nigh.

So do not be turned away from the station of vision by those who stubbornly reject (these realities), lest you fall from the station of proximity and intimacy and are left among those who are veiled by the sensory world. It may be that this is what Ibn al-Fāriḍ meant by his words:

I saw in the precinct a fire by night
and gave glad tidings to my people.
I said to them 'Wait. I shall go on ahead.
Perhaps I can find there guidance.'
Then I drew near, and there was a Fire
with which one had spoken before me,
and from it I was called to in a loud, clear voice:
'Bring back those nights of union.'
And when the time of meeting drew nigh,
my mountain was scattered to dust
in awe of the One unveiled before me,
and a hidden secret gleamed forth,
a secret which anyone like me will know:
To die in God: that is my life,
And in my life is my slaying.
And I became a Moses for my time
when what was a part of me became my totality.

'My mountain was scattered to dust' means 'the mountain of my separative existence was eclipsed in the light of the One Revealed, and *He is the Great and Sublime.*' This follows the subduing and death of the individual ego, which is then given new life by the vision of its Lord, a life after which there is no death. His words 'When what was a part of me became my totality' mean that, upon the effacement of his senses, when he was granted intimate communion (with God) and true nearness, his individual spirit was united with the all-encompassing Spirit, and that is the ocean of pure Spirit in which all vessels are subsumed. And in God is all success.

Then God recounts His words with His beloved interlocutor, Moses ﷺ:

17. *"And what is that in your right hand, O Moses?"* 18. *He said, "It is my staff. I lean upon it and beat down leaves for my sheep. And I have other uses for it."* 19. *He said, "Cast it down O Moses!"* 20. *So he cast it down, and behold, it was a serpent, moving swiftly.* 21. *He said, "Take hold of it, and fear not! We shall restore it to its former way.* 22. *And enclose your hand in your side. It*

will come forth white, without blemish, as another sign, 23. That We may show You some of Our greatest signs.

[17] God, the Truth 🏵 says: *"And what is that in your right hand, O Moses?"* He asks him this in order to show him the power of what He is about to do with the staff, turning it into a living serpent. So this question is in order that Moses 🕊 might affirm that at that moment it is indeed his staff. But it has also been said that this question was a way to create ease and familiarity with Moses, who then answers, *it is my staff*, affirming both that it belongs to him and that it is in his right hand.[25]

This staff has been said to have originally belonged to Adam 🕊 and had been given to Moses by Shuʿayb when he began to work for him as a shepherd as mentioned in *Sūrat al-Qasas* ...[26] It has also been said that the top of the staff was forked and the bottom pointed and that, according to Muqātil, its name was *Nabaʿa*.[27]

'I lean upon it for support when I walk, or when I am weary, or when I am standing at the head of my flock, and with it I *beat down leaves* for my sheep....[28] *And I have other uses for it.'* Ibn ʿAbbās said: "Moses 🕊 would carry his food and water with this staff and it was made to come to him and guard him. If he struck the earth with it, there would emerge from that spot a day's sustenance, and if he drove its pointed end into the ground, water would flow forth until he raised it back up. He would also use it to ward off predators from his flock, with the permission of God, and when a foe would approach, the staff would drive him away. When he wished

---

25. In *al-Tafsīr al-Kabīr*, Imām al-Rāzī explains that after Moses had been shown the tree illuminated with a light that reached far into the sky, and had heard the angels glorifying God, and had been allowed to hear even the voice of God, he 🕊 was so overwhelmed by awe and bewilderment that he no longer knew his right hand from his left. So God Most High asked him this simple question that he could answer without error. "Even thus," continues Rāzī, "will it be for the believer when he dies and comes into the Presence of the All-Mighty so overwhelmed with awe and shame that he cannot speak—even thus will he first be asked a question about a matter concerning which he never erred while in the world, and that is the Oneness of God."

26. Q. 28:22-28

27. This word may mean 'spring' or 'source,' but also refers to a type of tree whose wood was used to make bows.

28. Ibn ʿAjība notes that the word, *ahushshu*, translated here as 'I beat down leaves,' is sometimes read *ahussu*, 'I herd my flock,' for when the Arabs herded animals, they would say, *Hass! Hass!*

to draw water from a well, he would extend the staff down into it and it would lengthen to the depth of the well. Then its forked end would become like a bucket to bring up water. At night there would appear upon that same end what was like two candles to give him light, and when he came to a tree and desired to eat of its fruit, he would drive the staff into the ground near it and the tree would put forth a branch from which would emerge leaves and then fruit. Such were its *other uses.*[29]

Here, it is as if Moses ﷺ had understood that the point of the question was for him to explain what the staff was and to detail its uses, and so his speech became somewhat verbose, but when marvels came forth through it, he knew it was a clear sign from God and an astonishing miracle. Also, 'Verbosity between good friends is laudable.'

[19-20] God Most High says to him: *'Cast it down, O Moses... so that you might see things about it you never imagined.'* It has also been said that Moses ﷺ was ordered to cast it down to end the comfort he derived from it and from its 'other uses,' and for that same reason, God Most High went so far as to turn it into a snake that Moses ﷺ would fear... *So he cast it down* upon the earth, *and behold, it was a serpent, moving swiftly.* It has been related that when he cast it down, it became a yellow serpent as thick as the staff and then began to swell in size. Thus, it is called *ḥayyatun* here, and elsewhere *jānn* [27:10 and 28:31] and *thʿubān* [7:107], each name reflecting a change in its appearance and size...[30] Then after (God) had taken away the comfort (Moses) had found in it and had so removed it from his heart that he fled from it, He returned it to him, saying: "*Take hold of it,*" O Moses, "*and fear not!*" Ibn ʿAbbās ﷺ said that when it changed to a viper (*thʿubān*), it began to swallow up every bush and stone (around it) and it was when Moses ﷺ saw this that he *became afraid and turned to flee* [27:10]. The fear and shock that befell him is what would befall any human being in the face of something terrifying, for sainthood does not preclude human

29. Ibn Kathīr considers all this to be *Isrā'īliyāt* (see introduction p. xii). He also reasons that if Moses ﷺ had known that the staff was capable of such miraculous things, its subsequent transformation into a snake would not have shocked him as it did. Regardless of whether one accepts Ibn Kathīr's reasoning, virtually the same passage is quoted in a number of the earliest *tafsīrs* including Zamakhsharī, Rāzī, Bayḍāwī, and al-Khāzinī.

30. The Arabic words refer to different types of snakes, somewhat analogous in English to 'snake,' 'viper,' and 'serpent.'

traits. *We shall restore it to its former way.* 'As soon as you grasp it, We shall restore the staff to its original state.' It is said that when he heard this, Moses ﷺ gained such fearlessness and confidence that he put his hand in the serpent's mouth and took hold of its fangs, at which moment it turned back into a staff. It is also said that the reason that God transformed it into a snake and then commanded Moses to take hold of it was so that he might gain confidence and calmness for the moment he would confront Pharaoh and show neither surprise nor fright...

[22] Then God showed him yet another miracle, saying *And enclose your hand in your side,* meaning under your upper arm. The word *janāḥ* literally means 'wing,' and for a human being, this 'wing' is the side of his body under his arm. *It will come forth white.* That is, 'If you thrust your hand beneath your arm it will come out glowing white *without blemish,*' meaning that its white color will not be due to some disease such as leprosy.' And it has been related that Moses ﷺ was of a dark, ruddy color but when he brought forth his hand, it was white with rays like the rays of the sun. This was *another sign,* a miracle in addition to the staff, *that We may show you some of Our greatest signs.* That is, 'We have done what We have done in order to show you some of Our mightiest signs,' or 'In order to show you the greatest of Our signs,' or 'In order to show you, from among Our signs, the single greatest one,' and Ibn ʿAbbās ﷺ said, "The hand of Moses was His greatest sign." And God Most High knows better.

Spiritual Allusion

It is said to the *faqīr*, '*And what is that in your right hand?*' and he answers, 'It is my world. I depend on it for my living, and spend of it for my dependents, and through it, I fulfill other needs: beauty, charitable works, acts of piety.' Then it is said to him, '*Cast it down* from your hand, O *faqīr*: get yourself out of it, or get it out of your heart, if you can, and be detached from it.'

So he casts it down and gets away from it *and behold,* it is a serpent which was biting him and seeking to destroy him while he was unaware. Then, when he is granted stability in his certitude and equilibrium, it is said to him, '*Take hold of it, and fear not!*' for by having rejected the world of secondary causes, you have come to know the ultimate Cause of All,[31] so that whether you have (the world) or not, whether it is given to you or withheld from you, becomes equal in your eyes. Then *We shall restore it to its former way.* You will find your uses in it, and it will labor for you, not you for it, even as God Most High says: *O My world, serve whoever serves Me and make weary whoever serves you.*[32] ....

As for the *ḥadīth* which quotes God as saying [to the world]: *Be bitter to My friends, not sweet, lest you tempt them away from Me,*[33] the bitterness mentioned is from tribulations and illness, the fatigue of journeying, and injury at the hands of the vicious. Indeed, some of them have found in outward poverty the honor expressed by the Prophet ﷺ when he said, "Poverty is my pride and by it I am honored."[34]

About these sayings, my master al-Būzīdī ؓ said, "The first.. (*serve whomsoever serves Me*) concerns the pious seekers from among the folk of outward knowledge, while the second (*be bitter to My friends*) concerns the gnostic saints from among the folk of inward knowledge.'

And it is also said to the *faqīr*—if he withdraws from the workaday world and casts it from his hand and his heart—'*Reach* with the hand of contemplation into your heart and *it will come out white*, luminous and pure, undiluted and undiminished, and this is *another sign*, along with withdrawal from the world and patience in the face of hardships.

---

31. 'The world of causality' (*al-asbāb*, literally, 'causes' or 'means') refers to the everyday world. For the Sufis, it is generally taken to mean 'working for a living,' with the implication that this is only the illusory means by which one's sustenance comes, while in truth, God is the true Provider and the ultimate Cause.

32. In some collections, this has been related as a *ḥadīth qudsī*, but is more likely a saying of one of the saintly.

33. This is close in wording to a *ḥadīth* in Bayhaqī, *Shuʿab al-Imān* (9800), narrated by Qatāda who said:

The Messenger of God ﷺ said: "God sent down Gabriel in the most beautiful form I had ever seen and he said to me, 'Truly God conveys to you salutations, O Muḥammad, and says to you: In truth have I said to the world through inspiration, Be bitter and turbid and a loss and a hardship to My friends in order that they might love the meeting with Me, for truly have I created the world as a prison for My friends and a paradise for My foes.'"

34. This is sometimes narrated as being a *ḥadīth*, but is more likely a saying of one of the pious.

It is written in *al-Lubāb*,[35] "The *hand* is the hand of contemplation and the *pocket*[36] is the pocket of comprehension from which the hand emerges white with gnosis." And al-Wartajibī said: 'God showed Moses ﷺ His greatest sign in his hand, for He enrobed it with lights from the Hand of His Power (*Qudra*) so that the hand of Moses was the Hand of God's Power' in its form and attributes, as in the *ḥadīth*: 'For him I am his hearing, his sight, his tongue, and his hand.'[37] And in God is all success.

Then God mentions the beginning of Moses' message.

> 24. *"Go to Pharaoh! Truly he has become a tyrant!"* 25. *(Moses) said, "My Lord! Expand for me my breast!* 26. *Make my task easy for me,* 27. *And untie a knot from my tongue,* 28. *That they may understand my speech.* 29. *And appoint for me a helper from among my family,* 30. *Aaron, my brother.* 31. *Through him, increase my strength,* 32. *And make him a partner in my task,* 33. *That we may glorify You much* 34. *And remember You much.* 35. *Truly You are ever seeing us."*

[24] God, the Truth ﷻ says to His prophet Moses ﷺ: 'Go to Pharaoh with the mighty signs you have seen, call him to worship Me Alone, and warn him of My wrath.' *Truly he has become a tyrant,* that is, 'He has transgressed all limits in pride, intransigence, and arrogance and has even attributed to himself divinity.'

[25-26] Seeking the help of his Lord ﷻ, Moses says, '*My Lord, expand for me my breast.*' That is, 'Make it broad enough to bear the weight of this message.' *And make my task easy for me* so that nothing I intend to do is too hard.'... The moment he is charged with this mighty task, he humbles himself before his All-Mighty Lord, acknowledges his own powerlessness and weakness, and asks his Lord to expand his breast, grant him understanding of people's ranks and conditions, and make him forbearing and lenient so that if he confronts their hardness and rejection, he can do so with the beauty of patience, magnanimity, and calm. And along with this, he asks that the task he is facing—which is the greatest (a human

---

35. *Lubāb fī mushkilāt al-kitāb* is a *tafsīr* by the Moroccan Sufi Abū ʿAbdallāh al-Shṭaybī (see biographical index).

36. In 27:12 and 28:32, Moses ﷺ is told to put his hand into the fold of his robe, *jīb*, or 'pocket,' which covers his breast. A number of traditional garments have this simple sewn pocket at the breast.

37. See note 152 above.

being can face) involving the most difficult discourse—be made easy for him by removing any obstacles (he might encounter). The addition of the particle *lī* ("for me") in his [first two supplications] even while they are comprehensible without it, stresses how important these first two were to him.

[27] Then he says, *And untie*, that is, untangle *a knot from my tongue* and make it more intelligible. It has been related that there was a scar on his tongue from having put an ember in his mouth as an infant. [This happened] one day when he was in Pharaoh's chambers, and slapped him and pulled his beard. Pharaoh said to his wife Āsīya, 'This one is my enemy!' She replied, 'Do not be so severe! He is but an infant who does not even know the difference between an ember and a ruby.' [To test her point], two trays were brought, one bearing an ember and the other a ruby. Then Gabriel came [unseen], took the hand of the enfant Moses, and (caused him) to raise the ember to his mouth and place it on his tongue. This is what left the scar. ....

In respect to whether this scar ever disappeared completely, there are [two] views. Those who say that it did cite as evidence the words *You have been granted your request, O Moses* [20:36], while those who say it did not cite the words of Moses about his brother Aaron, *[he] is more eloquent than I in speech* [28:34] and the words (of Pharaoh), *This one... who can scarcely speak plain* [43:52]. They also point out that in Moses' supplication, he did not ask God to remove the knot from his tongue completely, but only enough so that people could understand his speech. So in response to his supplication, the impediment was lessened, but was not all together removed. Thus, this verse could be read, '(*Untie*) *a* knot that is in my tongue so that people can understand what I say.'

[29-32] *And appoint for me a helper from among my family, Aaron, my brother,* 'who will support and strengthen me in conveying the message.' *Through him, strengthen my back,*' that is, 'Give me strength through him, *and let him share my task* as my partner, so that we might help one another in conveying the message as it should be conveyed.'

[33-35] [So] *that we may glorify You much...* This is the object of the last three supplications, beginning with the words *appoint for me a helper*. Without a doubt, to gather with others for worship and in-

vocation is a way of maintaining them as a practice and increasing in them. A *ḥadīth* states: "The Hand of God is with the assembly,"[38] and so much has been related that encourages gathering with others for *dhikr* and offering the prayer in assembly so that the strong may strengthen the weak and energetic may inspire the lazy. The word *much* (*kathīran*) can mean either in quantity or time. That is, 'That we may affirm in abundance Your transcendence above all that is not fitting to Your Majesty and Beauty, including whatever Pharaoh and his wanton entourage may claim, ascribing partners to Your divinity.'

[34-35] '*And* [so that we might] *remember You much* and mention You with the attributes of perfection that are fitting [to Your divinity]. *Truly, You are ever seeing us*: You know our states and know we are asking You for what will benefit us and strengthen us in the task we have been given...' And God Most High knows better.

Spiritual Allusion

O *faqīr*, when you have removed from yourself the two worlds and have thrown down your staff in the valley in between,[39] then go to the pharaoh of your ego and your sensory nature, *for he has become a tyrant* over you, veiling you from witnessing your Lord. For there is no veil between you and Your Lord except the veil of your ego and the veil of having stopped [your journey] at the level of your sensory nature (*ḥissik*). This is the biggest of the pharaohs you must face. Raze him to the ground and drown your perception of him in the ocean of the Truth, by passing away [from all else] in the perception of your Lord. And if this task becomes hard for you, seek help from your Guardian Lord and say, O God, *expand for me my breast* until it is vast enough to bear the direct knowledge of You. Make my task of journeying to Your Sacred Presence easy for me, and untie the knot of created beings from my heart and *my tongue*, until I am not bound to anything except Your Love, nor speak except to invoke You and thank You, even as the poet has said:

> And if I speak, I speak of no one else but You,
> And if I am silent, it is You who binds my *thoughts*

38. *Ḥadīth* in Bukhārī and Muslim.

39. *Wādī al-bayn* is understood by the Sufis to mean either the abode between beginninglessness and endlessness or the perfect distinction between the Lord and the servant.

And appoint for me a helper from among my family, that is, my shaykh. *Through him, increase my strength,* and let him share my task, that he might turn wholeheartedly towards my innermost soul and we might together affirm Your transcendence abundantly, until we see nothing else beside You, *and remember You much*, for we shall not cease to remember You through invocation with our hearts, souls, or innermost beings. *Truly, You are ever seeing us.*

Al-Wartajibī says about the words of God Most High, *Go to Pharaoh...*: 'When Moses knew that God wanted him to experience suffering at the hands of adversaries and return from contemplation to effort, he asked Him to expand his breast, to loosen his tongue, and ease his task so that he would be strong enough to bear the world of opposites and the tribulations they bring. Thus, he sought Divine strength and mastery with his words *My Lord! Expand for me my breast*! He knew that it was God's right upon him to place him in the abode of servanthood (*al-ʿubudiyya*), and to test him through it, and that in the course of that test, he might become veiled from the One Who was testing him. So fearing that, he asked that his breast be expanded, meaning, 'When I am in the cloud of the *sharīʿah* which may hide the *ḥaqīqah*, expand my breast with the lights of Your unveilings so that You are not hidden from me.' Do you not see how the master of the prophets and saints ﷺ spoke of that cloud and complained of being in the abode of opposites in order to deliver the message when he said, "A veil descends upon my heart so I seek forgiveness from God seventy times a day.."?[40] About this, however, it has been said that he meant a veil of light, not a veil of "otherness."[41] So reflect upon this. And God Most High knows better.

And God, the Truth ﷻ, answers his prayer.

> 36. *He said, "You have been granted your request, O Moses!* 37. *And We have indeed shown You favor another time,* 38. *When We revealed to your mother that which was revealed:* 39. *'Cast him into the ark and cast it into the sea. Then the sea will throw him upon the bank. An enemy to Me and an enemy to him shall take*

---

40. *Ḥadīth* recorded by Muslim and Abū Dāwūd.

41. It is related in *Laṭāʾif al-minan* that Shaykh Abū'l-Ḥasan al-Shādhilī pondered long about [this *ḥadīth*], but its meaning remained unclear to me until I saw the Messenger of God ﷺ and he said to me, 'O blessed one! I was speaking of a veil of light, not a veil of "otherness!"'" *Laṭāʾif al-minan*, pp 86-87 and also Roberts, *The Subtle Blessings*, p. 110.

> *him.' And I cast upon You a love from Me, that You might be formed under My eye.* 40. *When your sister went forth and said, 'Shall I show you one who can nurse him?' Thus We returned you to your mother that she might be comforted and grieve not. And you slew a soul, but We saved you from sorrow. And We tried you with trials. Then you remained some years among the people of Midian. Then you came [to this meeting], as determined, O Moses.* 41. *And I have selected you for Myself.*

[36] God, the Truth ﷻ, says to Moses ﵇ "*You have been granted your request, O Moses!*" ... That is, 'You have been given what you asked for and have been brought to what you were seeking.' The (verbal form of) *al-ītā'* (which carries the meaning of coming forth, and also of being carried out) signifies that [what Moses prayed for] concurred with the Divine Will, even if some of it would occur in the future, for God says to Moses elsewhere, *We will strengthen your arm with your brother* [28:35]. Through God's words *O Moses*, he is honored by being called by name after having been honored by having his prayer answered.

[37-38] Then God reminds him ﵇ of the graces he had received in the past, saying: '*And We have indeed shown you favor another time.* That is, 'We favored you before you ever asked Us, so how could We not answer you (now), after you have asked Us?' That favor was '*When We revealed to your mother,* in her desperation and fear for your life, *that which was revealed.*' That is, 'We showed her in a dream, or by inspiration, or by one of the noble angels ﵇ [that she should] "*Cast him into the ark,*" meaning, 'Place him in the cradle, then close it so no water gets inside, and cast the cradle into the *sea.*'

[39] *Then the sea will throw him upon the bank*, that is, cast him upon the shore. When bearing the cradle to the shore became the object of the Divine Will, this became a commandment and the sea a discerning and obedient creature. 'Then, when (the cradle) is cast upon the shore, *an enemy to Me and an enemy to him,* Pharaoh, *shall take him*. But do not fear, for *We shall surely return him to you and make him one of the messengers* [28:07].' That [the word] 'enemy' is repeated twice conveys the sense that no matter how extreme the enmity was, no harm would come (to the baby). On the contrary, the result would be Pharaoh's loving him. Being cast into the sea

and falling into the hands of an enemy, either of which could have resulted in (Moses') death, show how all this was a hidden grace and a gift from God concealed beneath what appeared outwardly to be a tribulation.

The shore (al-sāḥil) referred to was not the bank of the Nile, but ... rather a channel in the middle that brought water to Pharaoh's garden. It is related that Moses' mother had lined the cradle with carded cotton, then placed him in it, and covered the outside with pitch. It has also been said that the cradle was made of reeds that she had woven together, while al-Muqātil says that the reeds had been woven by a believing man named Ḥazkīl and that then Moses' mother covered it with pitch and cast it into the sea.[42]

From the sea to Pharaoh's garden was a large channel and its water carried the cradle to the garden where he was sitting with Āsīya bint Mazāhim. (Upon seeing the cradle), he bade her take it from the water, and inside there was the infant and the people rejoiced. Pharaoh loved the baby as soon as he saw him with a love so strong he could scarcely control it, and thus does God Most High say to Moses, *And I cast upon you a love from Me.* Concerning this, Ibn ʿAbbās said, 'God loved him and made him loveable to His creatures,' and Qatāda adds that, 'The beauty and charm in the eyes of (the baby) Moses were such that no one could look at him without loving him.' (Thus, God says) '*I cast upon you* a great love that came from Me and which I sowed in people's hearts such that anyone who saw you could scarcely resist you, and in this way did I make one who was My enemy and his family love you so that they might care for you.'

And that you might be formed under My eye, that is, 'Raised with kindness and compassion and nourished in My protection and care ...' This began *when your sister went forth* following your cradle ... and said to Pharaoh and Āsīya when she saw them seeking a nursemaid whose breast the baby would accept, '*Shall I show you one who can nurse him?*' It is related that the news had spread in Egypt that the family of the Pharaoh had found an baby boy in the Nile but that he would not nurse, and so they were looking for nurse maids. So Miriam, the sister of Moses, came to them without telling them who she was, said to them what she said, and they accepted. Then she

---

42. The word translated as 'sea' in these verses and others which relate the story of Moses 🕮 and Pharaoh, is a Hebrew noun, *al-yamm*, which the commentators understand as a synonym for the Nile River or any large body of water.

returned with Moses' mother, and the baby accepted her breast.

God Most High then says: '*Thus We returned you to your mother*, keeping Our promise to her, *that she might be comforted* by being reunited with you *and grieve not* and be saddened no more by her separation from you.'

Then, much later, *You slew a soul*, an Egyptian, when an Israelite sought Moses' help against him in a fight. Kaʿb said, "This happened when Moses ﷺ was twelve years old." *But We saved you from sorrow*, that is, from the sorrow of having slain a man and the fear of God's punishment, by forgiving you, and 'We saved you from Pharaoh's machinations by inspiring you to leave that land. *And We tried you with* mighty *trials* throughout and rescued you time after time until you were ready to receive prophecy and scripture.' These trials included what befell him when he migrated from his homeland and was separated from those he loved, when he journeyed on foot and ran out of provision, and before that, when he was saved from the slaughter (of infant boys that Pharaoh had ordered), saved from the sea, and spared the retribution for having slain a man.

Ibn ʿAbbās was asked about (the words, *And We tried you with trials*) and said, "(They mean) 'We saved you from one trial after another.' For he was born in a year when all male babies were being killed, and that was a trial; then he was cast by his mother into the lake; and Pharaoh considered killing him; and he himself slew an Egyptian; then he indentured himself for ten years; and he lost his way (in the wilderness) and got separated from his flock on a pitch black night. All of these were trials." But following the order mentioned in the Noble Book, the next words are *Then you remained some years among the people of Midian*, mean that his indenture and what followed it, after his arrival in Midian, are to be not counted among those trials. Rather, his trials were all that had befallen him before he came to Midian.

Wahb said, 'He stayed twenty-eight years with Shuʿayb: ten years as a dowry for the hand of Shuʿayb's daughter, Ṣafrā', and eighteen more years until a child was born to him.' The word *labath*, 'a sojourn,' rather than *wuṣūl*, 'an arrival,' evokes the many tribulations and hardships which befell him there, each one of which was a trial (*fitna*).[43] Midian, the homeland of Shuʿayb ﷺ, was

43. The verb translated above as 'you remained', *labiththa*, might be better expressed as 'you stopped for a time,' carrying the notion of its being temporary.

eight days' journey from Egypt and Pharaoh's rule did not extend to it because he feared the awesome power of (Shuʿayb's) prophethood[44] and what might happen to the one who opposed it.

'*Then you came* to the place where you beheld the fire, saw the miracles, and were chosen to receive the Scripture *as determined* (*ʿalā qadarin*) for you in eternity and at the moment that I chose for you, that I might speak to you directly and send you to Pharaoh. Thus, you did not come except as determined by that decree, neither before it nor after it.' '*ʿAlā qadarin*' has also been said to mean, 'At the point in time determined for revelation to be sent to prophets,' meaning at the beginning of each forty-year cycle.

[41] *I have selected you for Myself.* That is, 'I have selected you for scripture, for My message, for My love, and to speak to you personally.' This is a reminder [to him] of God's words, I have chosen you [20:13] and how he was made ready [under God's eyes] to be sent to Pharaoh supported by his brother just as he had asked, after the reminder of all God's previous favors to him, so that his trust in God might be strenghtened. The change from the first-person plural of majesty ('*We tried you,*') to the first person singular ('*I have selected you*') emphasizes that this choice relates to God's Self (*al-Dhāt*). And God Most High knows better.

Spiritual Allusion

"*You have been granted your request*, O *faqīr*, when We brought you to someone who would take you by the hand, guide you to your Lord, and teach you. *And We have indeed shown you favor another time* when We brought you into existence from two Muslim parents, and placed you in the cradle of Islam, and then in the river of faith, and then threw you into the Ocean of gnosis.

And I cast upon you a love from Me, so that We loved you and you loved Us and We cast love for you into the hearts of our servants, *that you might be formed under My eye*, in Our protection and care. Then, after you left behind your kith and kin to attain to the direct knowledge of God and you were granted stability in that knowledge, We brought you back to them that you might inspire them towards God, and they might find comfort in obedience to the Lord.

And you slew a soul, the ego that was veiling you from your Lord,

---

44. The Qur'ān identifies Shuʿayb ﷺ as a prophet sent to the people of Midian in 7:85.

but We saved you from the sorrow of that veil (*ghammi 'l-ḥijāb*) and brought you out of the prison of created beings into the infinite space of contemplation and vision. *We tried you with trials* in your efforts against the ego: the trial of poverty, then the trial of lowliness, then the trial of leaving your homeland, until you were finally delivered from the confinement of created beings, and came to Us by a decree We ordained for you, at the moment We had chosen for your spiritual opening (*al-fatḥ*) to happen,

And I have selected you for Myself and chosen you to be in My presence, not by any strength or power from you, but purely by providence. For My providence towards you was there before anything else: "Where were you when Our providence confronted you and you met Our care face to face? In Our eternity there was neither the sincerity of actions nor the existence of states. There was nothing there except Pure Grace and Absolute Generosity' as it is said in the *Ḥikam*.[45] And thus do the Sufis sing:

> There was no deed from me to You by which I earned it—
> Only pure Grace—no other cause...

And as another said:

> I used to think that union with You could be purchased
> At the price of precious wealth and gain.
> In ignorance I deemed Your love was something easy
> For which noble souls could be given in exchange,
> Until I saw that it was You Who chooses
> Those to whom to give the subtlest gifts
> And realized You were not reached through ruses.
> So I placed my head beneath my folded wing
> And made my home in the nest of Your love
> To dwell there, to fly forth, and return.

Then God sends them to Pharaoh:

> 42. *"Go forth, you and your brother, with My signs, and tire not in the remembrance of Me.* 43. *Go, both of you, to Pharaoh! Truly he has rebelled!* 44. *Yet speak to him gently, that haply he may remember or have fear."* 45. *They said, "Our Lord! Truly we fear that he will deal hastily with us, or that he will transgress."*

45. Ibn ʿAjība is paraphrasing the 169th Aphorism of the *Ḥikam*. See the Danner translation, p. 89.

> 46. *He said, "Fear not! Truly I am with you both; I hear and I see.* 47. *So come to him and say, 'Truly we are two messengers of your Lord. So send forth with us the Children of Israel and punish them not. We have brought you a sign from your Lord. And may peace be upon him who follows guidance!* 48. *Truly it has been revealed to us that punishment shall come upon anyone who denies and turns away.'"*

[42-43] God, the Truth ﷻ, says to Moses *"Go forth, you and your brother, with My signs..."* That is, 'Go forth with the miracles I have shown you: the hand and the staff,' and if they are only two in number, yet each of them contained other signs.[46] The staff's transformation into a living creature was a sign, its becoming a massive viper was a sign, and the speed at which it moved even with its massive size was a sign. Likewise for the hand: its whiteness was a sign, its radiance was another sign, and its return to its original state was yet another... '*Go forth, both of you*, with My miraculous signs, holding firmly to them.

And tire not, that is, 'In the course of delivering My message do not lapse or fall short in your *remembrance of Me*.' In other words, 'Do not let the work of delivering this message distract you from My remembrance in whatever form fits your situation, whether it be through invocation, reflection, or contemplation. Do not let your involvement in carrying out My commandment distract you from the consciousness of My Presence, for that would make you both neglectful in My sight.'

[43] *"Go, both of you, to Pharaoh! Truly he has rebelled"* and has become tyrannical and haughty. Even though Aaron was not present at the time of this revelation, it is addressed to both of them because they were usually together. It has also been related that inspiration came to Aaron in Egypt to go to meet Moses (may peace be upon them both) and that Moses had heard his brother was approaching and had gone to meet him.

[44] *Yet speak to him gently*, for gentle words can break through the obstinance of a tyrant. Concerning this verse, Ibn ʿAbbās says it means, 'do not speak to him harshly, ' while others have said that 'gentle speech' refers to [the words in *Sūrat al-Nāziʿāt*], *Do you wish*

46. Here Ibn ʿAjība is explaining why the signs are referred here in the plural form, *āyāt*, and not the dual form, *āyatayn*.

to be purified? [79:18], which would mitigate the harshness of their later words: *We are two Messengers of your Lord so send with us the Children of Israel*; or that 'gentle speech' meant using one of his given names, Abū'l-ʿAbbās, Abū'l-Walīd, and Abū Marra; or that it meant, 'Promise him that if he accepts faith, he will have youth that will not fade and a kingdom that can only be taken from him by death, and that the sensual delights of food, drink, and intercourse will stay with him up to death.' It has also been said to mean, simply, 'speak to him kindly, for he is your master, and he is still the one who raised you well, so he has the right of a father over you.' This is in order *That haply he may remember* what you convey to him, and aspire towards it, *or have fear* of God's chastisement.

The import of the sentence is thus: 'Speak both of you to him with hopes that he will be reminded.' That is, 'Approach the task of exhorting him hopeful that his knowledge will bear fruit and preserve him from a wasted life,' leaving the question [of whether it was actually possible to guide him] unclear as a way of encouraging them in their task. Such is the view of Sibawayh concerning this paradox: that God Most High knew that (Pharaoh) would not believe and yet says (to Moses and Aaron), *That haply he may remember*, that is, 'with hope that he will.' Al-Warrāq's view is that Pharaoh did, in fact, remember when he was about to drown. And al-Zujāj said, "God spoke to them according to what they could understand." The fact that God Most High knew Pharaoh would not believe is among the mysteries of destiny (*al-qadr*) and the Supreme Truth (*al-haqīqah*) not to be revealed in this world. The Prophets were brought forth in order that the Divine Laws might appear and so He spoke to them about what concerned delivering the message in the realm of Divine Wisdom (*al-Ḥikma*),[47] and God Most High knows better. It may also be that God sent them to Pharaoh even while knowing [that it was impossible that he would believe] as a way of proof (against him) and of removing any means of excuse.

[45] *They said, "Our Lord! Truly we fear that he will deal hastily with us."* That is, 'We fear that he will hasten to punish us and not wait for us to complete our message or to see the miracles (we bring).... Or, 'We fear that out of pride and fear for his dominion, he will act in haste *or that he will transgress* even more by saying something about

47. See footnote 151 above.

You that should not be said.' Repetition of the word *that* conveys their concern and fear. These words may have been spoken by Moses ﷷ alone and included Aaron as a follower connected to him in what he said or did, or it may be that Aaron ﷷ also said this once they were reunited and God related what both of them said when the verse was revealed, similar to His words *O messengers! Eat of the good things* [23:51] which is in the plural even though each one of them was being addressed individually and it was impossible for them to have been together in one place and time.

[46] God Most High said to them, *"Fear not!"* These words are as if in response to someone who asked, 'What did their Lord say to them both when they humbled themselves before Him? He said, 'Do not fear what you are imagining, either his excess or tyranny, for *Truly I am with you both* through My protection, My care, My support, and My help. *I hear and I see* the words and deeds that will come to pass between you both and [Pharaoh] and in every state I will do what is fitting in order to shield you from harm and evil, and bring you benefit and goodness.'

[47] *So come to him.* The verb *atā* expresses the act of coming into [Pharaoh's] presence after they had been commanded to go to him (*idhhabā*), so it is not redundant. *And say* to him, *'Truly we are two messengers of your Lord...'* They are commanded to begin in this way so that the tyrant might know their roles and answer accordingly. *So send forth with us the Children of Israel.* The verb *send* (*arsal*) in this context does not mean to send the Children of Israel with them to Shām, because they then say, *and punish them not*. Rather, it means 'Release them from their bondage and captivity and take them out from under your oppressive hand.' Under Egyptian rule, the Children of Israel were forced to do all the hardest labor: digging, carrying stones, churning milk, threshing, and building cities. Added to that, their male children were being slain every other year. So the message of Moses ﷷ to the Pharaoh was first to believe in the One God and then to set free the Children of Israel.

It has been related that when Pharaoh was told of eternal life in Paradise for him and his family and an everlasting Kingdom, it attracted him and he began to incline towards belief. Then he called for his advisor Hāmān, who had not been there initially, and when he told him (of what he intended), Hāmān said, 'I used to think you were intelligent! You are a Lord who is now going to be lorded over? You are worshipped and now you will worship another?' And thus did he convince him [to change his mind].

Moses ﷺ said to him, '*We have brought you a sign from your Lord,*' and Pharaoh replied, 'What is it?' Then Moses reached his hand into the pocket of his robe and brought it forth white and gleaming with rays like the sun, and Pharaoh was amazed. Al-Thaʿlābī says, "He did not show him the staff until after that, on the feast day." But what seems to be the case from *Sūrat al-Shuʿarā'* is that he showed him both the staff and the hand, and if only the hand is mentioned there, it is because the focus is not to enumerate the signs but rather to affirm the proof of the message. So it is similar to God's words elsewhere: *I have come with a sign from your Lord* [3:49], or *And if I bring you a thing that is manifest?* [26:30]. And as for His words *If you have come with a sign, then bring it, if you are of the truthful ones* [7:16], it is clear that they mean 'one of the signs.'

And then Moses ﷺ said to him, '*And may peace be upon him who follows guidance!*' That is, 'Peace from God, the angels, and the faithful, which brings safety in this world and the Next, is upon the one who follows God's guidance, affirming the signs which guide to the truth, but not upon the one who follows error and caprice. *Truly it has been revealed to us* from our Lord *that punishment*, both in this world and the Next *shall come upon anyone who denies* the signs of God...' *and turns away* refusing to accept them. With these words, Moses ﷺ exhorts him with the gentlest language possible, [speaking of a general truth]: the punishment would be unleashed, but not only upon him. And God Most High knows best.

Spiritual Allusion

It is incumbent on the people of knowledge and the people of exhortation and reminder to help one another in the spreading of knowledge and in exhorting God's servants, and to go to them in every corner of the land. This is a *farḍ kifāya* upon the knowledgeable.[48] But the spreading of knowledge should not distract them from the remembrance of God, and reminding people should not distract them from the contemplation of God, just as God Most High says (in these verses): *And tire not in the remembrance of Me.*

48. A *farḍ kifāya* is a religious obligation which, if some people fulfill, suffices for everyone. The funeral prayer is the most common example of this. If some people offer it, not everyone in the community has to.

That is, 'Do not neglect My contemplation as you give My servants instruction.'[49]

And if you meet arrogant people and pharaohs, speak to them with gentle words and call them to the easiest way, for that will be the most attractive for them to follow. [Thus, we] disagree with those who say that this verse, (*Yet speak to him gently*), was only for the community of Moses ﷺ, while for the community of Muḥammad are God's words, *And say, "It is the truth from your Lord! So whosoever will, let him believe, and whosoever will, let him disbelieve."* [18:29]. Conveying the Truth should never be without kindness and generosity. And if a preacher fears the authority of the one to whom he speaks, (let him remember that) God is with him guarding and protecting him, hearing him and seeing him. Even if those to whom he is speaks do not heed his exhortation, still he has delivered the message entrusted to him and should say, either with the tongue of his state or in words, 'May *peace be upon him who follows guidance!*' And in God is all accord.
Then God speaks of Pharaoh's response:

> 49. *He said, "So who is the Lord of you two, O Moses?"* 50. *He said, "Our Lord is He Who gives everything its creation, then guides [it]."* 51. *He said, "What, then, of former generations?"* 52. *He said, "Knowledge thereof is with my Lord in a Book—He errs not, nor does He forget—* 53. *The One Who made the earth a cradle for you, and threaded paths for you therein. He sent down water from the sky, wherewith We brought forth diverse kinds of vegetation [saying],* 54. *'Eat and pasture your cattle.'" Truly in that are signs for those possessed of intelligence.* 55. *From it We created you, and unto it We shall bring you back, and from it We shall bring you forth another time.*

[49] ... Pharaoh said, *"So who is the Lord of you two, O Moses?"* This was his response to Moses ﷺ and his brother when they had come to him and delivered the message their Lord had commanded them to deliver. In his obstinacy and despotism, Pharaoh is careful to refer to God as *the Lord of you two*, not as his Lord, and [what he is quoted as saying] in the Chapter of the Poets [26:73]—*And what is the Lord of the worlds?*— conveys an even more condescending tone. The fact that he used only Moses' name, even though he was ad-

49. Teaching and preaching to people are outward practices which should not supplant the inward practice of contemplative invocation of the Divine.

dressing them both, shows that he knew that Moses was the source while Aaron was only his helper.

[50] *"Our Lord is He Who gives everything its creation..."* This is Moses' answer [to Pharaoh]. It has been said to mean, '[Our Lord is the one] who gives His creatures what they need and depend on to maintain their bodies and survive;' or 'He is the one who gives every creature its particular nature and form; He does not place the human form in animals nor the animal form in humans, but rather, creates everything *measured out with due measure* [25:2];' or 'That our Lord is the one who gives to each thing its own particular action and purpose, so that the hand is made for grasping, the foot for walking, the tongue for speech, the eye for vision, and the ear for hearing;' or, 'That He is the one who created for each creature a mate: for a man, the woman; for a camel, the she-camel; for a stallion, the mare; for an ass, the jennet.' *Then He guides* [them] to the way which will best serve them in using what they are given, and He endows them with the knowledge of how they might live and be completed, so He inspires[50] them with how to nurse, to eat, to drink, to mate, and to avoid harm. And because creation, which refers to the structure and ordering of the body, precedes guidance, which refers to endowing that body with the powers of motion and perception, the two are connected by the word "then" (*thumma*) which indicates a sequence of time.

This response is both eloquent and concise. It expresses the fact that God Most High is omniscient and omnipotent in His essence, the Creator of all that is in existence, the Source of all manner of blessings which encompass His creatures, and the One Who guides them to the paths by which they might develop.

[51-52] Pharaoh asks, *"What, then, of former generations?"* That is, 'What is their state after death and what has God done with them?' To which Moses answers, *"Knowledge thereof is with my Lord,"* meaning that this pertains to the unseen which none knows except God. (Pharaoh's question has also been said to mean,) 'What happened to those generations of the past and nations which have vanished?'

50. *Alhama* in this context means "inspire," and recalls verse 16:68, *And Your Lord revealed* (awḥā) *to the bee, "Take up dwellings among the mountains and the trees and among that which they build..."* In other words, what from a scientific perspective might be called "natural instinct," is seen as a kind of revelation from God to His creation.

That is, 'What are the details of the events that befell them?' If this latter is the meaning of these words, then Moses' answer means that the knowledge of such details is part of God's infinite knowledge but has no relevance to the message he is bringing. It is as if the enemy of God, fearing that he would be disgraced and fearing the proofs that Moses ﷺ would show people, wanted to divert him toward something irrevalent, tales that had no bearing on the message, and for this reason, Moses ﷺ refused [to answer him directly] and said instead, *Knowledge thereof is with my Lord.*

This (latter explanation) is, in fact, preferable to the former, for if the question had been about their states after death, it is possible that Moses would have said in response, 'Those among them who followed guidance are safe and blessed, and those who turned away from it are punished,' as his words (elsewhere) state: *And peace be upon him who follows guidance!*

It has also been said that when Pharaoh asked *What, then of former generations?* he meant 'Why were they not brought back? Or 'Why did they not follow your way?' Or, 'Why, when they rejected the message, were they not punished?' But these explanations are unlikely. It is evident that the tyrant understood Moses' words, *And then guides,* to mean 'guides to faith,' and so he challenged him by asking, '*What, then, of former generations* who did not believe and were destroyed?' And Moses ﷺ simply answered, *The knowledge thereof is with my Lord* and *He knows best who has strayed from His path and who is guided* [16:125].

God's words *in a Book* mean 'in the Guarded Tablet,'[51] where it is recorded in detail. They may also be understood to mean that everything in God's knowledge is confirmed and exact, as if it were entrusted to someone who records it in writing, as the words which follow confirm: *My Lord does not err,* that is, He does make some mistake in the beginning, *and does not forget* [later] so that He needs reminding. In other words, if something is recorded in the Guarded Tablet, it is not because God needs it to be, either at its

51. *Al-Lawḥ al-Maḥfūẓ,* the Guarded Tablet, is mentioned at the end of *Sūrat al-Burūj: Nay, it is a glorious Quran, upon a Guarded Tablet* [85:21-22]. In the commentary of Ibn Abī Ḥatim on 3:29, Ibn ʿAbbās is quoted as having said, "God created the Guarded Tablet which would need a journey of a hundred years to traverse. Then He said to the Pen before He created the world and He was upon the Throne, 'Write!' to which the Pen answered, 'What should I write?' And God said to it, 'Write My knowledge of My creation until the Day of Resurrection.' And the Pen flowed forth with all that exists in God's knowledge until the Day of Resurrection..."

beginning nor its end. (It has also been said) that Moses ﷺ used the words *My Lord* here instead of a pronoun so that he could taste the sweetness of mentioning Him as well as express the sublimity of this pronouncement, for it is a necessary attribute of the Lord that He be without forgetfulness and error.

Moses ﷺ responded to (Pharaoh's) question with skill and eloquence, for while answering the question, he also described the divine nature, using attributes that would be impossible for His adversary to claim for himself, either literally or figuratively,[52] for if (Moses) had said, 'God is creator and provider,' Pharaoh could have claimed those qualities for himself.

[53] The discourse continues in a manner that is more specific to the one being addressed with words which may be understood either as God speaking (of Himself) or as the speech of Moses ﷺ: *The One Who made the earth a cradle for you*. That is 'He made it like a cradle, level and smooth enough to dwell upon, and made each place upon it a cradle for each one of you.' *And* [*He*] *threaded paths for you therein*, 'so that you can go from one land to another in search of what you need, and to benefit from one another's company, and He made these paths run between mountains and through valleys so that you might know them by their landmarks.'

And He sent down water from the sky, the rain, *wherewith We brought forth diverse kinds of vegetation.* These latter words may be understood as the direct speech of God and what preceded them as the speech of Moses ﷺ, or all of it may be taken as God's speech being quoted by Moses ﷺ to note the perfection of Divine Power and Wisdom and to declare that none could bring this about except an omnipotent sovereign. 'We brought forth by way of that water various forms of plant life,' referred to as *azwāj*, 'pairs,' because they are paired to one another and yet differ in form, color, taste, smell, and use, some for human beings and others for animals.

[54-55] It is part of God's perfect blessings that human beings obtain their provision using animals (to plow) and that what is left (after harvest) and is not considered human food becomes feed for those animals. Such is the meaning of God's words, *Eat and pasture your cattle.* This sentence is thus adverbial and means, 'We bring forth from the earth varieties of plant life, saying *Eat and pasture your cattle*, thus giving you permission to do both.'

52. To be without error or forgetfulness cannot be said of any human being.

Truly, in what has been mentioned of God's tasks, acts, and favors *are signs,* clear and evident proofs, of God's greatness in His
Essence, His Attributes, and Acts. They are also proofs of Moses'
and Aaron's prophethood (may peace be upon them both) *for those
possessed of intelligence (nuhā).* This last word, the plural of *nuhyat,*
is a name for human intelligence because it prohibits (*nahā*) someone from following what is false and abominable such as what the
oppressor was claiming and what his wanton entourage accepted.
The signs are said to be *for those possessed intelligence* in particular,
even while they are for all the world, because the intelligent are
the ones who benefit from them the most.

'*From* the cradle of the earth *We created you* by creating your
father, Adam 🕮, in whom you were contained,' for his primordial
perfection (*fiṭra*) was not limited to himself but rather was a model
which contained and recapitulated the primordial perfections of
all other individuals of his species: their creation was contained
in his.

These words have also been said (to mean): 'Your bodies are
created from the union of cells born from nutrients which themselves are born from the earth.' ʿAṭā said, "The angel charged with
the womb goes forth to the place where (that person) will (eventually) be buried and takes from it some earth which he sprinkles
upon the union of cells. Thus is the fetus created from both the
union of cells and the earth."

And unto it We shall bring you back by death and dissolution, but
this is speaking of the body, not the soul, which, after being ques-
tioned (in the grave), ascends to the heavens as will be explained
in the commentary on God's words *Then, if he is among those brought
near* [56:88].[53] Also note that the verse does not say 'and *to* it (*ilayhā*)
do We return you,' which would mean 'to remain there.' '*And from
it We shall bring you forth another time,* assembling your fragments
that had been scattered and mingled with earth into their original
form and returning to them the souls.[54] It is described as *another
time* because the [first] creation [of man] was a coming forth from

---

53. See our translation of this in *The Immense Ocean,* p. 74 ff.

54. It is related in the *Musnad* of Imām Aḥmad and *al-Sunna al-Kubra* of Bayhaqī
that when the body of the Prophet's daughter, Umm Kulthūm, who died at the
age of 27, was placed in her grave, he recited this verse (*From it We created you...*),
and then said, "In the Name of God, in the way of God, and in the religion of the
Messenger of God" (*Bismi Llāh, wa fī sabīli Llāh wa ʿalā millati Rasūli Llāh*).

the earth, and so his resurrection is coming forth once again.

Spiritual Allusion

Our Lord is He Who gives everything its creation according to what has been apportioned it for it in eternity, *then guides it* to the means by which it will reach that portion. Of these, there are people whose portion in eternity was the nourishment of their bodies, and they are led to the means (of doing that). Such are the people at the station of remoteness. And there are those whose portion was the nourishment of their hearts and they are led to spiritual effort through physical acts of devotion and other means of approach. These people, too, vary. Some of them God has occupied with the teaching of knowledge, refining people's understandings, resolving issues, and simplifying religious questions, and God guides them to the means by which to do that. If they are sincere and their intentions are pure, they become the bearers of the Sacred Law. And some of them God has occupied with accomplishing devotional acts and filling their moments with worship, and He guides them to the means to do that and strengthens them to meet its challenges. Such are the devotees and the renunciants.

And some of them God has occupied with giving food and companionship to people, filling zāwiyas, and receiving gifts, and He guides them to the means of doing that. Such are the righteous (*al-ṣāliḥūn*).

And there are those whose portion is the nourishment of souls (*al-arwāḥ*). These are the aspirants who travel the path, the people of spiritual effort and purification, of ridding (the soul of vice) (*al-takhlīya*) and adorning (*al-taḥlīyya*) it (with virtue), of self-discipline and refinement. And God guides them to the means of doing that by bringing them to a complete master who explains to them the Way and sets them on their journey. In this, too, their stations differ in proportion to their sincerity and their (personal) experience (of God).

And there are those whose portion is the nourishment of their innermost beings (*al-asrār*). Such are the greatest of the gnostics, the Foremost, those Drawn Nigh, people of self-effacement and subsistence in God, of deep-rootedness and stability, and He guides them to what they had hoped for and had been seeking. May God benefit us by them and allow us to join them in their journey. *Amen*!

In [Pharaoh's] question, *"What, then, of former generations?"* is a caution to aspirants not to get overly involved with stories from the past, for they can be a distraction from God other than those which contain teachings that truly bring us nearer. For *That is a community that has passed away. Theirs is what they earned and yours is what you earned* [2:134].

Then there are God's words, *the One Who made the earth a cradle for you.* That is, He made the earth of the individual soul (*al-nafs*) a cradle in which to maintain the formal aspects of servanthood, *and threaded paths for you therein* which lead those who follow them by effort and practice to the witnessing of God's Divinity. And *He sent down from the sky* of the *Malakūt* the *water* of spiritual inspirations by which souls are revived. From it, *diverse kinds of* knowledge and wisdom spring forth, so *'Eat and pasture* your hearts among the luminous blossoms of its unveilings, and nourish your physical forms on the fruits of its outward dimension.[55] *Truly in that are signs for those possessed of intelligence..*

From the earth of your lower souls *We created you* and brought you forth by a vision of the Divine immensity, *and unto it We shall bring you back* to maintain the forms of servanthood, *and from it We shall bring you forth another time*, so that you might belong totally to God and to nothing else.

Or, *from (the earth) We created you,* that is, brought you forth from the darkness of your ego into the Light the One Who created it, by means of your self-effacement, *and unto it We shall bring you back* to the world of forms in the station of subsistence in God, *and from it We shall bring you forth another time* by the liberation promised you in the station of subsistence, so that you might be one of God's eternally grateful servants. And in God is all accord.

But Pharaoh did not benefit from Moses' exhortation nor from the miraculous signs he saw.

> 56. *We indeed showed him Our signs, all of them; yet he denied and refused.* 57. *He said, "Have you come to us in order to expel us from our land with your sorcery, O Moses?* 58. *But we shall surely produce for you sorcery like it. So appoint a tryst between you and us at a neutral place, which neither we nor you shall fail*

55. The Shaykh uses here the word *nawwār*, blossoms, which is from the same root as the word *nūr*, light, to evoke inward unveilings (*al-tajalliyāt*) while "the fruits of its outward dimension" refers more to the physical benefits one might derive from a devotional practice.

to keep." 59. *He said, "Your tryst shall be on the Day of Adornment; let the people be gathered when the sun has risen high."*

[56] God, the Truth ﷻ, says *We indeed showed him*, that is, Pharaoh, *Our signs*, when he said, "*Bring [them], then, if you are among the truthful.*" *So Moses cast his staff, and behold, it was a serpent manifest. Then he drew out his hand, and behold, it was white to the beholders* [26:31-33]. These signs are referred to in the plural even while they were only two in number[56] because of the many extraordinary things they contained, each of which was a sign in itself... It has been said that when (Moses) ﵇ cast down the staff, it turned into a [gigantic] serpent covered by armor-like scales, with a gaping mouth that measured eighty yards between its upper and lower fangs, and then that it set its lower fangs into the earth and its upper fangs into the palace wall and turned in the direction of Pharaoh, who ran off breaking wind. The people, too, ran to escape it and twenty-five thousand were killed in the stampede. Pharaoh called out, "I will praise the One who sent you if only you will take [this monster] away!" Then Moses took hold of it and it turned back into a staff. It is also related that when it turned into a serpent, it rose a mile into the sky and it was then that Pharaoh began to say to Moses, "O Moses! Command me as you will." After this Moses ﵇ took his hand out from the pocket of his robe, and it was white, glowing with a brightness not of this world. So enclosed in each of the two miraculous signs were others not specifically mentioned but affirmed by God's words: *all of them*. This amounts to saying 'We showed him Our signs along with all they entailed' in order to make it clear that there was no excuse left to him.

It has also been said that these words mean, 'We showed him Our nine miraculous signs,'[57] but this explanation is unlikely since the other signs appeared after the defeat of the sorcerers over a period of twenty years. Of course, it may also be that the words mean that 'eventually the nine signs were shown to Pharaoh and

56. That is, they are referred to as *āyāt*, in the plural form of the noun, rather than *āyatayn*, the dual form.

57. In *Sūrat al-Aʿrāf*, seven afflictions are mentioned: *And We indeed afflicted the House of Pharaoh with drought and a shortage of crops, that haply they would be reminded.... and We sent against them the flood and the locusts, and the lice and the frogs and the blood—signs expounded* [7:130-133]. If the miracles of the staff and the hand are added to those, this could be the nine mentioned in *Sūrat al-Isrā'*: *And We indeed gave unto Moses nine clear signs* [17:101].

yet he still rejected faith,' and then God completes the narrative.

Even less likely is the explanation of those who would include among these signs what was done to destroy Pharaoh's people—nay, to direct them to faith—such as the parting of the sea, and even what came to pass for the Children of Israel after Pharaoh's death, such as the raising of the mountain and the rock.[58] Also improbable is the view of those who would count among them the evident signs that came by way of [earlier] prophets ﵈ which Moses ﵇ recounted to Pharaoh, for they did not form part of the discourse at this time and are far from the present context.

God Most High says, *Yet* Pharaoh, in his obstinacy and pride, *denied Moses'* [message] *and refused faith* and obedience to God even as he witnessed the miraculous signs that (Moses) brought which bore witness to the truth [of his message]. It has also been said that these words mean he denied all the signs and refused to accept any of them.

[57] *He said, "Have you come to us in order to expel us from our land...?"* These words resume Pharaoh's speech and show the way in which he chose to reject Moses, regardless of whether he said them mockingly or in earnest. They mean, '*Have you come* from your place amongst us, which was that of a lowly shepherd, *in order to expel us out of our land*?' Or '*Have you come before us in order to expel us* from Egypt by way of the sorcery you have shown us?' Either of these, which represent a desperate attempt [to repudiate the Messenger], could not have been said by a person of sound mind. Rather, they were said only to incite hatred and repulsion in the minds of the people towards Moses by pretending that his real purpose was to remove them from their land, steal all their possessions, and destroy them completely, so that not one of them would have the least inclination to follow him ﵇. But *God prevails over His affair* [12:21].

[58] Then he made a pretense of opposing him, saying *But we shall surely produce for you sorcery like it*. That is, 'If [you are trying to expel us with sorcery], then we will come with sorcery like yours. *So appoint a tryst between us and you*,' that is, 'an appointment which neither we nor you shall fail to keep.' Pharaoh gives the decision

58. These two miracles are referred to in 7:171—*And when We lifted the mountain above them, as if it were a canopy, and they thought it would fall upon them*—and in 2:60—*We said, "Strike the rock with your staff" Then twelve springs gushed forth from it.*

to Moses ﷺ in order to hide his own faint-heartedness and fear, to appear tough, and appear to be the one in control from beginning to end. For this same reason, he mentions himself first, then Moses, with a negation between them.[59]

At a neutral place (*makānan siwā*) means 'at a place that is equal in distance between us and you, so that neither of us will be disadvantaged in getting to it...'

[59] Moses said to them, *"Your tryst shall be on the Day of Adornment..."* 'The Day of Adornment' has been said to mean a place that was well-known for gatherings upon that day, which was a yearly holiday when people would don their finest garments and congregate. It has been said that this refers to their new year, or to the day of ʿAshūra,[60] or simply one of their market days.

"Let the people be gathered when the sun has risen high" may be understood to mean either 'gather the people in the early morning of this day' or that 'this is a day when they will be gathered.' In either case, Moses' ﷺ intention was that the proofs and refutation of [Pharaoh's] lies be seen in broad daylight, at a time when the greatest number of people could gather. And God Most High knows better.

Spiritual Allusion

If someone is destined to remain distant from the All-Merciful, then neither miracles nor proofs will avail him. If pride and arrogance have so removed him from God, he will even invoke what is false to defend himself against what is true. We seek refuge in God from the morasses of being forsaken.

Then God speaks of their gathering and what transpired for them.

> 60. *Then Pharaoh turned away and devised his scheme and then came [to the tryst].* 61. *Moses said to them, "Woe unto you! Do not fabricate a lie against God, lest He should destroy you with a punishment. Whosoever fabricates [lies] has failed."* 62. *So they debated their affair among themselves and kept secret their intimate discourse.* 63. *They said, "These two are sorcerers who wish to expel you from your land with their sorcery and to do*

59. The last part of verse 58 literally reads, "...us and not you" (...*naḥnu wa lā anta*).

60. Ashūra is the tenth day of the first lunar month. It was recognized as a special day in the pre-Islamic period and continues to be so.

away with your exemplary way of life. 64. So gather your plot, then come in ranks. Today, whosoever gains the upper hand will surely have prospered. 65. They said, "O Moses! Either you cast, or we shall be the first to cast." 66. He said, "Nay, you cast." Then, behold, their ropes and their staffs appeared to him, through their sorcery, to move swiftly, 67. Whereat Moses conceived a fear in his soul. 68. We said, "Fear not! Truly you are uppermost. 69. Cast what is in your right hand; it will devour what they have produced. They have produced only a sorcerer's trick. And the sorcerer prospers not, wherever he may go."

[60-61] God, the Truth 🕮, says *Then Pharaoh turned away...* That is, he left the gathering and returned to his dwellings to devise *his scheme,* meaning the ruses and sorcerers he would use to trick Moses 🕮, *and then* [he] *came* with them all to the tryst.

And when they had gathered, Moses admonished them, saying *Woe unto you!* 'If you make up lies against God, He will bring upon you everlasting woe. *Do not fabricate a lie against God,* by taking someone as a partner in His Divinity as you have done with Pharaoh, or by pretending that what is false is true, *Lest He should destroy you with a punishment* of unimagineable severity ...*Whoever fabricates [a lie]* against God, in whatever form it might take, *has failed;*' or 'By fabricating a lie against God, Pharaoh has failed, and do not imitate his failure.'

[62] When they had heard Moses 🕮, the sorcerers *debated their affair among themselves.* They argued about the task they had been given... exchanged opinions about best how to confront him, encouraged one another, and conversed back and forth. And they *kept secret their intimate discourse,* meaning from Moses 🕮, lest he discover their plan and devise a defense against it.

[63] *They said, 'These two'*-- Moses and Aaron -- '*are powerful sorcerers who wish to expel you from your land,'* from Egypt 'by using the sorcery they have already shown you and then to take power and *to do away with your exemplary way of life,* that is, your rites (*madhhabukum*), which are the best and most imitated... by spreading their rites and propagating their religion.'

Ibn ʿAṭiyya said "The word *ṭarīqah* (way) in this context means 'way of life and kingdom,' while *al-muthlā* (exemplary),[61] means

---

61. *Muthlā* is the feminine form of *al-amthal,* "examples."

'superior.'" Others have said that *tarīqatikum al-muthlā* refers to the highest ranking and noblest people among them who are called *al-muthlā* because they were considered examples or models for the rest. Following this interpretation, the verse would mean, '(Moses and Aaron) intend to win over your noblest and highest-ranking people and to do away with all that you believe in.' Of this, Qatāda said, "The highest ranking people of that time were the Children of Israel, who were greatest in number and possessions, and so what Pharaoh meant was that 'They want to take them away for themselves.'" But it is unlikely, as some *tafsīrs* have suggested, that this means 'taking the Children of Israel out from their midst while leaving Pharaoh and his people safe in their dwellings.'

[64] *... So gather your plot, then come in ranks.* This proclaims what is being sought. That is, 'If it is indeed the case that these two are sorcerers seeking to put you out of your land, then be united in carrying out your plot. Do it in unison and let no one deviate from it so that the arrow will be shot from a single bow.' *... Then come in ranks,* that is, in lines, for the sight of line upon line of sorcerers advancing would be more terrifying and awe inspiring to the on-lookers. Some (*tafsīrs*) say the sorcerers numbered seventy thousand, each of them with a rope and a staff, and that they approached (Moses) as one body, while others say that they numbered only seventy-two, two of them being Egyptian and the rest Israelites, and others, that there were nine hundred of them -- three hundred Persians, three hundred Romans, and three hundred Alexandrians, and yet others, that there were fifteen thousand. And God Most High knows best.

It has also been said that if that meeting place was a large open field, then Moses ﷺ must have spoken to them from one end of it and the sorcerers must have debated their strategy at another, after which they met in the middle as mentioned.

When they had completed their secret council, the sorcerers said, "*Today, whosoever gains the upper hand will surely have prospered!*" that is, 'Whoever defeats (the other) will gain the reward and approval of Pharaoh,' or 'will win high rank, honor, and fame.' Some *tafsīrs* have said that after they had heard Moses' address ﷺ, they said to one another privately, 'These are not the words of a sorcerer.' And according to some, they said '*whosoever gains the upper hand*' because they had already resolved amongst themselves that if Moses were victorious, they would join him. It has also been related that they said, 'If (what he brings) is sorcery, we will defeat him, and if it is from heaven, then he will win the day,' which would mean that when they kept their discourse secret, it was not from Moses ﷺ but rather from Pharaoh. It can also be understood that they said, '*These two are sorcerers* (*who wish to expel you from your land*),' only after they had disagreed amongst themselves concerning [Moses and Aaron] and had argued about the [best] way to confront and defeat them. And God Most High knows best what transpired.

[65-66] When they wanted to begin, they said: '*O Moses! Either you cast* what you both are going to cast first *or we shall be the first to cast,*' giving Moses ﷺ the choice both out of respect after having seen signs of his goodness and also to show confidence.

He said, "Nay, you cast..." answering their gesture of courtesy with one that was better, showing that he was not intimidated by their sorcery, and also allowing them to think that the advantage was in being first so that they might expend their greatest efforts before God (be He glorified) manifested His power and "cast truth against falsehood, and crushed it,"[62] for this is what he had come to expect from his Lord.

So they cast down what they had and *behold, their ropes and their staffs appeared to him, through their sorcery, to move swiftly ...* That is, Moses was surprised and perceived their ropes and staffs to be moving. According to many commentators, this was because the sorcerers had daubed them with mercury so that when the sunlight played upon them, they shimmered and appeared to be writhing. But the more acceptable explanation is that these movements were produced by tricks of the eye, like those used by charlatans. In fact, [the knowledge of how to produce the illusion of movement] is something well-known in the art of magic. This latter explanation is also strengthened by what is conveyed elsewhere, where the ropes are described as "turning into serpents moving on their stomachs" in Moses' direction, an illusion that could not be produced using mercury. Of this verse, Ibn Juzayy said, "Some use it as proof that sorcery is pure illusion devoid of anything real."

62. This paraphrases 21:18: *Nay, but We cast truth against falsehood, and it crushes it, and, behold, it vanishes.*

[67] *Whereat Moses conceived a fear in his soul ...* That is, some degree of fear arose in his soul, for it is human nature to have an aversion to snakes and to avoid their harm. But al-Muqātil said, "Moses was afraid because what Pharaoh's magicians produced was like what he was about to produce, and so the people might doubt him and not follow him, and even those who followed him might be cast into doubt." *We said, "Fear not"* what you imagine. "*Truly you are uppermost*, the one who will defeat them,' and this is stated in the most forceful way possible using the emphatic form (*innaka*) followed by the pronoun (*anta*).

[69] Then God said to him, *Cast what is in your right hand*, that is, 'your staff.' It has been said that the indefinite pronoun here, "what" (*mā*), conveys a sense of the staff's awesome nature: that this is no ordinary staff, but rather something beyond description.[63] But it has also been suggested that it is to belittle the staff itself, as if to say, 'Pay no heed to their many ropes and staffs; just cast down that paltry stick you are holding, for it contains the power of God Most High which will swallow all of them up no matter how many they are and how small it appears...' The words of God Most High, *It will devour what they have produced,* complete the imperative: ["*Cast what is in your right hand.*"]. The verb *talaqqafa* ['*devour*'] literally means 'to snatch or snap up a piece of food.' So the phrase means that the staff 'will swallow up in an instant all they have produced using ropes and staffs which you imagined [to be real].' This explains to him ﷺ how he will defeat them and also eases his fear. If his staff will swallow up all their tricks, about which *he conceived in himself* what he had conceived, then the reason for his fear is completely removed. You can also see from this that his fear was not as al-Muqātil is reported to have said—that people would doubt him and cease to follow him—because the promise of God's help was enough to insure to him that they would. So think about this, which was pointed out by Abū al-Saʿūd. It is also a clarification that there is no ambiguity in this verse. God's words, *It will devour what they have produced* are clear. There is nothing ambiguous about the act of his staff swallowing up theirs! Think about it.[64] *They have produced only a sorcerer's trick.* That is, all they have

63. That is, instead of referring to it as a staff, it referred to as '*what*,' implying that it is more than a staff.

64. Ibn ʿAjība appears to be responding to the view of an earlier *tafsīr* that the phrase, *what they have produced*, is somehow ambiguous or indefinite.

produced is a sorcerer's trick and a ruse...[65] *And the sorcerer prospers not, wherever he may go.* That is, wherever he is and in whatever direction he turns, he is utterly without power. And God Most High knows better.

Spiritual Allusion

It is said from the direction of the Truth to the *faqīr* who turns to God, *Either you cast* down the world that is in your hand *or we shall be the first to cast* it down for you. That is, either you give it up by choice, or it will be taken from you by force. For it is God's wont, with a sincere aspirant, to protect him from worldly preoccupations. If his heart is sincere, he will say '*Nay, cast* it down, I really do not need it.' Then God, the Truth, Most High will cast it down, taking it out of his hands as a way of protecting him, for in reality, its preoccupations and attachments were seeking to destroy him, to ruin his heart, and waste his life. And when he *conceived a fear in his soul* of being overcome by weakness and loss, *We said: Fear not*, for your aspiration is towards your Guardian Lord, *And God provides without measure* and (even) without intermediaries.[66] *Cast that which is in* the *right hand* of your heart, which is the certitude you have of God, and *it will devour what they have produced*, that is, what passing malevolent thoughts and demons can produce within you, for *Satan threatens you with poverty and commands you to indecency* [2:268], and that is what such thoughts produce: they are frightening but illusory, containing nothing real, just like the tricks of a sorcerer—*and the sorcerer prospers not, wherever he may go.*

Then God speaks of the submission of the sorcerers.

> 70. *Then the sorcerers were cast down in prostration. They said, "We believe in the Lord of Aaron and Moses."* 71. *He said, "Do you believe in Him before I give you leave? He is indeed your chief, who has taught you sorcery. Now I shall surely cut off your hands and your feet on alternate sides, and I shall surely crucify you on the trunks of palm trees. And you will surely know which of us [inflicts] a more severe and lasting punishment!"*

[70-71] God, the Truth ﷻ, says when Moses had cast down his staff

65. Ibn ʿAjība adds there that these words may be seen as the complement of *it will devour*: that is, 'It will swallow them up *because* they are only a sorcerer's ruse.'

66. That is, his provision can come to him without his even having to work for it or seek it.

and it had turned into a huge serpent that swallowed up their ropes and staffs, *The sorcerers were cast down in prostration,* for they realized that what had happened had nothing to do with sorcery but was a sign from God. It is related that their leader said, 'We would trick the eyes of people but the tools of our craft would always remain with us. If this is sorcery, then where are those tools?'

Thus were they convinced by what they had seen that Moses' message was real, and witnessing this threw them down upon their faces in a gesture of utter humility, repenting and affirming their faith. And it has been said that they did not raise up their heads from prostration until they had seen Heaven and Hell and reward and punishment. According to ʿIkrima, during the time they were in prostration, God Most High showed them their places in Heaven, and this in no way contradicts their words, *Truly we believe in our Lord, that He may forgive us our sins.* Rather, it was because they knew those places in Heaven were their places that uttered those words.

They said: "We believe in the Lord of Aaron and Moses." They mention Aaron before Moses (may peace be upon them both) either because he was the elder or because Pharaoh could have been considered the 'Lord' of Moses when he was a child,[67] and had they mentioned Moses first, the accursed one and his people might have imagined that they meant him...

[71] *He said: You believe in him*, that is, in Moses, *before I give you permission?*[68] That is,

> 'Without my giving you permission?... *He*, meaning Moses, *is indeed your chief*, that is, 'your teacher and the most knowledgeable of you in your craft, the one *who taught you sorcery* and led you to do what you have done.' This was surely a far-fetched claim, for where was Moses ﷺ and where were these sorcerers that he could have taught them? Yet these were the words that Pharaoh spoke out of fear that people would follow Moses ﷺ and do as the sorcerers had done. This was delusion on his part, given that they were been destined to be among the lost

Then he turned to the sorcerers in menace and said *Now I shall*

67. The literal meaning of *rabb*, usually translated as "lord," is 'the one who raises or nurtures something.'

68. Ibn ʿAjība notes that the *lam* in the question, *āmantum lahu...* (Do you believe in Him...?) gives the sentence the meaning of "Do you humbly submit to Him?"

surely cut off your hands... and your feet alternately, meaning the right hand and left foot, speaking with such detail either to stress how real his threat was and how surely it would be carried out, or else because that was the established punishment for anyone who disobeyed his command. *And I shall crucify you on the trunks of palm trees*, and it has been said that Pharaoh was the first use crucifixation as a punishment. *And you will surely know which of us*, he or Moses ﷺ, *has a harsher and more lasting punishment...*When the sorcerers were awestruck by the staff and accepted faith, the accursed one assumed that it was not because of a miracle but rather out of the fear of seeing his staff swallow up their ropes and staves. *Which of us* may also be understood to mean 'me or the Lord of Moses and Aaron in whom you have professed belief?'

It has been said that neither the Qur'ān, *ḥadīths*, nor other narrations confirm whether Pharaoh carried out his threat, but according to Ibn ʿAbbās and others, he did. It has also been related that Pharaoh's wife had asked, 'Who was victorious?' and when she was told it was Moses, she said, 'I believe in the Lord of Moses and Aaron.' Whereupon Pharaoh sent someone to threaten her, saying to him, 'Find the largest stone you can, and if she persists in what she is saying, throw it down upon her.' It was when the stone was about to be thrown down upon her that she lifted her gaze heavenward and was shown her house in Paradise,[69] continuing to proclaim (her faith) until her soul left her body and the stone fell upon a lifeless form. (All) this is related by al-Thaʿlabī, and God Most High knows better.

Spiritual Allusion

Anyone destined for salvation through God's eternal providence (*al-ʿināya*) will not be harmed by the sins (*al-jināya*) of the past. The sorcerers came to the tryst as enemies of God and his messenger and ended as friends. It is (also) related than when Moses ﷺ said to them *Cast what you have to cast* [26:43], he heard a voice say 'Cast, O friends of God!' and he became perplexed. It was then that he

69. Pharaoh's wife, although not mentioned by name in the Qur'ān, is cited in 66:11, along with Mary, mother of Jesus ﷺ, as an example of a woman whose faith remained strong in the face of worldly trials. Her supplication to God is quoted in that same verse: "*My Lord, build for me a house near to You in the Garden, deliver me from Pharaoh and his deeds, and deliver me from wrongdoing people.*" In a *ḥadīth* in the collection of Bukhārī and elsewhere, she is referred to by name, as Āsīya.

conceived in his mind a fear and said to himself, 'How can I oppose God's friends?' Then, when he cast down his staff, their sanctity became manifest. For 'how many of God's saints (*al-khuṣūṣ*) have been brought forth from the ranks of robbers (*luṣūṣ*).' This is an example to strengthen the hopes of those guilty of transgressions to still seek God's providence and the station of the saintly. For this same reason, al-Qushayrī begins his *Risāla* by mentioning those saints who had begun as transgressors, people such as Fuḍayl, Ibn Adham and others, may God be well pleased with them all.

Then God speaks of the firmness of the sorcerer's faith and their imperviousness in the face of Pharaoh's threats.

> 72. *They said, "We shall never prefer you to the clear proofs that have come to us, nor to Him who originated us. So decree whatsoever you decree; you only decree in the life of this world.* 73. *Truly we believe in our Lord, that He may forgive us our sins and the sorcery that you compelled us to perform. And God is better and more lasting!"* 74. *Verily, whosoever comes to his Lord guilty, surely his shall be Hell, wherein he neither dies nor lives.* 75. *But whosoever comes unto Him as a believer and has done righteous deeds, those shall be of the highest ranks—* 76. *Gardens of Eden with rivers running below, abiding therein. That is the recompense of one who purifies himself.*

[72] ... (The sorcerers) said in answer to Pharaoh and impervious to his threats, "*We shall never prefer you,*" by choosing to follow you instead of *the clear proofs* that were contained in the staff and *have come to us* from God by the hand of Moses ﷺ nor prefer you *to Him who originated us,* Who created us and all other creatures...' That is, 'We will not choose you instead of the proofs shown to us that Moses is a true prophet, nor will we prefer you to the One Who created us, by following you and abandoning the truth.' They thus spoke of two [kinds of] proofs: the first was a physical sign, and the second a rational one.

So decree whatsoever you decree; You only decree in the life of this world. That is, "Do what you are going to do, order what you are going to order.' Such was their response to his threat: 'Whatever you decree is part of the ephemeral life of this world, and what is most important to us is not how to remain in it, but rather how to die as believers and dwell in the Eternal Abode.'

[73] *"Truly we believe in our Lord, that He may forgive..."* 'our sins of disbelief and the transgressions we committed in the past and not hold us to account for them in the Hereafter. We are no longer deluded by this fleeting life and would even prefer what you have threatened us with [to continuing in error]. We also believe that our Lord will *forgive us for the sorcery that you compelled us to perform* against Moses 🕊 and for which you gathered us from the distant towns.'

The fact that they mention, in particular, the sorcery they performed among all their other transgressions shows how completely they had come to hate it and how sincere was their repentance, and to say that they were *compelled* [to do it] is a way of offering an excuse in hopes of (God's) forgiveness.

It has also been suggested that these words mean they had been forced to *teach* sorcery. This is based on a narration that says that their leaders numbered seventy-two -- two Egyptians and the rest Israelites -- and that Pharaoh had compelled them all to teach sorcery, or that they had been compelled to come to the tryst. For they had said to Pharaoh before it, 'Show us Moses while he is asleep,' and when he did, they found that his staff was guarding him. They said, 'This is not sorcery! When the sorcerer sleeps, his sorcery ceases!' So they had refused everything except to confront him. This explanation, however, seems to be contradicted by the fervor reflected in their words, *Surely there will be a reward for us* [7:113], and *By Pharaoh's might, truly we are doubtless the victors!* [26:44].[70] But it has also been said that they spoke that way because when they saw Moses' power, they grew greedy and were seeking more payment.

"And God is better and more lasting!" That is, 'God's reward is better than anything in this ephemeral world and more enduring in the eternal abode,' or that 'God Himself is better and His recompense—be it favor or punishment—is more enduring.'

[74-75] Then they explain this further, saying, *Verily, whosoever comes to his Lord guilty,* as one who dies in disbelief and sin, *surely his shall be Hell, wherein he neither dies,* and is given respite from the torment, *nor lives* a life from which he could benefit. This is

---

70. Ibn ʿAjība points out concerning the second verse quoted that the use of the double emphatic, *innā ... la,* gives the words an extra sense of emphasis and certainty.

thus a statement of how God's punishment is more enduring, '*But whosoever comes unto Him as a believer* in God Most High and in the miracles which have come from Him, which include those we have witnessed,' *and has done righteous deeds,* meaning everything established by the revealed Law and in accordance with [orthodox] belief, *those shall be of the highest ranks.* The fact that they are referred to here using the plural demonstrative of distance [*those*] just after having been referred to twice in the singular expresses a sense of how high their ranks are and how distant their abodes... But there is nothing in these words that indicates that faith alone, without actions, does not bring reward. Rather, it is by faith combined with righteous deeds that those high ranks are attained, [even while faith alone] has recompense.[71]

[76] Then God Most High explains what those ranks are: *Gardens of Eden...*[72] *with rivers running below, abiding therein. That is the recompense of one who purifies himself...* This is the result of having reached those highest stations, and the pronoun 'that' (*dhālika*), expresses high honor. Their success in reaching those ranks is the recompense of someone who purified himself from the stains of disbelief and sin through faith and good works, and this is another affirmation of how God's *recompense is better and more lasting* in response to Pharaoh's claim. It has also been said the words *Verily, whosoever comes to his Lord* begin the direct speech of God ﷻ, and God Most High knows best.

Spiritual Allusion

In these verses is encouragement for the *fuqarā'*, the people of affiliation and states that if opposition and threats are raised against them, they should pay them little heed, remain firmly on the path, and not be turned back, but rather say, as did Pharaoh's sorcerers, *We shall never prefer you to the clear proofs that have come to us, nor to Him who originated us. So decree whatsoever you decree; you only decree in the life of this world.* ...Many Sufis, in fact, have suffered injury because of their affiliation. Some were killed, some were subjected

71. This comment, which Ibn ʿAjība conveyed from the *tafsīr* of Abū al-Saʿūd, is a rather oblique way of saying the faith alone can deliver the believer from hell, that being its recompense, but it is by faith combined with good works that the most sublime paradiasical ranks are attained.

72. Ibn ʿAjiba adds here that the word *ʿadn* (Eden) itself means 'residing in perpetuity.'

to public ridicule,[73] some were exiled from their land, and others underwent other trials. Still this did not turn them back from the path, for they had reached the presence of God Most High and tasted what they had tasted. In fact, only someone who is still traveling can be turned back. As for those who have arrived, they can never be turned back, even if their bodies are rent asunder. And God is the Protector of the pious.

God then speaks of the departure of the Children of Israel for Shām.

> 77. *And We indeed revealed unto Moses, "Set forth with My Servants by night and strike for them a dry path through the sea. Be not afraid of being overtaken, and fear not."* 78. *Then Pharaoh pursued them with his hosts, and they were overwhelmed by the sea that enshrouded them.* 79. *Pharaoh led his people astray, and guided them not.*

[77] God, the Truth ﷻ, says *And We indeed revealed unto Moses, "Set forth with My servants by night..."* As we mentioned in our *tafsīr* of (*Sūrat*) *al-Aʿrāf,* this was revealed to Moses ﷺ after he had spent twenty years calling Pharaoh to God, had shown him evident signs, and bested the sorcerers. When Moses ﷺ gave up hope that they would come to faith, God inspired him to leave [Egypt]...saying ... 'Set forth with My servants to whom I have sent you in order to deliver them from the hand of Pharaoh,' that is, 'Flee with them by night from Egypt to the Red Sea.'... Referring to them as '*My servants*' expresses God's mercy and care for them and at the same time, the extreme iniquity of Pharaoh in inflicting upon them the torment he inflicted upon them and in making them his slaves when in reality they were the slaves of God ﷻ. *And strike for them*, that is 'make for them, or take them on' *a dry path through the sea*, a path where there would be no water.

Be not afraid of being overtaken, for you will be safe from your enemies catching up with you. *And fear not* being drowned by the sea.... They are told first not to fear being overtaken in order to quickly relieve them of this first fear, since ... *when the two hosts saw one another, the companions of Moses said, "Surely we are overtaken!"* [26:61].

[78] *Then Pharaoh pursued them with his hosts*, that is, he and his army

73. *Ṭuwwif*, literally, "taken around," means the practice of being paraded around town on a donkey, which was a form of punishment in Morocco at one time.

followed them, and he said to his army, 'Pursue them! Even if they are ahead of you, you will overtake them....' In some recitations, the verb is read *attabaʿhum*, which means that Pharaoh forced his army to follow them, driving them on from behind.

It has been related that Moses عليه السلام went forth with (the Children of Israel) in the early hours of the night and that they numbered seventy thousand and six hundred. When Pharaoh was told of this, he set out with his army in pursuit, following their tracks, and came so close to them that the two hosts saw one another. When the Children of Israel caught sight of the dust of (their pursuers' horses), they said, "*Surely we are overtaken!*" And Moses عليه السلام answered them, "*Nay! Truly my Lord is with me; He will guide me*" [26:61-62].

As Pharaoh's host drew near, the Children of Israel said 'O Moses! Where shall we turn? The sea is before us and Pharaoh's horses are behind us!' Then Moses struck the sea with his staff and it parted into twelve parts, *and each part was like a great mountain* [26:63] of water.

When the Children of Israel, all of whom were cousins to one another, began crossing the sea by these paths, they lost sight of one other and began to say 'Our brethren have drowned!' Then God inspired the mountains of water, saying to them, 'Become as nets!' and the mountains became nets of water so that the people could see one another and hear each other's voices. When Pharaoh reached the beach, he found the waters thus parted and said, 'Moses has bewitched the sea!' And the people around him said, 'If you are a lord, enter it as he has done!' [but he hesitated]. Then Gabriel came mounted upon a mare in heat and Pharaoh was mounted upon a stallion. When Gabriel rode past him into the water, Pharaoh lost control of his mount and it raced into the water after the mare. Then all the Egyptians followed him, until, when the mountains of water loomed above them, God Most High inspired the sea to rise up over them and drown them all.

And so Moses عليه السلام and the tribes who were with him crossed safely, but as for Pharaoh and his army, *they were overwhelmed by the sea that enshrouded them.* That is, it rose up over them and drowned them in a catastrophe beyond reckoning and words. Al-Qushayrī says, "All of them were drowned, and it was when Pharaoh beheld this devastation that he professed his faith, but after [a life of intransigence], it was to no avail." And al-Kawāshī says, "*They were overwhelmed by* the divine wrath, by drowning, and by other calamities that no one knows except God Most High," but the indefinite pronoun indicates the magnitude of the destruction.[74] It has also been said that *they were overwhelmed* means 'By what you have heard concerning this story in another *sūrah*,' but there is nothing to this, since the indefinite pronoun here concerns not the question of having heard this story, but rather [the nature of] the destruction and its magnitude, which were beyond comprehension and description.

[79] *Pharaoh led his people astray*, that is, he led them down a path of loss and destruction, for they all died in disbelief. He brought them to a devasting torment in this world and to eternal punishment in the Next. *And* (he) *guided them not*: he did not direct them at all to anything of value in this world or the Next. They express emphasis and affirmation but are also a sort of ironic response to the words of Pharaoh [quoted elsewhere]: [*And I am only showing you what I, myself, see*] *and only guiding you to the right way.* [40:29]... And God Most High knows better.

Spiritual Allusion

Behold what can happen for someone who holds fast to his religion and endures with patience the hardships of his time: how miraculous things can come to pass for him and such honor and providential aid that it causes him to forget all those hardships. And (behold) how God can bring to ruin those enemies who were harming him and can lead him along the road to guidance and salvation. Such is God's way with His friends: first they are strengthened by trials and tribulations, and then they are given honor, divine aid, and all manner of blessings.

Thus, God next reminds the Children of Israel of the favors He gave them after they crossed the sea.

> 80. *O Children of Israel! We have saved you from your enemies and have appointed a tryst for you on the right side of the Mount. And We sent down to you manna and quails.* 81. *Eat of the good things We have provided you, but exceed not the limits therein,*

74. He means here the indefinite pronoun "what" (*mā*). The Arabic text – *fa ghashiyahum mina'l-yammi mā ghashiyahum*—literally says, "Then there covered them up from the sea *what* covered them up," as if the actual details of the event were too terrible to mention specifically.

> *lest My Wrath be unleashed upon you. And he upon whom My Wrath is unleashed has been cast into ruin.* 82. *And surely I am most forgiving toward the one who repents and believes and works righteousness, and thereafter is rightly guided.*

[80] God says to the Children of Israel after He had saved them from drowning and bestowed upon them myriad blessings both in their religion and worldly lives, *O Children of Israel! We have saved you from your enemies*, meaning Pharaoh and his people, *who inflicted a terrible punishment upon you, slaying your sons and sparing your women* [2:49]. *And We have appointed a tryst for you on the right side of the Mount* through the intermediary of your prophet, whom We brought to that side of the mountain, the side that was on his right, to speak to personally and so that he might be given the Torah.' As to whether it was on this same mountain that he had seen the fire and where the message [first] descended upon him or another, there are differing views. Also, [the tryst] is described as being for all the Children of Israel, even though it directly involved only Moses ﷺ, or him and the seventy who had been chosen to go up the mountain with him, because all of them were connected to it and all would benefit from it. It also gives [Moses' meeting] its full worth, and is thus similar to God's words, *Indeed, We created you, then We formed you* [7:11], which relate God's creation and formation to all human beings even though the only one He created was Adam ﷺ.

And We sent down to you, when you were wandering and lost in the wilderness, *manna*, which [was a food that] looked like frost, stayed from the time of *fajr* until sunrise, and was enough for each righteous person, *and quails*, carried to them by the south winds which God had raised, and of which each man could slaughter what sufficed him.

[81] And We said to them, *Eat of the good things We have provided you...* That is, eat what is wholesome and lawful. In the mention of these blessings—beginning with the blessing of being saved [from their enemies], then of being given their religion, and then of being given their sustenance—there is a beautiful order. '*But exceed not the limits therein* by forgetting to be grateful, or by acting in ways which transgress the boundaries [of morality], such as by being extravagant, or by arrogantly flaunting what you have, or by denying it to someone who deserves it.' Al-Qushayrī says: "'Ex-

ceeding the limits' means going beyond what is lawful into what is unlawful, or taking more than is necessary for life, or eating heedlessly and without thinking." Others have said that it means not to horde, and others, that it means not to use [what God gives you] for sin.' *Lest My Wrath be unleashed upon you.* The verb *yaḥill* ('unleashed') gives these words the tone of a debt whose time for repayment had come. *And he upon whom My Wrath is unleashed has been cast into ruin*, that is, has been brought low and destroyed, or has fallen into the abyss (*al-hāwiya*).

[82] *And surely I am most forgiving...* That is, God abounds in forgiveness *towards the one who repents and believes and works righteousness*, who repents from polytheism and sin, both of which are forms of transgressing the limits mentioned, believes in what it is necessary to believe in, and accomplishes the virtuous deeds instituted by the religious law. This is an exhortation and encouragement to anyone who has lapsed or fallen into sin to repent and have faith. *And thereafter [he] is rightly guided* and walks the path of righteousness according to [divine] guidance and perseveres in it until death. This also signifies that someone who does not do this risks being deprived of God's forgiveness. Al-Kawāshī says, "*And thereafter is rightly guided* means he knows that all of this is purely by God's accord."

Spiritual Allusion

When the days of trial have passed and days of blessings arrive, let the servant of God bring to mind what has passed and consider his present state, so that he might be increased in gratitude and humility, which will, in turn, bring him ever more of God's gifts. But if he forgets those times of trial and is not grateful for the blessings he now enjoys, then he risks having them taken away and being returned to his previous state.

Let him bring to mind as well the *ḥadīth* about the leper, the bald man, and the blind man as recounted in the *Ṣaḥīḥ* collections.[75] Both the leper and the bald man, after they had been

75. This long *ḥadīth*, recorded in both Muslim and Bukhārī, begins: "There were three people among the Children of Israel—one had leprosy, the other was bald-headed, and the third one was blind." It then goes on to recount how God tested them by sending each an angel who cured him and gave him what he most desired in life. When the angel returns years later in the form of a poor traveler, the first two deny that their wealth and goodness in life was by the grace of God,

cured by God and enriched by His grace, denied their past conditions, and so were returned to them, while the blind man acknowledged his and gave thanks for the state he was in, and the blessings he had been given stayed with him and were increased, for gratitude is what binds to us God's gifts and keeps us from losing them. And so to the people who have been given God's bounty and who are constant in their gratitude for it, God says: *Eat of the good things We have provided you, but exceed not the limits therein.* Do not misuse them and do not deny them to the deserving, *lest My wrath be unleashed upon you..*

Concerning God's words *And surely I am most forgiving*, al-Qushayrī said, "God is most forgiving of the lapses that may occur to *the one who repents... and believes* and who does not see good deeds issuing from himself, but rather sees that everything comes to pass from God, the Truth. And along with them, he *works righteousness* by not falling short in fulfilling what God has made obligatory upon him, *and thereafter is rightly guided* to what is orthodox." He also said of the words *And thereafter is rightly guided*: "They mean 'by Us to Us.'"

Al-Wartajibī said, "The repentant is the one devoted to God. The believer is the one who knows God. To work righteousness is to give up everything that is apart from God. Someone like this is guided by God to God, enveloped in God's Mercy, and protected by God's protection."

Then God speaks of how the Children of Israel were tried by way of the calf.

> 83. *"What has made you hasten from your people, O Moses?"* 84. *He said, "They are close upon my footsteps, and I hastened to You, my Lord, that You may be content."* 85. *He said, "Truly We tried your people in your absence, and the Samaritan led them astray."* 86. *Then Moses returned to his people, angry and aggrieved. He said, "O my people! Did your Lord not make you a goodly Promise? Did the pact seem too long for you? Or did you desire that the anger of your Lord be unleashed upon you, such that you failed your tryst with me?"* 87. *They said, "We did not fail our tryst with you of our own will, but we were laden with the*

refuse to help the traveler, and so are turned back to the state they had been in, while the man who had been blind says, "I was blind and God restored my vision; take whatever you like and leave whatever you like..." Ibn ʿAbbād al-Rundī quotes this *ḥadīth* in the context of gratitude. See Ibn ʿAbbād, *Fatḥ al-Tuḥfa.*

burden of the people's ornaments. So we cast them [into the pit], and thus did the Samaritan also throw." 88. *Then he brought forth for them a calf as a mere body that lowed, and they said, "This is your god and the god of Moses, though he has forgotten."*

[83-84] Moses عليه السلام had gone to the Mount to keep his tryst and the covenant he made and he had chosen seventy of the Children of Israel to be with him to receive the Torah by God's command. But when he approached the mountain, yearning for his Lord made him hurry on ahead, leaving the others below. Thus, God, the Truth ﷻ, asks him, *"What has made you hasten from your people O Moses?"* That is, 'What has caused your haste and made you rush ahead of your folk? I commanded you to be with them, and perhaps coming yourself without them means you do not care about them.' To this Moses عليه السلام answers, *"They are close upon my footsteps,"* meaning, 'They are near me; in fact, they are with me. I am only a few steps ahead of them—not enough to come between us—and it never occurred to me that I was leaving them behind.'

Al-Kawāshī said, "Since the Lord's question to Moses had two aims -- one to rebuke him for his haste and the other, to ask the reasons for it—the most important of the two for Moses عليه السلام was to present his excuse, and so he answered apprehensively, 'I am only a few steps ahead of them,' not any more than the leader of a delegation would be to its members, and then he answered the other question: *I hastened to You, my Lord, that You may be content.*' That is, 'That You may be more content with me because of how quick I was in carrying out what You commanded and how careful I was to keep the tryst with You,' for he supposed that his haste was more pleasing to God. This is thus a proof that the Prophets عليهم السلام are permitted to interpret (God's commandments). And so, what he means is 'I hastened to You, dear God, that You might know that I truly love You and that there is no place of rest for me with anything except You.'

Al-Qushayrī said that the words, *"They are close upon my footsteps"* mean 'I did not leave them behind in order to lose them, but rather *I hastened to You, my Lord, that You may be content.*' And God said, 'O Moses, My contentment is in your being among them, not in your being ahead of them nor behind them, but rather in your being *among* them, among the weak and among those whom you have chosen to be with you seeking My contentment."[76]

[85] God Most High said to him, *Truly We tried your people in your absence.* That is, 'After you left them, We tried your people through the worship of the calf.' It has been related that [the Children of Israel] kept to what Moses ﷺ had commanded for twenty nights after his departure, and reckoned those twenty nights, along with their days, as forty. Then they said, 'We have completed the allotted time but still have not seen the least trace of Moses!' Moses had promised them that he would be gone for forty days and had left Aaron in charge of the six hundred thousand who stayed behind, and of those, all but twelve thousand fell into worshipping the calf.

The meaning of God's words, *And the Samaritan led them astray,* is that through him they were tempted. For he had said to them, 'Moses ﷺ has not kept to what he promised you because of the jewelry you have, which God has forbidden you....' God tells Moses ﷺ of this trial as soon as he arrives before Him, which was before it actually happened, because it was already affirmed in His knowledge. This way of speaking about what will happen in the future as if it were past is similar to His words, *The inhabitants of the Garden will call out* [7:44].[77] It may also have been because the Samaritan had resolved to bring temptation upon the people as soon as Moses ﷺ left them and had already taken the first steps, so that it was already coming to pass when Moses ﷺ was being told about it.

The Samaritan was from one of the tribes of the Children of Israel called Sāmara, and it has been said that he was from Kerman.[78] Ibn ʿAbbās said, "His name was Moses, son of Ẓafar, and he had come from a village where they worshipped the cow but had entered among the Children of Israel and pretended to be a monotheist, even though love of worshipping the cow remained in his heart. Thus did he become the means by which God tried the Children of Israel."

[86] *Then Moses returned to his people.* After Moses ﷺ had completed forty days on the mountain and had received the Torah, he returned , but this was not because he had heard from God that

76. See *al-Ḥāshiya*, v. 1, p. 491.

77. The verb in this verse, *nādā*, is grammatically in the past but expresses something that will take place in the future. See also footnote 22.

78. Kerman is a city in southern Iran that was said by some commentators to have been a place of cow worship.

his people had been tempted, as some *tafsīrs* suggest based on the words, *angry and aggrieved,* for his stay of forty days is well-known and confirmed. The word *asaf* (in this context) has been said to mean 'extreme anger,' but it has also been said to mean 'sadness and grief' over his people's having gone astray.

He said, "O my people! Did your Lord not make you a goodly Promise?" 'for He gave you the Torah containing light and guidance, *Or did the pact seem too long*? That is, 'Did the period of my separation from you become too long for you..., such that you erred on account of it?' *Or did you desire that the anger of your* Lord, the Sovereign of all your affairs, be *unleashed upon you* in all its severity *such that you failed your tryst with me?..."* That is, 'Did you forget the promise because the time grew long and so you (broke it) mistakenly, or did you truly want God's wrath to be unleashed upon you and so you (broke it) intentionally?'

[87] *They said, "We did not fail our tryst with you our own will ..."* That is, 'We did not break our promise to remain steadfast by our own authority and ability... If we had been left alone and the Samaritan had not tempted us, we would not have broken our word, but we were overcome, and the Samaritan deceived us, and circumstances helped him do so.'

Al-Qushayrī said, "This means, 'We did not start out intending this, nor knowing what its outcome would be. What brought us to this was the jewelry and ornaments of the Egyptians. The Samaritan used them to plate the calf, and then it led to the evil that resulted.' Thus, in what is forbidden there are always portents of the tribulation and evil [it will bring]."

[87] ... *But we were laden with the burden of the people's ornaments.* These words continue the Children of Israel's excuses for how they fell into error. That is, 'We were laden by the weight of the Egyptians' jewelry which we had borrowed from them when we were planning our escape from Egypt, telling them that it was for a marriage celebration.' This has also been said to mean that they had borrowed the jewelry for a holiday celebration and had not returned it, fearing that their plan would be discovered, or that when the sea washed up the bodies of the (drowned) Egyptians, most of their garments were of gold and silver, and the Children of Israel had gathered them up. Such were *the people's ornaments* with which the calf was plated. It may be that they are referred to here

as *the burden* because they were liabilities and sins, for (to take) booty was not lawful for them.

'So we cast them into the fire hoping to rid ourselves of the punishment they would bring,' or 'We cast them to the Samaritan and he cast them into the fire.' *And thus did the Samaritan also throw* what he had, as we had done.' This has also been said to mean, 'He cast the soil he had picked up from the hoofprints of Gabriel's horse which he was keeping in his turban. For the Devil had told him that anything he mixed it with would come to life. So when he cast the soil into the mouth of the calf, it began to low.

It has been related that he said to them, 'Moses has not returned to you because of the burden you bear. In my view, we should dig a pit, build a fire in it, then throw into it all the jewelry we have.' And that is what they did.

[88] *Then he brought forth for them a calf....* When they [had cast the jewelry into the pit], the Samaritan fashioned from that melted jewelry a calf, that is, the form of a calf. It is described *as a mere body*, meaning a physical body of flesh and blood or else a body made of gold, without spirit, *that lowed* with the sound of a calf. And the Samaritan and those who had been tempted by him then said, *"This is your god and the god of Moses, though he has forgotten."* That is, 'He has forgotten your real god and has gone (instead) to seek Him on the mountain.'

The words (beginning) *Then he brought forth for them...* are the speech of God Most High recounting the result of the Samaritan's having tempted them in word and deed. They emphasize its folly and also introduce (the words which follow) expressing God's condemnation of them. (Contrary to what some *tafsīrs* state), they are not the speech of those offering an excuse (to Moses), for in that case they would have said, 'And he fashioned for *us*...' And God Most High knows better.

Spiritual Allusion

During a journey, the leader of a people should walk with them in their midst or at the rear, but not at the head of the group or hurrying on before them. "Slowness is from God and haste is from the devil,"[79] and it is best for a leader to remain with the weak and the

79. This *ḥadīth* is found in the *Musnad* of Abī Yaʿlā al-Mawṣilī, *Shuʿab al-Īmān* of Bayhaqī, *Musnad al-Shāmiyyīn* of Ṭabarānī, and several other collections.

poor as if he were one of them. But should he need to separate from them (to tend to) something important, then let him appoint in his place someone who can be trusted in his religion and let him depend upon his Lord in doing so, always with a view of God's care and protection. Al-Kawāshī said that according to Ibn ʿAṭā', "God Most High spoke to Moses through inspiration saying, 'Do you know how this befell you?'[80] Moses answered, 'No, my Lord.' God said, 'When you said to Aaron, "*Take my place among my people* [7:142]," and depended upon him totally, where was I?'"

All the tribulations and mistakes that befall *fuqarā'* happen because they are not with people who truly know the way, or because of how rarely they listen to them. And should some trial in respect to their livelihoods come upon them and they begin to depend upon some worldly thing during the shaykh's absence, let him return to them *angry and aggrieved* and say to them, *Did your Lord not make you a goodly Promise,* the great opening (*al-fatḥ al-kabīr*) which will come to you if you can be patient with the journey with a life apart from the workaday world (*al-tajrīd*)? *Did the pact seem too long for you,* for there have been aspirants who remained in the service of a shaykh for twenty or thirty years, *or did you desire that the anger of your Lord be unleashed upon you,* leaving you remote and veiled from God, when you broke the pledges you gave your shaykhs? If they offer their excuses, accept them, but if they revert to worshipping the calf of this world, then take it away from them and say, "*Now behold your god, to whom you remained devoted: we shall surely burn it and scatter its ashes in the sea!*" [20:97] And with God is all accord.

Then God mentions His rebuke to them for their worship of the calf.

> 89. *Did they not see that it did not respond to them with words, and that it had no power over what harm or benefit may come to them?* 90. *And Aaron had indeed said to them earlier, "O my people! You are merely being tested by this, and truly your Lord is the All-Merciful. So follow me and obey my command!"* 91. *They said, "We shall not cease to be its devotees till Moses returns to us."* 92. *He said, "O Aaron! What hindered you, when you saw them going astray,* 93. *That you did not follow me? Did you disobey my command?"* 94. *He said, "O son of my mother! Do not*

80. That is, the temptation of his people.

seize me by my beard or my head. Truly I feared that you would say, 'You have caused division among the Children of Israel, and you did not heed my word.'"

[89-91] God, the Truth ﷻ, says in rebuke of their worship of the calf and to show how ugly their vision had become, *Did they not see...?* That is, did those who were misguided themselves and misguiding others not reflect enough to know that the calf *did not respond to them with words* nor answer them in any way because it was an inanimate object? How could they have taken it as a god? To connect the faculty of sight[81] with something that does not exist stresses the extent of their abomination and folly. 'And did they not also see that the calf *had no power over what harm or benefit may come to them,* that it could not defend them from harm nor attract to them benefit, that it could neither harm them if they did not worship it, nor benefit them if they did?

[90] *And Aaron had indeed said to them earlier*, counseling and exhorting them towards the truth before Moses' return: "*O my people! You are merely being tested by this.*" That is, 'You have fallen into tribulation because of the calf,' or 'You have been misled by it. It has brought you tribulation, not direction.' Then, trying to guide them to the truth after having reproached them for what is false, he continues: '*Truly your Lord is the All-Merciful* alone, not the calf.' His mention of God's name (*al-Raḥmān*) shows the care he took to gently lead them to the truth which would take them to God's all-inclusive mercy. (Thus, these words mean,) 'The Lord who is worthy of your worship is the All-Merciful and none other. *So follow me* in being steadfast in religion *and obey my command* to give up worshipping what you know to be a false (idol).'

[91] *They said* in answer to Aaron ﷺ, "*We shall not cease to be its devotees.*" That is, 'We shall continue to worship it "*till Moses returns to us.*" They made his return a limit until which they would keep worshipping the calf, but did not promise to abandon it. Rather, it was a way of procrastinating, for behind their words, and based on what the Samaritan had told them, they did not believe that Moses ﷺ would return to them with anything that would falsify what they were doing. It has been related that when they said this, Aaron ﷺ withdrew from their midst to be with the twelve thou-

81. In the question, *Did they not see?*

sand people who had not taken to worshipping the calf.

When Moses returned and heard their shouts and clamor as they danced around the calf, he said to the seventy who had been with him on the moutain, 'This is the sound of tribulation.' And when they had arrived in their midst, he said to them *"O my people! Did your Lord not make you a goodly Promise?* and he heard from them in response *"We did not fail our tryst with you of our own will."*

[92-94] When Moses ﷺ saw Aaron, he angrily grabbed him by the hair on his head with his right hand and his beard with his left and said *"O Aaron!"* This phrase begins without the particle *waw* ('and') because the discourse here returns to the main narrative, which is what Moses said to Aaron when he had heard his [his explanation]: "*What hindered you, when you saw them going astray*" by worshipping the calf and reveling in sin before you? Is it *"that you did not follow me?"*[82] That is, 'When you saw them going astray, what prevented you from following me in what I had told you to do, which was to battle against them with those who remained with you?'... It has also been said that the question, *what hindered you*, means, 'What prevented you from coming to me and telling me that they were going astray. In that case, leaving them would have been a way of reproaching them.' This is the most accepted meaning.

Did you disobey my command to stand firm and defend the religion, for when he had said to his brother, *"Take my place among my people,"* [7:142] that included commanding them. Representation (*al-khilāfa*) necessitates that the representative (*al-khalīfa*) be empowered to do what the one he represents would have done had he been present.

He said, "O son of my mother! He mentions in particular their mother in hopes of touching his brother's heart, but not, as some *tafsīr*s have suggested, because they had different fathers, for the majority agree that they were full brothers. *Do not seize me by my beard or* by the hair on *my head*, which was how Moses had taken hold of him in his anger for the sake of God, for Moses ﷺ was staunch and rigid in all matters, and when he saw them worshipping the calf, he was unable to control his rage and did what he did.

Then his brother sought his pardon, saying: '*Truly I feared* that if I had fought with some of them against others and they had be-

---

82. Omitted here is Ibn ʿAjība's mention of whether the word *Lā* before the verb *tattabiʿani* (*"follow me"*) is truly a negation or a particle of emphasis.

come divided, *you would say 'You have caused division among the Children of Israel,'* for they were descendants of a single man, which is why they were called "the Children of Israel" and not 'the folk' or something similar. By 'division,' Aaron ﷺ meant the division which leads to battle, following which there is no reconciliation. 'And I feared that you would say, *You did not heed my word,* which was: *Take my place among my people and set matters aright* [7:142]. I saw that it was best to avoid bloodshed and to indulge them until you returned. In that way, I would leave it in your hands for you to do what you saw fit, not to mention the fact that they were at the pinnacle of their strength while we were weak and few in number,' as (his words elsewhere) state: *Truly the people deemed me weak and they were about to kill me* [7:150]. And God Most High knows best.

Spiritual Allusion

Anything someone depends upon instead of God, or inclines towards with love apart from God is for that person the calf of the Children of Israel. And it is said to him: 'Are you looking for your support in something that *has no power over what harm or benefit may come to* you? Surely *you are merely being tempted by this* to give up the journey to your Lord and stay veiled from the Sacred Presence. But *Your Lord is truly the All-Merciful*, the Generous, and the Giver of every grace, so keep to the worship which has been commanded, be His servant in every state, and you will belong to God alone and be free from all else. And in God is all accord.

Then God mentions Moses' reproach to the Samaritan.

> 95. *He said, "What was your purpose, O Samaritan?"* 96. *He said, "I saw that which they saw not. So I took a handful [of dust] from the footsteps of the messenger, and I cast it. Thus did my soul prompt me."* 97. *He said, "Be gone! In this life it shall be yours to say, 'Touch [me] not!' And truly for you there is a tryst that you cannot fail to keep. Now behold your god, to whom you remained devoted: we shall surely burn it and scatter its ashes in the sea!"* 98. *Your only god is God, besides whom there is no other god. He encompasses all things in knowledge.*

[95] God, the Truth ﷻ says: (*Moses*) *said* in rebuke to the Samaritan, *"What was your purpose?"* That is, 'What was your role in this and what did you hope to gain by tempting the people as you did?' He asks him about this so that he might show the people the

Samaritan's deceptiveness by his own admission and also so that the punishment he would receive might be an example for others who were similarly tempted from among them and from among the peoples to come.

[96] He—that is, the Samaritan—said: "*I saw that which they saw not*," which has been said to mean, 'I knew what they did not know, and realized what they did not realize,' or, 'I physically saw something they did not see,' and this latter is more correct. For he had seen Gabriel ﷺ come mounted on a horse, and had seen that every place the horse's hooves touched the barren ground, it would turn verdant with plant life. He understood that (the soil in those places) had some special property and so he gathered some of it up, referred to by God's words which quote him as saying, "*So I took a handful [of dust] from the footsteps of the messenger*," that is, from the tracks of the messenger's horse, the messenger being Gabriel ﷺ, 'who had been sent to accompany you (O Moses) to the mountain.'

The author of *al-Lubāb* says, "The Samaritan had been among those close to Moses ﷺ and he saw Gabriel ride his horse into the sea when it parted. It was then that he took (some of the soil) from the places where the horse had left prints. No one would have seen this except those who were with Moses (at the head of the people)." Qatāda said, "The Samaritan was a person of high repute among the Children of Israel, from a tribe called Sāmira, but (became) an enemy of God and hypocrite after the Children of Israel had crossed the sea. When they passed near the land of the ʿAmālakites[83]—and they were a people *given up to the worship of idols which they had* and who worshipped cows—*they said, O Moses, make for us a god even as they have gods* [7:138]. So the Samaritan took advantage of [their weakness] and made the calf [as an idol for them]."

Al-Kawāshī says, "The Samaritan recognized Gabriel among all the people because his mother had given birth to him in a year when all male babies were being killed and she had placed him in a cave to save him. Then God Most High sent Gabriel to raise him so that the tribulation that was destined to arise by his hand might come to pass." Ibn ʿAṭiyya, however, considers this narrative unreliable. I would say that that might be true of its chain of transmission, but as to whether it could have happened as described, it is entirely possible for God to fulfill His decree in such as way.

83. The land of the Amālakites is said to have been along the southern border of Canaan.

Then he said: '*So I took a handful [of dust] ... and I cast it* into the mouth of that statue plated with the gold of their jewelry, and it began to low.' *Thus did my soul prompt me*, that is, 'Thus did my soul make it fair-seeming in my eyes.' His answer shows that what he did was purely because he was following his own egoistic desires and nothing else, neither rational proof nor divine inspiration.

[97] Moses ﷺ said to him, *"Be gone!"* meaning 'Leave the company of people.' *In this life, it shall be yours to say: Touch [me] not!* That is, 'For the rest of your life, you will say to people "Touch me not" and you will be completely set apart from them, not by choice, but because of the necessity to protect them from you.' For God Most High afflicted him with an incurable illness, and none could touch him nor could he touch another without that one being instantly seized by a violent fever. And so he shunned people and they shunned him, and he would shout at the top of his voice, *Lā misās!* (*Touch [me] not!*)

And it is also said that Moses ﷺ exiled him from his folk and ordered the Children of Israel not to mingle with him or even come near him. Al-Ḥasan said, "God made the Samaritan's punishment that he would not touch people nor they him. This was his punishment and the punishment of anyone like him until the Day of Judgment: a heavy tribulation to bear as punishment in this world." It has also been said that he was afflicted by whisperings, and that all human whisperings come from that time.[84] Qatāda said, "Those who are like him today still say 'Touch me not!'" And it is said that Moses ﷺ considered slaying him, but that God Most High said to him, 'Do not slay him, for he is a generous man.' And it may be that the lesson in his receiving such a punishment is that the tribulation he wrought arose from his intermingling with people, so his punishment was to be shunned and removed from their midst.

And truly for you there is a tryst in the Next World *that you cannot fail to keep*, that is, 'Which God will not allow you to miss and which you will surely be brought to after having been chastised in this world.' Or: 'You will not be able to pass it up nor make any mistake

84. "Whisperings" (*waswās*) in this context mean demonic suggestions. These can take the form of promptings towards evil, dark thoughts, or simply doubts about whether one has completed an act of devotion correctly, which may lead to repeating that act again and again. In modern psychological parlance, this latter is close to obsessive-compulsive behavior, but from the traditional point of view of Islam, it originates from a devil or jinn.

concerning it. Rather, you will have no choice but to come to it.

"*Now behold your god*," that is, the calf, "*to whom you remained devoted. We shall surely burn it* in the fire," or according to some, in a coldness so extreme that it burns.... *and scatter its ashes*, taken by the winds *into the sea* in particles like motes of dust...so that not the least trace [of it] remains. The imperative *behold* signifies that Moses ﷺ actually carried this out at that moment.

[98] Then informing them of the truth, he said, "*Your only god is God...*" That is, 'The one who merits your worship is God' whom he describes with the words which follow... "*Besides whom there is no other god*," God Alone, with Whom nothing shares in divinity, *He encompasses all things in knowledge*....That is, His knowledge encompasses all that it is His concern to know... and (this can be said) of nothing else, whatever it might be, starting with the calf.

Thus, the speech of Moses ﷺ ends with a proclamation of God's Oneness (*al-tawḥīd*) just as the revelation to him had begun with the same proclamation: *Truly, I, even I, am God. There is no god except Me.*[85] And God Most High knows best.

Spiritual Allusion

Behold how the hoofprints of Gabriel's horse gave life to dead forms. So how would you not be given life by kissing the footprints of the gnostics or even their feet? Indeed, the soul of anyone who humbles himself before them will be given new life, his lights will shine forth, and his deepest knowledge will be confirmed. And this is well known: humility towards God's saints is humility towards God inasmuch as they are the ones who lead you to God and remove you from everything else.

Behold, too, the Samaritan: when he humbled himself before what was other than God by following his passions alone, he was cast out and removed, and became an example for people.

The Sufis also say that the *faqīr* should flee from human company and be like the Samaritan who, when he saw anyone, would say, 'Touch me not.' Thus do they sing:

Be as fearful of people as you would of wild beasts.
Mix with them but keep a careful distance
And be like the Samaritan when you are touched

85. Verse 14 above.

And it is said to one who depends on something other than God Most High, be it his knowledge, or deeds, or station, or state, or even his effacement from creatures, "*Now behold your god, to whom you remained devoted: we shall surely burn it and scatter its ashes in the sea!*" In a narration that has been passed down, God says to His servant, 'O My servant. Do not depend on anything except Me. If you depend on your knowledge, We will render you ignorant; if you depend on your deeds, We will throw them back at you; if you depend on your state, We will leave you in it; if you depend on your gnosis, We will make it unacceptable from you. So what ruse do you have left, O My servant? Be Mine as a servant, and I will be yours as Lord.' To this do His words refer: *Your only god is God.*

Then He reminds His Prophet ﷺ of the graces He has bestowed upon him through these narratives.

> 99. *Thus do We narrate to you some of the accounts of those who have come before.*

[99] God, the Truth ﷻ, says *Thus*, that is, similar to the wondrous narration you have just heard, *do We narrate to you some of the accounts of those who have come before,* that is, from the histories of those past communities and by-gone eras, in order that they may give you insight, increase your knowledge, be a reminder to others, and a lesson for those who will come after you. And God Most High knows best.

Spiritual Allusion

The stories of the saintly and the lives of the gnostics are among the armies of the heart which inspire those who wish to emulate them, encourage them to strive towards their stations, and give comfort to those who have found in God something similar to what they found.

Then He gives a warning to those who turn away from the Qur'ān in which these beautiful narratives are contained:

> 99. ... *and We have given you a Reminder from Our Presence.* 100. *Whosoever turns away from it, verily he shall carry on the Day of Resurrection a load,* 101. *Abiding therein. How evil a burden for them on the Day of Resurrection—* 102. *The Day the trumpet shall be blown, and We shall gather the guilty on that Day, blind.* 103. *They will whisper among themselves, "You*

have tarried only ten [days]." 104. *We know well that which they will say, when the most exemplary of them in conduct will say, "You have tarried only a day!"* 105. *They ask you about the mountains. Say, "My Lord shall scatter them as ashes.* 106. *And He will leave it a barren plain.* 107. *You will see no crookedness or curvature therein."* 108. *On that Day they shall follow a herald from whom there will be no turning aside. And voices will be humbled before the All-Merciful, and you will hear naught but a murmur.* 109. *On that Day intercession will be of no benefit, save [that of] those whom the All-Merciful has granted leave and with whose word He is content.* 110. *He knows that which is before them and that which is behind them, and they encompass Him not in knowledge.*

[99-100] God, the Truth ﷻ, says: *And We have given you,* O Muḥammad, a mighty *Reminder from Our presence...,* from what is especially nearest to Us, a Noble Recitation that gathers within it all perfection, and conveys wondrous stories and parables.

Whosoever turns away from that Reminder, which leads to the happiness of this world and the Next, *... shall carry on the Day of Resurrection a load,* a heavy and severe punishment for his disbelief and other sins, referred to here as "a load" (*wizr*) because of how it weighs down the one who bears it and is so hard to carry, like a porter's burden which bends his back. It has also been said that it is called "a load" because [on the Day of Resurrection] it will be given physical form and be placed upon the back of the one who bears it on the way to the Gathering, but the first explanation better fits with the words that follow: *abiding therein*. That is, they will remain under that load which is itself the chastisement, or they will remain under that heavy weight even after they have entered the fire.

How evil a burden for them on the Day of Resurrection. That is, 'Evil is their burden on the Day of Resurrection,' with repetition of "*the Day of Resurrection*" emphasizing a sense of dread.

[102] *The day when the trumpet shall be blown...* which may be understood to mean, '*That is the day on which* the trumpet is blown,' or '*Make mention of* the day when the trumpet shall be blown with the blast of the Resurrection.' '*We shall gather the guilty,*' meaning the idolaters, *on that Day blind*, literally, "blue-eyed" (*zarqa*), for blue is the worst and most repulsive eye color to the Arab, and was even

considered by some to be a bad omen, as a poet once said:

> Your eyes have turned blue, O Ibn Muka'barin,
> Like any beast whose eyes turn blue with guilt.

It is also said to simply mean 'blind,' for in cases of extreme blindness, the whites of the eyes turn blue, or 'thirsty,' for in cases of extreme thirst, the pupil of the eye may turn blue. Here, too, the repetition of "that day" sustains a tone of dread.
[103] *They will whisper among themselves...*They will speak in lowered or concealed voices because of the fright that has overwhelmed their hearts, and in that whispered tone they will say, *"You have tarried only ten [days],"* that is, 'You have spent only ten days and nights in the world,' for time will appear short after it is gone. Or they may say this in regret at its passing when they witness the adversities and calamities before them. It has also been said to refer to the length of time they spent in the grave, and this explanation best fits the context. When they witness the Resurrection, which they had denied while in the world and considered beyond the realm of possibility, they will be unable to keep themselves from saying this in recognition of how soon it came to pass. So it is as if they were saying 'You have been resurrected after spending only the briefest time in the grave.' It has also been said [that this refers to] the time between the two Trumpet Blasts, which is forty years. It has been related that the punishment will be lifted from the non-believers during that time but that it will appear brief in their eyes when they see before them the calamities of Resurrection Day, for while they underwent the punishment of the grave, they were unaware [of time].

[104] God Most High says: *'We know well that which they will say...* concerning how long they tarried,' or 'We know well the Day on which they will say this before it occurs.' *When the most exemplary of them in conduct,* that is, those whose views are the most just and minds the most trustworthy, *will say, "You have tarried only a day!"* That these words are attributed to *the most exemplary of them* is not because what they say is the most correct, but rather because [what they say] is the most indicative of how severe the calamity [of that day will be].

[105-107] *They ask you about the mountains*, that is, about what will become of them. Some *tafsīrs* mention that this was asked by a man

from Thaqīf,[86] and others, that it was asked in derision by the idolaters of Mecca. *Say* to them *"My Lord shall scatter them as ashes.* 'He will make them like sand and then send the winds to spread them far and wide,' or 'He will level them and cast them into the seas like scattered dust.' *And He will leave* the earth that was beneath them a level *barren plain* so that the places where mountains had stood will be level with all the other places on earth, and all will be transformed into a single plain...

(The words) *qāʿ* and *qīʿa*[87] mean level and solid ground, similar to the word *al-sahl*.[88] It has also been said to mean "ground devoid of vegetation." As for the word *ṣafṣaf*,[89] it describes ground which is level and smooth because all its tracts are running in the same direction.

You will see therein, that is, in the earth after the mountains have been scattered, *no crookedness or curvature* (*lā ʿiwajan wa lā amtan*), which can also mean 'no downward or upward slopes.' Ibn ʿAbbās said, "ʿIwaj are valleys and amt hills." And al-Mujāhid said, "ʿIwaj is ground that slopes downward and amt is ground that slopes upward." The meaning here is that were you to examine it with the tools of a surveyor, you would find it level in every direction, and the "you" refers to anyone with eyes to see.

[108] *On that Day,* when the mountains are leveled, *they shall follow a herald* calling human beings to the Place of Gathering. That herald will be Isrāfīl 🌺,[90] who will beckon to people after the second Trumpet Blast, standing upon the Rock in Jerusalem,[91] 'O you people, hasten to your Lord!' This will be after he has called them forth from their graves saying: 'O crumbled bones! O rent joints! O scattered flesh! Arise to the Exposition and the Reckoning!'[92] And

---

86. The tribe who live in the mountainous area of Ṭāʾif, about 56 miles from Mecca.

87. Translated in the verses as 'plain.'

88. Another word for "plain" in Arabic. *Sahl* also means "easy." Flat, level ground is easier to cross.

89. Translated in the text as "barren."

90. The angel Isrāfīl 🌺 is identified in several *ḥadīth* as the one who blows the trumpet signaling the Hour. See al-Suyūṭī, *al-Ḥabāʾik*, items 85-106.

91. The Rock (*al-ṣakhra*) lies under what is now called the Dome of the Rock.

92. *Yawm al-ʿarḍ*, the Day of Exposition, is one of names for the Day of Judgment. It refers particularly to the fact of all people being shown or exposed before God. See also Winters' translation of al-Ghazālī's *The Remembrance of Death and the Afterlife*, pp. 173 ff.

they will come forth from every direction in hordes like locusts, not knowing where they are going, and then they will be called from the Rock to gather for the Reckoning, as the *ḥadīths* and traditions affirm.

God's words *from whom there will be no turning aside* mean that no one who is called will be able to turn aside or turn away from the herald. All will head towards his voice, from east to west and every other direction, and it will be directed towards each person and reach each person regardless of where he is.

And voices will be lowered before the All-Merciful, that is, humbled and silent in awe, *and you will hear naught but a murmur*, a half-hidden sound. The word *al-hams* ("murmur") has been said to refer to the sound of their footsteps as they head to the Place of Gathering. So voices will be silenced in fear and awe, and all that you will hear is the shuffling of feet walking towards the Gathering.

[109] *On that Day intercession will be of no benefit*, that is, on the day when these calamities come to pass, no intercession will avail *save (from) those whom the All-Merciful has granted leave* to intercede—the Prophets, the saints, the learned, and the deeply pious—*and with whose word He is content*, that is, whose speech on behalf of the one being interceded for is accepted, or *with whose word He is content* in this world, that word being *Lā ilāha illā Allāh*, said with totality from the heart. It has also been said to mean 'Except the one whom the All-Merciful allows to intercede and whose words of intercession are pleasing (to Him),' and this most fits that station of calamity. But as for the one who has made himself an enemy to God, his intercession will not avail even if it takes place, as His words elsewhere state: *Thus, the intercession of the intercessors will avail them not* [74:48].

[110] *He knows that which is before them*, meaning the states or matters of this world they have gone through, *and (He knows) that which is behind them*, that is, what they are heading towards or the matters of the Next World. *And they encompass Him not in knowledge*, that is, their knowledge cannot encompass God's Essence so that they could fully comprehend His Divinity. This may also be understood to mean that the totality of their knowledge does not encompass what is known to God, be He exalted. Al-Qushayrī said: "His words *And they encompass (Him) not in knowledge* may refer either to *that which is before them and that which is behind them* or to God, the Truth

(He be glorified!).[93] This latter explanation is what the earliest believers meant when they would say, 'God, the Truth, is known, but knowledge does not encompass Him,' even as they would say, 'He is seen, but vision cannot comprehend Him.'"

Spiritual Allusion

And We have given you a Reminder from Our Presence, a Recitation which gathers hearts to God and directs them to the consciousness of God. *Whosoever turns away,* that is, whoever turns away from God and does not seek Him with the totality of his being, *shall carry a load* which will weigh him down, prevent him from ascending to the station of the gnostics, and leave him forever in the depths of heedlessness. This will be on a Day when God gathers together the first and the last, when the God-fearing will be honored, and the guilty will be brought low by the weight of all that they had been given, their comfort and ease having disappeared, as if they had not tarried in the world more than an hour.

They ask you, O gnostic, *about the mountains* of the rational mind when the sun of gnosis rises upon the light of its moon. *Say, "My Lord shall scatter them as ashes,* leaving the earth of the ego when it is overcome by the mysteries of the Spirit *a barren plain*, for it will be one with the vastness of the Spirit. When the diverse forms of creation vanish, *You will see therein* neither descent or ascent, but rather seamless Being and an Effacing Ocean, wherein there is neither distance nor nearness, neither height nor depth. It is of this reality that a poet has said:

> He who sees creation as a mirage has gone past the veils
> To Being Itself, seamless, with neither distance nor nearness
> Nor anything besides it.
> When someone has been guided to what is real,
> There is no speech from him to Him, and no allusions left to make.

By the word "creation," he means every existing thing. There is no speech from the servant to his Lord because the servant is effaced in the extremity of his nearness, nor are there any allusions left for him to make. As it is said in the *Ḥikam* [77]: "The gnostic is not one who, when making a symbolic allusion, finds God nearer to himself than his allusion. Rather, the gnostic is the one who, because of his

93. If the verse is understood as referring to God, then the pronoun in parentheses would be "Him," and if to God's knowledge, then "it."

effacement in God's being and absorbtion in his contemplation of God, has no allusion left to make." Thus, they say, "When someone truly knows God, his tongue grows weak," and to this alllude God's words: *Voices will be humbled before the All-Merciful, and you will hear naught but a murmur.*

This is after having followed *a herald* calling to God and after having journeyed with him without turning aside or parting from him until he says: "Here you are and here is your Lord!"[94] At that moment, in the Presence of the Generous king, there is such awe and veneration that no one is able to raise his voice. Such it is for the Sufis: all their speech is hidden or secret because they are overwhelmed by awe.

On that Day intercession will be of no benefit in entering the Sacred Presence *save for the one to whom the All-Merciful has granted leave* both to teach others and guide them along the path and *with whose word He is content*, this word being the invocation of God (*dhikru Allāh*) which is enjoined upon anyone to whom God wishes to grant intercession. Then the lights of invocation will overcome him, and he will enter into the company of the beloveds, sit upon the carpet of nearness, and be granted knowledge by God, not by way of evidence and proofs, but by way of taste, ecstasy, and vision.

In God's words, *And they encompass Him not in knowledge,* is an allusion to the impossibility for those who enter God's Presence to fully comprehend His Divinity, for if that were possible, there would be no more ascent left for them to make, and how could that be when they are eternally and endlessly ascending the mysteries of the Essence and the Lights of the Attributes, in this world and the Next? At every instant, the delights of contemplation and the lights of spiritual unveilings are renewed for them in a way that neither minds can grasp nor tongues express.

And even though they might be granted necessary knowledge of the Sublime Essence, and they might perceive the unveilings of its mysteries and lights, and their meditations might roam the ocean of Firstness, Lastness, Outwardness and Inwardness, the immensity of the upper realms and of *what is beneath the soil,*[95] and they might be plunged into the Seas of Oneness and contemplate

94. This is paraphrased from the well-known definition of the spiritual master (*al-shaykh*) which appears at the end of Ibn ʿAṭā'illāh's *Laṭā'if al-Minan*, page 204. See also Nancy Roberts' translation of that book, pp. 372-373.

95. Echoing verse 6 of this *sūrah.*

the lexicon of the God's Divinity without fear or boredom—even after all this, as we have said, their understandings will still not encompass [God's divinity]. And God Most High knows best!

Thus, when they return to the formal world, their faces are humbled before the Living, the Self-Subsisting.

> 111. *Faces will be humbled before the Living the Self-Subsisting. And whosoever bears wrongdoing will have failed.* 112. *But whosoever performs righteous deeds and is a believer, he shall fear neither wrong nor deprivation.*

[111-112] God, the Truth ﷻ, says *Faces will be humbled before the Living, the Eternal...*Faces [of all creation] will be abased and humbled with the humility of a captive (*ʿānin*) in the hands of a conquerer. Of this did Umayya ibn Abī al-Ṣalt say:

> A King upon the Throne of Heaven, a Guardian—
> Before His might faces are humbled and prostrate.

Faces may be understood to mean those of transgressors, similar to God's words elsewhere, *The faces of those who disbelieved shall be stricken* [67:27], and this meaning is supported by God's words which follow: *And whosoever bears wrongdoing will have failed.* That is, 'Faces will be humbled in failure and loss when they are presented with their wrongdoings to bear.' Ibn ʿAbbās ﵄ said of this verse, '[It means] ruined are those who join partners to God and do not repent.' They are the ones whose faces shall be humbled, while as for the people of Unity, to them do God's words refer, *but whosoever performs righteous deeds...*

If, however, we understand the phrase *faces will be humbled* to mean absolute humility or prostration, then it applies to everyone. All created beings will be humbled before God at that time, and then separated into groups, *and whosoever bears wrongdoing will have failed* and lost, while *whosoever performs righteous deeds and is a believer,* inasmuch as faith is the condition upon which devotions and good works are accepted, *he shall fear neither wrong*, that is, the wrong of being kept from the recompense he is promised or of being punished for sins he did not commit, *nor (shall he fear) deprivation*, that is, that the recompense for the good he accomplished will be diminished.

Spiritual Allusion

When meditation has ranged the farthest reaches of the *Malakūt* and the mysteries of the *Jabarūt* and has affirmed their limitlessness, it returns to the nest of sevanthood and humbly submits to *the Living, the Eternal.* Someone who does not reach this station has failed inasmuch as he bears the wrong of inclining towards what is other than God and of being overcome by his physical nature and desires. As for the one who ascends towards his Guardian Lord and occupies himself with works that will bring him closer to the divine Presence, that one *shall fear neither wrong nor deprivation.* For God elevates the servant in proportion to his aspirations, and graces him to the measure of his obedience. It is for this that revelation and inspiration came, even as the verses continue:

> 113. *Thus have We sent it down as an Arabic Recitation, and We have varied the exhortation therein that haply they may be reverent, or [that] it might occasion for them remembrance.* 114. *Exalted is God, the Real Sovereign. Be not in haste with the Qur'ān before its revelation is completed for you, but say, "My Lord! Increase me in knowledge!"*

[113] God, the Truth ﷻ, says *Thus*, that is, like those previous revelations, *We sent it down.* The entire Qur'ān is referred to here by the pronoun "it" without antecedent, giving the sense that its eminence, centrality, and presence dispense with the need to name it (in minds of those who read it). And it is *an Arabic Recitation,*[96] that the Arab might understand it and come to know that its miraculous verses are beyond the realm of human effort (to produce), but are rather revelation from an omnipotent Creator.

And We have varied warnings therein, that is, 'We have repeated therein certain warnings, or passages that are like warnings, *that haply they may be reverent,* and stay clear of disbelief and transgression, *or [that] it might occasion for them remembrance*, that is, exhortation and reflection that leads to what is higher. *Exalted is God* above what unbelievers attribute to Him and above the abasement of the sinful, those for whom the Qur'ān is neither a restraint nor a warning. Exalted be God in His Essence, Attributes and Acts beyond all comparison to created beings. He is *the* (*True*) *Sovereign,*

96. We have chosen here to use the literal meaning of *Qur'ān*, 'a Recitation,' in keeping with the context of the *tafsīr*.

able to carry out what He commands and what He prohibits. He is One whose promise is hoped for and whose threat is feared. He is the *True* in the Divinity of His Essence, or He is the *Absolute* Whose non-existence is eternally and forever impossible.

Be not in haste with the Qur'ān before its revelation is completed for you. That is, 'When We send down to you this Qur'ān in Arabic, displaying to you its varied forms of admonition, stay silent until the Angel has finished reciting it to you and do not be in a hurry.' For when Gabriel was conveying to him the revelation, the Prophet ﷺ was so concerned with receiving and remembering it that he would repeat it after him sound by sound, word by word. (This verse) prohibited him from doing that, because perhaps in pronouncing one word, he would be unable to hear what followed it, and the purpose of the utterances is that their meanings, which contain limitless knowledge, be understood. Thus, God commands the Prophet ﷺ to seek ever more knowledge in the words that follow: *But say "My Lord! Increase me in knowledge!"* That is, 'Say either to yourself or aloud, "*My Lord! Increase me in knowledge!*"' Or, 'Ask God ﷻ to increase your knowledge of Him as well as of His commandments, for there is no limit to this knowledge just as there is no limit to His Essence, and it will bring you what you seek without needing to hasten it.' And God Most High knows better.

Spiritual Allusion

Thus have We sent it down as an Arabic Recitation which articulates (*yuʿrab*) the perfection of the manifestion of God's Essence and the lights of His Attributes. *We have varied exhortation therein* to anyone who lags behind on [the journey towards] witnessing God after the completion of His manifestation, *that haply they may be reverent* by staying clear of whatever may veil them from that vision, *or [that] it might occasion for them remembrance*: a yearning which will inspire them to set out towards the Divine Presence and union. But *Exalted is God, the True Sovereign*, beyond any notion that His Essence could be joined to anything or that anything could be joined to Him. Rather, union with God [means attaining] the knowledge of His All-Encompassing Nature and of His Essential Oneness.

Be not in haste, O gnostic, *with the Qur'ān* which is being sent down to your heart by Divine Inspiration, before this inspiration has been completed for you. For divine inspirations come all at once, after which will come their elucidation, as God's words elsewhere say, *So when We recite it, follow its recitation. Then surely it is for Us to explain it.* [75:18-19]. But seek from your Lord increase in God-given knowledge and Divine unveilings. That is, 'Do not be concerned with how soon inspirations will come to you or how long they stay, but rather, be concerned with both formal knowledge and gnosis.' For formal knowledge can be a means to gnosis, and thus to arriving in the presence of the Living, the Eternal. And in God is all accord.

Then God explains the warnings against disobeidience and speaks of its origin.

> 115. *And We indeed made a pact with Adam aforetime, but he*
> *forgot. And We found no resoluteness in him.* 116. *And recall the*
> *time We said to the angels, "Prostrate yourselves before Adam,"*
> *they prostrated, save Iblīs; he refused.* 117. *We said, "O Adam!*
> *Truly this is an enemy to you and your wife. So let him not expel*
> *the two of you from the Garden, such that you would be wretch-*
> *ed.* 118. *Truly it is for you that you shall neither hunger therein,*
> *nor go naked,* 119. *And that you shall neither thirst therein, nor*
> *suffer from the heat of the sun."* 120. *Then Satan whispered to*
> *him. He said, "O Adam! Shall I show you the Tree of Everlasting-*
> *ness and a kingdom that never decays?"* 121. *So they both ate*
> *therefrom. Then their nakedness was exposed to them, and they*
> *began to patch together the leaves of the Garden.*

[115] God, the Truth ﷻ, says: *And We indeed made a pact with Adam aforetime* concerning the deceptions and enmity of Satan, and warned him not to be fooled by him. *We said, "O Adam! Truly this is an enemy to you and your wife,"* 'so do not be deceived by what he advises you to do.' *But he forgot* that pact and did not respect it [as it should be] and so became heedless of it. And he was misled by the literal sense (of that commandment), interpreting it as mild disapproval or as applying only to that one particular tree and not to its species, and so he ate from another.

We found no resoluteness in him, that is, no firm determination (to sin), for if there had been, Satan would not have needed to deceive him with his whisperings. But this occurred when Adam was at the beginning of his life, before he had any experience of things, before he had felt their heat and coldness, or tasted their bitterness and sweetness, [but it was not because he lacked intelligence], for the Prophet ﷺ said, "Were the intellects of all the Children of

Adam to be weighed against Adam's intellect, his would outweigh them all."[97]

The words *We found no resoluteness in him* have also been explained to mean 'We found no resolve on his part to commit sin.' He erred or misinterpreted [the commandment] but did not intend to commit a sin. Indeed, God's words *Adam disobeyed his Lord...* [20:121] could be taken to mean that because of Adam's sublime station and nearness to God, this (error) was reckoned as a sin (in the same sense that the Sufis say): 'The good deeds of the pious are the sins of those brought near.'

Then, in explanation of what that pact was, of how Adam ﷺ forgot, and of his lack of resolve, God says *And recall the time We said to the angels, "Prostrate yourselves before Adam...."*[98] That is, 'Remember what came to pass at that moment from Us and from him so that you might clearly understand (how) he came to forget and how he lost his resolve, for We had commanded the angels to prostrate before Adam and all of them did so *save Iblīs; he refused* to prostrate and waxed proud, or made some gesture of refusal.

We said, cautioning Adam against Satan's advice—and this is the pact We made with him—"*O Adam! Truly this one* that you have seen do what he has done *is an enemy to you and your wife*, for he would not prostrate before you, *So let him not expel the two of you from the Garden.*' That is, 'Do not let him become the means by which the two of you are put out of the Garden.' Thus, God had prohibited them both from letting themselves be deceived by him. *Such that you would be wretched, ...* that is 'You would be wearied by the hardships of the world, by hunger and thirst, poverty and injury, and the physical exhaustion of having to search for sustenance and clothing, for your lives would then be by the toil of your hands.'

Ibn Jubayr said, "There was sent down to Adam a red ox, and with it he would plow the earth and then wipe the sweat from his brow. Such was his toil and wretchedness (*shaqā'*)." Note too that even though these words are addressed both to Adam and Eve, the masculine singular form is used because man's toil in the world was to be greater.

97. This *ḥadīth* is mentioned in the commentary of al-Ṭabarī (d. 310/922) and al-Suyūṭī attributes its transmission to Ibn al-Mundhir (d. 317/930).

98. This is a linguistic explanation of the word *idh*, usually translated as "when," but which is literally the beginning of the imperative form of the verb *dhakara*, "remember, recall, or mention."

[118] God Most High said to him, *Truly it is for you,* O Adam, *that you shall neither hunger therein, nor go naked* for lack of clothes, nor thirst, nor suffer from the heat of the sun which would harm you, for in that paradisiacal Garden there is neither sun nor the freezing cold of the moon (*zamharīra*).' Here, instead of speaking [to them] of the many delights of the Garden—its foods and drinks, its splendid garments and pleasant abodes— God speaks [to them] of being spared the conditions which come from their lack—hunger, thirst, nakedness, and exposure—as a way of warning them to avoid whatever would lead to those conditions. In fact, they had already been encouraged to enjoy all that exists [in the Garden], with the exception of the Tree, in the words of God Most High ... *"O Adam, dwell you and your wife in the Garden and eat freely thereof, wheresoever you will* [2:36]... and because [that encouragement] is mentioned elsewhere, it is only abbreviated here. Encouragement [towards one thing] always includes within it discouragement [from something else]. Indeed, hunger and its like is inconceivable in respect to the people of Paradise for they are free from needing food, drink, and shelter. Each time they enjoy one of [heaven's] bounties, it is followed by something like it or better, without ever approaching a limit imposed by need.

[120] *...Then Satan whispered to him...* That is, 'the whisperings of Satan became apparent to him,' or 'he said to him in a low voice:' *"O Adam! Shall I show you the Tree of Everlastingness,* the tree from which he who eats lives forever, never dies, whether it be in his own [human] state or because he will become an angel, *And* shall I show you *a kingdom that never decays?* a kingdom that will not pass away or fade in any sense of the word?

[121] *So they both ate therefrom. Then their nakedness was exposed to them...* Ibn ʿAbbās, ﷺ, said, "They were stripped of the light with which God Most High had clothed them and their nakedness appeared to one another." *And they began to patch together... the leaves of the Garden....*

Spiritual Allusion

'*And We indeed made a pact with Adam aforetime* not to forget Us, nor become distracted from his vision of Us by the delights of Our Garden.' But he forgot that vision and became attracted to the ornaments of the Garden, and so We sent him down to the earth of servanthood to be purified of the remnants [of his fallen nature] and perfect therein his virtues. Then did We cause him to reside in Our nearness, and unveiled to him the Presence of Our Beauty, by granting him eternity in Our abode.

Jaʿfar al-Ṣādiq said: "*And We indeed made a pact with Adam aforetime* not to forget us, *but he forgot* and became distracted by the Garden. So, he was tried by his having ignored the prohibition (of the tree) and by becoming distracted by the gift from the Giver. Then he fell from grace into tribulation and was removed from the Garden and its bounties, that he might learn that the (real) gift is not in the delights of food and drink, but in being near the Giver. So let no one look towards what is other than God, and may God Most High sustain us with His Accord and Infinite Care."

One of the sages said, "Adam forgot the covenant because when his mate was created for him, God placed a sense of intimacy and familiarity with her in Adam's heart and then tried him through his ego's desires for her so that when he saw in her face the tree of perfect beauty, he became overcome by wanting her." That is, he turned away from his vision of spiritual beauty and became absorbed by [a vision of] physical beauty and this led to his loss of comportment [with God] and to his being tied [to a life of] toil." So let the aspirant beware of inclining towards his ego's designs and of the heedlessness which can occur when they present themselves to him. And all safety comes from God.

Concerning the words of God ﷻ, *And We found no resoluteness in him,* (Ibn ʿArabī) al-Ḥātimī said, "(*And We found no resoluteness in him*) to transgress what was forbidden. Rather, there befell him what had been written in destiny which caused him to forget the path to what he was seeking ..." About this, the master of our masters, Sīdī ʿAbd al-Raḥmān al-Fāsī, said: "The meaning of [Ibn ʿArabī's words] 'what had been written in destiny' will be clear to you if you consider the words of the Prophet ﷺ, "Adam won his dispute with Moses."[99] But this is for no one else (to claim) if he is not truly

99. Here he is referring to the *ḥadīth* found in both Muslim and Bukhārī: The Prophet ﷺ said, "Adam and Moses argued with each other. Moses said to Adam. 'You are Adam whose mistake put you out of Paradise.' Adam said to him, 'You are Moses whom God selected as His Messenger and to whom He spoke directly; yet you blame me for a thing which had been destined for me before my creation?' Then the Prophet said twice, 'So, Adam won his dispute with Moses.'

In another version, the Prophet ﷺ said, "Adam and Moses met, and Moses said to Adam 'You are the one who brought people to misery and got them expelled

constrained (to sin). This decree distinguishes what might befall a saint from what might befall someone else and is what Junayd was referring to (when he quoted the verse), *And God's Command is a decree determined* [33:38][100], alluding to the overwhelming and constraining force of destiny without any resolve (towards sin) on the part of the servant.[101]

The dispute between Adam and Moses (may peace be upon them both) does not take place in the formal world, which is subject to the [religious] law, but rather in the spiritual world, which is the place of inner truths. So any view into that world pertains to the mystery of the Supreme Truth (*al-Ḥaqīqah*), which has no relation to anyone's actions or omissions. So someone who disputes based on inner realities may win against someone who debates based on the physical world, where it is unacceptable to cite divine determination [as the reason for one's sin], for to do so rends the cloak of the revealed laws.[102] So reflect upon this.

(Ibn ʿAṭā'illāh) said in the *Tanwīr*, "Know that Adam's eating of the tree was neither out of obstinacy nor in opposition [to God's command]. Rather, it may have come about because he had forgotten the commandment, and was offered the food in that state, which we can understand from the words of God ﷻ, *But he forgot.* If, however, he took the food while remembering the commandment, then it was because (Satan) had said to him [and his wife] *Your Lord has only forbidden you two this tree, lest you should become angels, or among those who abide [forever]* [7:20]. And because of his great love and passion for God, he wanted whatever might allow him to be eternally near Him, forever in His Presence, or whatever might give him the angelic state, for he had seen with his own eyes the nearness to God that the angels enjoyed and believed that if he ate from the tree, he would attain their state, which he considered to be higher than his own. Moreover, God

---

from the Garden.' Adam said to him, 'Are you not the one whom God chose for His message and singled out for Himself and the one to whom He revealed the Torah?' Moses said, 'Yes.' Adam said, 'And did you not find there that my destiny was written before my creation?' Moses said, 'Yes.' So Adam won his dispute with Moses."

100. This was Junayd's answer when he was asked if it were possible for a saint to commit adultery.

101. Al-Fāsī, *al-Ḥāshiya*, I:495.

102. That is, on the level of the Supreme Truth (*al-Ḥaqīqa*), all that happens is by God's decree, but this may not be invoked as an excuse for a sin or transgression committed in the realm of human beings and legal responsibility.

says [of Satan], *He swore unto them, 'Truly I am a sincere adviser unto you* [7:21].' And Adam ﷺ said, 'I could not imagine that anyone could swear by God and lie.' It is for this reason that God says, *Thus he lured them on through deception* [7:22]."[103]

Ibn ʿAṭā was asked about the words *O Adam! Shall I show you the Tree of Everlastingness* and he said, "Adam ﷺ said, 'O Lord, why have You chastised me? I only ate from the tree wishing to be ever in Your Presence.' And God answered him, 'O Adam, you sought eternal life from a tree, not from Me, and eternal life is in My Hand and belongs to Me. So you attributed to another My divinity without realizing it, and to make you ever aware of that error, I am expelling you from the Garden so that you might never forget Me again.'"

In a word, the forgetfulness (mentioned in the verse) may be understood either in its literal sense, and (Adam's) eating from the tree was by the ineluctable design and constraint of destiny. If that was the case, then the words *Your Lord has only forbidden you two this tree, lest you should become angels, or among those who abide [forever]* [7:20] do not contradict this because what was destined was inward and hidden. Otherwise, the forgetfulness mentioned may be understood as (a conscious) omission because he thought the prohibition was not absolute, and so consciously ate from the tree thinking it would make him eternally near God, which for him took precedence over all else. Such is the view of the author of *al-Ḥāshiya.*[104]

His words, *Then Satan whispered to him*, close any door of interpretation which might (appear) to allow what is prohibited by the religious law. If something is partly permissible and partly forbidden, there is no room for discussion. To give up what is allowed (*mubāḥ*) is better than falling into what is forbidden, and among the pious ancestors (*al-salaf*), there were people who would give up a hundred portions of what was allowed out of fear that they would fall into [the one portion] that was forbidden. And God is the Guide to the straightest of paths.

> ... *Adam disobeyed his Lord, and so he erred.* 122. *Then his Lord chose him, and relented unto him and guided [him].* 123. *He said, "Get down from it, both you together, each of you an enemy to*

103. Ibn ʿAjība notes here that this was conveyed by Ibn ʿAbbās and Qatada.
104. See al-Fāsī, I:496.

> *the other. And when guidance comes to you from Me, then whosoever follows My Guidance shall not go astray, nor be wretched. 124. But whosoever turns away from the remembrance of Me, truly his shall be a narrow life, and We shall raise him blind on the Day of Resurrection." 125. He will say, "My Lord! Why have You raised me blind, when I used to see?" 126. He will say, "Thus it is. Our signs came to you, but you forgot them. Even so, this Day shall you be forgotten!" 127. Thus do We recompense whosoever is prodigal and believes not in the signs of his Lord. And surely the punishment of the Hereafter is more severe and more lasting.*

[121] ... *Adam disobeyed his Lord* by eating from the tree and *so he erred*, that is, he lost the way to what he was seeking, which was eternal life, and found instead its opposite. In fact, seeking immortality is both futile and wrong since it is contrary to destiny. *He erred* may also be understood to mean '(He was turned) from the right direction,' misled by the words of the Foe.' Al-Kawāshī said, "(These words mean) 'He did something that he should not have done, or mistook the way to the Truth, when he sought immortality by eating what was forbidden to him. So he failed and did not reach his goal.'" The fact that (God) calls what Adam did 'disobedience' and 'error,' even while his offense was small, shows how grave it actually was and warns his children away from anything that resembles it.

Then his Lord chose him ... and brought him near by leading him to repentance and Divine Accord, and by the words "*his Lord (Rabbuhu)*," Adam ﵇ is further honored. Then God *relented towards him*, which means that He accepted the repentance of Adam and his wife when they said, "*Our Lord! We have wronged ourselves.*' [7:23] *And* (God) *guided* him to be resolute in his repentance and to hold firmly to the means by which he would be protected. If only Adam ﵇ is mentioned as being chosen by God and having his repentance accepted, [without mention of Eve], it is because [he was God's] original creation and accepting his repentance meant accepting hers as well—and *men are the supporters of women* [4:34].

[123] *He said, "Get down from it, both you together.* This address continues God's words to Adam ﵇ [stated] as if in response to someone who asks, 'And what did God say after He accepted their repentance? He said to them both: *Get down from it.*' That is, 'Descend, both of you, from the Garden to the earth, where your state shall

be that *each of you* shall be *an enemy to the other*, living in mutual enmity concerning matters of survival.' This, then, is the source of all human strife, wars, and religious conflicts. And (if the discourse shifts to) the plural, even though it is addressed to Adam and his wife,[105] it is because those two were the source and progenitors of all the generations to come.

It is said in *al-Lubāb*, "When they were cast down to the earth, Adam placed his hand beneath his cheek and wept for a hundred years and Eve placed her hand atop her head and began to wail and moan, and such is still a way women grieve. Adam continued to weep until furrows formed beneath his cheeks from his many tears, and from his eyes there began to flow two streams which will continue flowing until the Last Hour. He was cast down upon one of the leaves from the Garden which he had used to cover himself and in his hand was a bunch of the Garden's sweet-smelling herbs (*rayhān*), and as he wept, the winds carried those herbs to India. Thus are most of the plants of that land aromatic."

God's words *And when guidance comes to you from Me* mean 'Guidance from a Messenger and a scripture that will show you the way to reach Me.' ... These words were addressed to both [Adam and Eve] but are in the plural [rather than the dual form] because of all the future generations which they bore within them. *Then whosoever follows My Guidance*, believing in the messengers and in what they brought from God, *shall not go astray* in this world *nor be wretched* in the Next. God's words [describing this guidance as] *from Me* and *My guidance* ennoble it and stress the necessity to follow it. Ibn ʿAbbās ﵄ said, 'Whoever reads the Criterion and follows what is in it, God will keep from going astray and protect from a woeful reckoning on the Day of Resurrection, for He has said, ... *Then whosoever follows My Guidance*, that is, My book and My messenger, *shall not go astray* in this world *nor be wretched* in the Next." He also said, "God will protect the one who follows the Qur'ān from going astray in this world and from being wretched in the Next." And Ibn ʿArafa said, "The particle *fa* ('then') at the beginning this verse signifies that it is because of human enmity that messengers would be brought forth, by the grace of God, to guide human beings to

105. In the phrase *get you down from it, both of you*, the pronoun and verb are in the dual form. Then with the words *each of you an enemy to the other*, the pronouns and nouns change to the plural.

the path of truth...[106]

[124-125] *But whosoever turns away from the remembrance of Me* meaning 'from the Qur'ān,' or 'from the guidance of one who bids them to remember Me and calls them to Me,' *truly his shall be a narrow life (maʿīshatan ḍankan)...*, because all his thoughts and concerns will be directed towards the things of this world, and he will wear himself out trying to gain more of them and live always in fear of losing them. But for a believer seeking the Next World, the light of faith will bring him contentment (*al-qanāʿa*), and that is the greatest wealth, the means to inner peace, and *a life that is good and pure.*[107] It has also been said that (the words) *a narrow life* refer to the punishment in the grave, even as the Prophet ﷺ said, according to Abū Saʿīd al-Khudrī, "His grave will grow narrow until his ribs are reversed and ninety-nine serpents are unleashed against him." It has also been said (that *a narrow life* means) 'enduring *zaqqūm*, *ḍarīʿ*, and *ghislīn*.'[108]

And We shall raise him blind on the Day of Resurrection, having lost his vision—as in God's words elsewhere *And We shall gather them on the Day of Resurrection upon their faces—blind, dumb, and deaf* [17:97]—but not blinded to the proof. They will say, "*My Lord! Why have You raised me blind, when I used to see* while in the world?

[126] And God will say: *Thus*, meaning, 'This is what you yourself did: *Our signs came to you*--luminous proofs brought by Our messengers—*but you forgot them*, you turned a blind eye to them, ignored them entirely and never brought them to mind. *So this Day shall you be forgotten*, left in blindness and suffering, *a fitting recompense* [78:26].'

But his blindness when he is brought to the Gathering will not last. It will be removed from him so that he might see the calamities of that station and his place therein, just as God Most High

106. He goes on to say that the fact the phrase in Arabic begins with the emphatic, *innā* [assimilated into the first word, *fa immā*], meaning "there will surely come to you.." rather than *idhā*, which would mean, "and if there comes to you.." eliminates the least doubt that this guidance must come.

107. This is an expression from 16:97: *Whoever works righteousness, man or woman, and has Faith, verily, to him will We give a new Life, a life that is good and pure and We will bestow on such of their reward according to the best of their actions.*

108. *Al-zaqqūm* is mentioned in 37:62 and 44:43 as *a tree that sprouts forth in the depth of Hell. Al-ḍarīʿ* is a thorny shrub mentioned in 88:06, and *al-ghislīn* is a purgative plant referred to in 69:36.

will remove deafness and dumbness, according to His words: *How well they will hear and how well they will see on the Day they come to Us* [19:38]. Thus, the Day of Resurrection will befall people in different ways.

[127] Then God Most High says: *Thus do We recompense whosoever is prodigal and believes not in the signs of his Lord.* That is, in this way does the recompense of those who are given over to excess and self-indulgence and who reject and oppose God's signs fit their sin. *And surely the punishment of the Hereafter,* that is the punishment of hell, *is more severe and more lasting* than having a narrow life, or than having a narrow life and being resurrected blind. From all this do we seek refuge in God!

Spiritual Allusion

Concerning His words, *And Adam disobeyed his Lord*, know that the real disobedience is that of the heart: being arrogant towards God's servants, demeaning anything in God's creation, opposing what is destined by God, and lacking contentment with what He decrees. One of the Sufis said, 'I committed a sin for which I have been weeping for forty years.' And when he was asked what it was, he said, 'I said about something that existed, "If only this were not."'

But a physical act of disobedience, if not persistent, can result in drawing nearer to God, the Generous and Forgiving, even as the *Ḥikam* states: "An act of disobedience that bequeaths humiliation and extreme need is better than an act of obedience that bequeaths self-infatuation and pride," and also, "Sometimes He condemns you to sin and it turns out to be a cause of arriving at Him."[109] Consider Iblīs's act of disobedience which came from within and brought about banishment and distance, and Adam's sin, which was a physical act and brought about nearness and repentance.[110]

In short, anything that brings you back to your Lord and confirms your servanthood and neediness is actually an honor and perfection, and anything, whatever it might be, that strengthens your egoistic nature and its control over you is a defect and leads

109. These are aphorisms 96 and 95 respectively in the Danner translation.

110. The sin of Iblīs was in not prostrating before Adam as God had commanded because he believed he was superior to Adam. The sin of Adam was in eating from the tree, but arose out of naivety or the desire to be eternally near to God as explained above.

to remoteness. So to be protected and preserved (from sin) means from the sins of the heart or from persisting in transgression. But a physical act of disobedience might occur as it is written for the servant without being a deficiency but rather a completion, as we have said. To transcend sin means to transcend the shortcomings which bring about distance from God, the Truth, not from the things which lead to perfection. In this way we can understand that what befell the Prophets 🙼 and appeared to be disobedience were not deficiencies but rather aspects of their perfection, similar to the lapses of the saintly. Reflect upon this well and do not be quick to dispute it until you have spent time in the company of people (of the way) that they might teach you the difference between defect and perfection.

Al-Wāsiṭī said, "An act of disobedience does not affect the state of election (*al-ijtibā'iya*).[111] God's words *And Adam disobeyed* (mean) that there appeared from him an action against God's commandment, but then he was overtaken by God's having chosen him (for vicegerency) which removed the offense. Do you not see how God shows His pardon in the words *He forgot and We found no resoluteness in him?*" Or as Shaykh Abū'l-Ḥasan al-Shādhilī 🙼 said, "How goodly the sin which resulted in vicegerency!"

Know too that the fall of Adam 🙼 to earth was before he was created. God Most High said, *I am placing a vicegerent (khalīfah) upon the earth* [2:30], which means He made him vicegerent before he created him, but He had decreed that he should be subject to intermediary causes (*al-asbāb*). So his eating (from the tree) was the means by which he was sent down to be vicegerent, receive the scripture, and populate the earth. Physically it was a descent, but spiritually it was an ascent. In a like manner does the lapse (*zilla*) of the gnostic send him down to the honored state of servanthood through which his place with God is elevated.

God's words, *each of you an enemy to the other* pertain to those whose natures are dominated by the sensual. As for those in whom the spiritual is dominant, they are brethren, loving one another, joined in friendship through reverence, for *Friends on that Day will be enemies to one another, save for the reverent* [43:67] ...

And when guidance comes to you from Me, that is, from someone who calls others to Me and guides them to knowing Me and to the

---

111. "Election" (*al-ijtibā'iya*). That is, if God has chosen to bestow sanctity upon a human being, lesser sins do not negate that state.

path leading to My presence, then whoever follows their spiritual guidance, *shall not go astray, nor be wretched*, but rather be guided and gladdened by the supreme happiness. *And whosoever turns away* from their reminder and exhortation and eschews their companionship, *truly his shall be a narrow life* full of cravings, greed, restlessness, and anxiety, *and We shall raise him blind* to the vision of Our Essence. He shall see nothing but the sensory world and its ornaments, not the mysteries of the Sacred Essence. And he shall say, *My Lord! Why have You raised me blind,* blinded to witnessing the mysteries of the spirit when I gaze upon Its vessels *when I used to see* in the world with physical vision. *He will say, "Thus it is. Our signs came to you*, these being the gnostic saints, *but you forgot them* and paid them no heed. *Even so, this Day shall you be forgotten!"* for "Each person dies the way he was living, and each shall be resurrected according to the state in which he dies."[112]

Al-Wartajibī said: "... *We shall raise him blind on the Day of Resurrection* means 'Ignorant of God's existence just as he had been in the world.' As ʿAlī, may God ennoble his countenance, said: 'Whoever does not know God in this world will not know Him in the Next.' And it has also been said that they are blinded from seeing God's saints and purified ones."

About the saying, "The state you were in is the one in which you will meet God," al-Qushayrī said, "So someone whose heart was blind in this world will be resurrected in that state, and someone who lived his life in ignorance will be resurrected in ignorance, and thus will they, "*Who has raised us from our place of sleep?*" [36:51] when their need to know has become most urgent. But even as they abandon any reflection upon God's signs today, tomorrow they themselves will be abandoned, left in torment, without mercy for the weakness of their states."[113]

Thus do We recompense whosoever is prodigal, who gives himself over totally to his passions and the pursuit of sensual pleasure until the days of his life have passed in vain and *We recompense him* with the anguish of being veiled and excluded from the presence of the beloveds. He did not believe in the existence of *the signs of his Lord*—meaning the saintly masters who call to God—And *surely*

---

112. The last phrase in this saying is a *ḥadīth* in the *Musnad* of Abū Yaʿlā, in Aḥmad, al-Ḥākim, and others. The first phrase is often mentioned along with this *ḥadīth*.

113. Al-Qushayrī relates this as a *ḥadīth*.

the punishment of being veiled in *the Hereafter is more severe and more lasting*, for it is permanent and perpetual. We seek refuge in God from the anguish of being veiled, from the worst of reckonings, and from being excluded from the presence of the beloveds. And in God is all accord.

Then God speaks of learning the lessons of this life.

> 128. *Does it not serve as guidance for them, how many generations We destroyed before them, amid whose dwellings they walk? Truly in that are signs for those possessed of intelligence.* 129. *And were it not for a Word that had already gone forth from your Lord and a term appointed, it would be inevitable.* 130. *So bear patiently that which they say, and hymn the praise of your Lord before the rising of the sun and before its setting, and in the hours of the night glorify [Him], and at the ends of the day, that haply you may be content.*

[128] God, the Truth ﷻ, says: *Does it not serve as guidance for them*, that is, 'Is not the outcome of their affairs clear to them when they think about *how many generations We destroyed before them ... amid whose dwellings they walk* as they journey to Shām? They pass through the inhabitants of al-Ḥijr,[114] and the Thamūd, and Pharaoh, and the people of Lot, and they see the ruins of their dwellings, knowing what befell them came to pass because they rejected (God's revelations). *Truly in that* dreadful sight is something that should impell them to seek guidance to the Truth and take heed so that what befell others does not befall them. (These words may also be understand to mean): 'Does it not serve as guidance to them how many generations before them We destroyed even in the security [they imagined they had] as they walked through their houses and their lands ... *and then the morning found them lying lifeless in their abode* [7:78]?

Truly in that terrible devastation are many powerful signs and clear direction that should lead them to the Truth *for those possessed of intelligence*, people whose minds prohibit them (*al-nāhiya*)[115] from

114. Mentioned in 15:80. In the commentary on that verse, Ibn ʿAjība and other exegetes generally say that the people of al-Ḥijr were the Thamūd tribe, and that al-Ḥijr was the river valley where they lived which ran between Medina and Syria. However, here Ibn ʿAjība seems to make a distinction between those people and the Thamūd.

115. *People possessed of intelligence* (*ūli al-nuhā*). The word *nuhā*, understood as 'intelligence,' is related to the verb *nāhiya*, 'to prohibit,' which expresses the no-

the ugliness of sin, the ugliest of which came from the disbelievers of Mecca who rejected God's signs, turned a blind eye towards them, and committed all manner of other transgressions as well.

[129] *And were it not for a Word that had already gone forth from your Lord*, by Divine Wisdom, that the punishment of this community would be delayed until the Next World , 'We would have hastened their destruction just as We did of those generations (through whose dwellings) they walk, heedless of the lessons to be learned from them, persisting in sin and disbelief.' Were it not for that destined period during which the punishment is delayed, *(it) would be inevitable*, that is, retribution for their wrongdoings would be inevitable and they would not be left in their sins for even an hour, just as it was inevitable for those of the past. Here, to refer to God as *your* Lord, meaning the Prophet's Lord, is a reminder that delaying (the punishment) is in honor of the Prophet ﷺ, as God's words (elsewhere) attest, *But God will not punish them while you are among them* [8:33] ....

... *And a term appointed*. That is, 'Were it not for a Word that had already gone forth to leave them until a later time and were it not for a term appointed for their lives, or for the punishment to come to them--and this ('term') has been said in some *tafsīrs* to be the Day of Resurrection and in others to be the day of Badr[116] — then the punishment would not have been delayed at all ....

[130] *So bear patiently that which they say* ... That is, 'If the situation is as We have said, and the fact that the punishment has not befallen them is not an oversight but rather a respite from what will inevitably come to pass, then bear patiently their words of disbelief,' and truly, for him to know that their end was coming would bring relief and patience. Or, 'Bear *patiently that which they say* and be occupied with God, not with them, and pay no heed to whether they perish or remain, for God knows best concerning them.' *Hymn the praise of your Lord* and exalt Him above all they ascribe to Him not fitting to His Sublimity. Praise Him and give thanks that He has chosen you for guidance, and recognize that He is truly the source of all blessings.

---

tion that an intelligent mind is one that keeps someone from sin by being able to understand its implications in advance.

116. The battle which took place on the 17th of Ramadan in the second year of the Hijra (624 CE) which was key to the survival of the first community of Muslims.

Al-Wartajibī said, "It is distressing to hear abusive language, so God [directs the Prophet ﷺ] to what will relieve him of that distress, saying *And hymn the praise of your Lord.* That is, 'If hearing their words grieves you, celebrating Our praises will relieve you.'

(The verse may also be understood to say), 'Offer the prayer in praise of your Lord who has brought you to the perfection of your guidance.' This meaning is supported (by the words which follow), *before the rising of the sun and before its setting,* for to affirm God's transcendence (with formulae of glorification) is not limited to any fixed time.[117] Thus, *before the rising of the sun* means at the time of *fajr,* and before its setting, at the times of *ẓuhr* and *ʿaṣr*, or according to some, the time of *ʿaṣr* alone.

And in the hours of the night glorify [Him]... That is, offer the prayers of *al-maghrib* and *al-ʿishā'* ... In the word order of this verse, mentioning *the hours of the night* first, there is a reminder of the added merit (of worship at these times), for at night the heart is more collected but the ego more inclined to rest, and so worship at that time may be harder. Even thus, does God Most High say elsewhere, *Truly the vigil of the night is firmest in tread and most upright for speech* [73:6]. *And* also glorify Him *at the ends of the day*. This mention again of the prayers of *al-fajr* and *al-maghrib* stresses their particular excellence, ... But these words may also be understood as referring to the prayers of *fajr*, *maghrib* and *ẓuhr*, for they mark the end of the first half of the day and the beginning of the second, or to any supererogatory worship offered during the day.

If we understand (this verse), however, to be referring to the affirmation of God's transcendence through invocations such as *Subḥān Allāh* (Glory be to God!) or *Lā ilāha illa Llāh* (There is no god except God), or any other formula of transcendence, then these times of day and night are singled out for invocation because of a particular honor they contain. There are many *ḥadīths* that recommend the invocation of God at the beginning and end of the day and during the small hours of the night upon awaking from sleep. Anyone who awakens from sleep should first invoke God with *Subḥān Allāh, Lā ilāha illa Llāh,* and *Allāhu akbar* before going back to sleep. Such was the practice of the vigilant among the pious ancestors.

That haply you may be made *content* by what God will give you in return when you praise Him at these hours, or 'that you may be

117. Whereas the prayer is.

made content by your intercession on behalf of all creatures that will gladden your heart.'

There is a *ḥadīth* in the *Ṣaḥīḥ* collection of al-Bukhārī which says, "You will see your Lord as you see the sun on a cloudless day, so try not to get too tired to offer the prayers before sunrise and sunset." And then he recited, "*And hymn the praise of your Lord before the rising of the sun and before its setting.*"[118] This (also) supports the explanation that the verse refers to the prayer and signifies that the prayer is invocation, drawing near to God, and devoting oneself to Him, all of which sows the seeds for the contemplation and vision (of God) in the Next World. Thus, it has been said concerning the people of Garden, "They will see their Lord morning and evening." This applies to the generality of the faithful, while for the elect of the elect, they will see their Lord with every glance and at every moment. And God Most High knows best.

Spiritual Allusion

Does it not serve as guidance to the people of faith and reflection, and the people of vision and insight *how many generations We destroyed before them*, (how many) communities of the past, *amid* the ruins of *whose dwellings they walk* and look upon the traces they left behind: how they traded their spacious palaces for narrow graves, and the comfort of their beds for the hardness of an earthly pallet and the covering of the tomb. So let them take a lesson (from that) and prepare to meet them, for they are surely like them or even worse. Their fame had spread far and wide, their places were exalted, and then, just as their moon waxed full, it was eclipsed, and it was if they had never existed. They were separated from those who were near and dear, and hastened on towards what they had sent before them, bound and led in submission towards the judgement. *Truly in that are signs for those possessed of intelligence*. But for hearts that have grown hard, neither threats nor reminders avail. *And were it not for a Word* of mercy and forbearance to delay the chastisement *and a term appointed* for their lives, the reckoning would be rushing

---

118. The wording of this *ḥadīth* in Bukhārī, *Muwāqīt al-ṣalāt*, according to Jarīr, is, "We were with the Prophet when he looked at the full moon and said, 'Certainly you will see your Lord as you see this moon with nothing obstructing your vision. So if you can avoid missing the *fajr* prayer and the *'aṣr*, then do so.' He then recited the words of God: *And hymn the praise of your Lord before the rising of the sun and before its setting.*" 20:130 and 50:39...

towards them.

So you who are turned towards God, devoted to your Guardian Lord, *bear patiently what they say* when they say things which are troubling to your heart, and occupy yourself with the invocation and glorification of your Lord at sunrise and sunset and during the hours of the night and day, until you are effaced in the Presence of the Knower of the Unseen, *that haply you may be* made *content* by the vision of the Beloved. And with God is all accord.

Then, inasmuch as reflecting on these lessons entails turning our aspirations away from this world, God says:

> 131. *Do not strain your eyes toward the enjoyments We have granted certain classes of them of the flower of the life of this world, that We may test them concerning it. The provision of your Lord is better and more lasting.* 132. *And bid your family to prayer and be steadfast therein. We ask no provision of you; We provide for you. And the end belongs to reverence.*

[131] God, the Truth ﷻ, says to His Prophet ﷺ: *Do not strain your eyes*, that is, 'Do not gaze with longing *toward the enjoyments*, the deceptive ornaments of this world that *We have granted certain classes of* the disbelievers nor deem them worthy to pursue, for truly they are ephemeral,' and for this reason are called *the flower of the life of the world* (*zahratu'l-ḥayāti al-dunyā*): they appear in their beauty then fade away and are extinguished, like a flower, so pleasing to behold, yet so quick to wilt and fade away.

'Such is what We have given them to enjoy when We gave them possessions and worldly power *That We may test them concerning it*: whether they will they be grateful for it, believe in your message, and spend (of their wealth) to strive by your side and (help) those who believe along with you, or not?' Or: '(We have given them wealth in this world) that We may punish them in the Next World because of their having misused it, so do not deem it of great importance. *The provision of your Lord* that awaits you in the Next World *is better*; or, 'Your provision in this world—which is to have sufficiency and guidance—is better than all their worldly gifts, because [though it might be small], it is safe from tribulation, while what they have been given is leading them to their reckoning and punishment. *And* (your provision is) *more lasting,* for neither it nor its effects ever end, while *the flower of the life of this world* is passing away.

[132] The essential is to be occupied with something which brings something lasting in return, and thus God says to (the Prophet ﷺ): *And bid your family to prayer*, that is, 'Enjoin prayer upon the people of your house or upon (all) those who follow you in your community.' This follows God's having enjoined it upon the Prophet himself ﷺ in His words *and hymn the praise of your Lord*, that they might help one another in their needs and not be anxious about their livelihoods nor impressed by the wealth of the rich. *And be steadfast therein,* meaning the prayer, and maintain it with patience and without worrying about your sustenance. *We ask no provision of you*, that is, 'We have not charged you with providing for yourself or for your family.' *We provide for you* and for them. So empty your heart of worry in order that you might witness Our mysteries. *And the end* that is worthy of praise *belongs to reverence,* that is, to the people of reverence. It is recorded that when some injury or need would befall his family, the Prophet ﷺ would tell them to offer the prayer and he would recite this verse. And God Most High knows better.

Spiritual Allusion

What is addressed to our Prophet ﷺ is also addressed to the elect of his community. So *do not strain your eyes*, O *faqīr*, towards what the people of this world have been given of its flowers and splendors. Rather, raise your aspirations above it, and refrain from admiring what they build and what they ornament, for in reality it is a kind of madness and illusion. When ʿUrwah bin al-Zubayr ؓ would see the rulers and their trappings, he would go inside his home and recite this verse: *Do not strain your eyes...*And Yaḥyā bin Muʿādh al-Rāzī once said to some scholars of his time, "O scholars of evil! Your homes are Hāmānian; your mounts are Qārūnian and your clothes are Pharaonic. Where is the way of Muḥammad?"[119]

And do not be taken up with seeking your provision. *The provision of your Lord*—which is what He brings forth for you in your time from the source of all grace, without intermediary causes or labor (on your part)—*is better and more lasting.* Certitude and happiness in God, and ever deeper knowledge of Him is better and more lasting,

---

119. Hāmān was Pharaoh's architect, mentioned in 40:36: *O Hamān build me a tower so that I might reach the gods.* Qārūn (Korah) is mentioned in 28:76 and 79: *Then he went forth before the people in his pomp and the people who were desirous of the things of this world said, 'O would that we had been given what Korah was given.'* They are the prime Quranic examples of pride and egotism attached to worldly wealth.

and the treasures of God are never depleted nor is the transformation of your heart by ever greater certitude and an ever stronger attachment to the Lord of the Worlds. These are the things which endure. *And bid your family to prayer and be steadfast therein*, for your provision is coming to you without doubt at the moment We will it to be. *We ask no provision of you*, neither for yourself nor your family. *We provide for you*, but with the provision of the reverent (*al-muttaqīn*) not with the provision of the dissolute (*al-mutrafīn*). *And the end belongs to reverence*, and in God is all accord.

Then God mention the things said by the disbelievers which the Prophet ﷺ is commanded to bear patiently.

> 133. *And they say, "Why has he not brought us a sign from his Lord?" Has there not come to them the clear proof of that which is in the scriptures of old?* 134. *Had We destroyed them with a punishment before it, they would have said, "Our Lord! If only You had sent us a messenger, we would have followed Your signs before being abased and disgraced."* 135. *Say, "Each is waiting, so wait! For you shall come to know those who are the companions of the sound path, and those who are rightly guided."*

[133-134] God, the Truth ﷻ, says: *And they say,* meaning the disbelievers of Mecca, *"Why has he not brought us a sign from his Lord"* to prove his veracity, something that they would consider to be a sign, such as the earth being rent asunder or the moving of mountains, for in their pride and intransigence, they did not reckon as signs the miraculous [verses] they had witnessed at which mountains fall prostrate.

God Most High says: *Has there not come to them the clear proof of that which is in the scriptures of old?* That is, 'Has there not come to them the Qur'ān with explanations of what is in the earliest scriptures—in the Torah, the Gospel, the Psalms, and all other heavenly revealed books? For the Qur'ān contains within it what was in them and adds to that other knowledge and other mysteries. This is God's answer to what they say as well as a rejection of what they insinuate by it. To say that no signs have come to them implies that they deny the coming of the signs and deny the coming of the Noble Qur'ān which is the most luminous of signs and the most sublime, mightiest, and enduring of miracles. The true meaning of a miracle is that it distinguishes the one claiming prophethood by something extraordinary, whatever that may be, and without a doubt, knowledge is the most magnificent and loftiest of things, for it is the source of actions, and (the Qur'ān) appeared bearing knowledge of the earlier and later peoples through an illiterate man who had had no involvement with formal knowledge nor learned from any scholar. So what miracle can match its revelation, and what other sign is needed? To call it a *clear proof of that which is in the scriptures of old*, that is, a witness to the truth of the doctrines and laws which they contain, and upon which the totality of the Messengers agree, further emphasizes its worth and its luminous proof, and is further affirmation that it is revelation. As a certain person of God said, "*Has there not come to them* clear proofs of *that which is in the* earliest scriptures, the accounts of peoples We brought to ruin when they asked for signs and then were given them, but rejected them. How quickly did their destruction follow. So how is it that these people, when there comes to them a clear proof, consider themselves secure from being like those before them?

Had We destroyed them in this world *with a punishment ... before it*, that is, before there had come to them the Quranic revelation and the advent of Muḥammad ﷺ, *they would have said, "Our Lord! If only You had sent us a messenger* to summon us to a book that would guide us, *we would have followed* the signs which had come to us *before being abased* by the chastisement of this world *and disgraced* by hell-fire on the Day of Resurrection. But 'We do not destroy them before they are warned,' and thus have no excuse. So on the Day of Resurrection, they will say, *"Indeed, a warner came to us, but we denied him and said, 'God did not send anything down; you are in naught but great error.'"* [67:9]

[135] *Say* to those who are recalcitrant in their rejection: '*Each* one of you and each one of us *is waiting* to see what is going to happen for us and for you,' *so wait! ...'* Or, 'Each of us is awaiting the cycles of time to see to whom victory will be given. *So wait! For you shall* soon *come to know who are the companions of the sound path,* the path of rectitude...[120] *and those who are rightly guided* away from error, you or we? And God Most High knows better.

120. Here, the Shaykh notes that a variant recitation of *al-ṣirāt al-sawiyyi* is *al-ṣirāt al-siwā'*, in which case it means "the path of equilibrium."

Spiritual Allusion

It should not be made a condition for gnostic saints, those who have direct knowledge of God and who are calling people to faith, to produce miracles. It is evidence enough that they are following clear proof from their Lord and that people are receiving guidance at their hands, along with their knowledge of the mysteries of Oneness and of the Way. Some of them may even be illiterate, and some may never have had a single formal lesson, as we, ourselves, have seen. God brings them forth in every age and their knowledge is by Him so that they are able to guide others to the mysteries of His Essence and the Lights of His Attributes by way of (their) direct perception, and be a proof for men.

When (those who reject the saints) are brought forth on the Day of Resurrection, still in ignorance of God, veiled from beholding His Essence, and excluded from the station of those brought nigh, they will say, 'If only You had sent to us a messenger by whom we would have come to know You and follow Your signs so that we could have reached You, rather than being abased, cast down from the station of those who are near, and disgraced by the lowering of the veils.

And God will then say, 'We brought them forth but you denied them.' Thus were they deceived and veiled by the words of those who said, "The time of spiritual training is past." Say, "*Each is waiting, so wait! For you shall come to know those who are the companions of the sound path, and those who are rightly guided.*

With God is all accord, and He is the Guide to the most beautiful of Ways. May He bless our master and guardian Muḥammad and his family and companions, and send them abounding salutations of peace.

Index of Quranic Verses Mentioned in the Commentary, other than those of the two principle *sūrahs*

Index of *Ḥadīths* Mentioned in the Commentary

Any Muslim who has lost three children to death will not enter hell except for what is sworn in [God's] oath. 88 n. 117

Each person dies the way he was living, and each shall be resurrected the way he died. 202

God sent down Gabriel in the most beautiful form I had ever seen and he said to me, "Truly

God conveys to you salutations, O Muḥammad, and says to you: In truth have I said to the world through inspiration, Be bitter and turbid and a loss and a hardship to My saints in order that they might love the meeting with Me, for truly have I created the world as a prison for My saints and a paradise for." 130 n. 33

Haste is from the devil, and slowness is from the All-Merciful. 101

I love to hear (the Qur'ān) recited by another. 76

O God! Fashioner of the heavens and the earth, Knower of the unseen and the seen, truly I pledge to You in this world that I bear witness that there is no god except You, one, without partner, and that Muḥammad is Your servant and messenger. So do not leave me to the power of my ego, for if You leave me under to power, You place me closer to evil and farther from good. I depend only on Your mercy, so please make for me a covenant with You that will grant me Your accord on the Day of Resurrection—Verily, You never break Your promise [3:194]. 103

May God be merciful to our brother Zachariah concerning his heir. 35

My face is prostrate before the One who created it, and formed it, and brought forth its hearing and sight by His power and strength... Dear God, write for me [by this prostration] reward, and remove from me sin. Make it a treasure for me in Your presence, and accept it of me as You accepted it from Your servant David ﷺ. 77

My servant cannot approach Me by anything more beloved to Me than what I have made incumbent upon him. 108 n. 152

My servant has lied about Me, and he should not have done so. And My servant has blasphemed against Me, and he should not have done so. 106

My servant will not cease to draw near to Me by supererogatory worship until he loves Me and I love him. 108

No servant turns with his heart towards God ﷻ except that God causes the hearts of the faithful to turn towards him with love and mercy and hastens to him every sort of good. 109

O God, make for me a covenant with You, and place love for me in the breasts of the faithful. 103

O God, make me among those who are humble before You, who glorify and praise You. I seek refuge from being one of the haughty who are too proud to follow Your commandments... 77

O Noah, you were the first of the messengers to the earth, and God called you a grateful servant. 74 n. 87.

Recite the Qur'ān and weep, and if you cannot weep, then try to weep. 76

The believer engenders love in the breasts of the pious and dread in the breasts of the wicked. 109

The believer will be brought near his Lord on the Day of Judgement until he is covered by God's protection. Then he will be asked 'Do you acknowledge [committing this sin]?' And he will say, 'My Lord, I acknowledge it.' 86 n. 112.

The Fire will say, 'Pass through, O faithful one, for your light has extinguished my flames.' 90

The most beloved to Me of those whom I love are those who make My servants beloved to Me, make Me beloved to My servants, and who walk the earth with good counsel. 112

There were three people among the Children of Israel—one had leprosy, the other was bald-headed, and the third one was blind. It then goes on to recount how God tested them by sending each an angel who cured him and gave him what he most desired in life. 168 n. 75

We, the prophets, do not leave [material] inheritance. 35

When death is brought forth in the form of a black ram with a white head... 57

When God loves a servant, He says to Gabriel, 'Truly I love this servant, so love him as well,' and Gabriel loves him and calls out to all the dwellers of the celestial realms, 'Verily, God loves this servant, so love him as well,' and they do, and then is love for him placed on earth. 108

When the people of Paradise enter Paradise, some will ask others, 'Did our Lord not promise us that we would come to [Hellfire]?' And it will be said to them, 'You did, but you came to it when it was quiescent.' 87

You are God's witnesses upon His earth. 109

You will see your Lord as you see the sun on a cloudless day, so if you can, do not get too tired to offer the prayers before sunrise and sunset. 206

Index and Short Biographies of Persons Mentioned in the Text

Only persons mentioned in the actual text of the *tafsīr* are listed below. Terms used in these entries: *Ṣaḥābī* (pl. *Ṣaḥāba*) = a Companion of the Prophet; *Tābiʿī* (pl. *Tābiʿīn*) = "A follower" = someone belonging to the generation following the *Ṣaḥābah* who had met one of them; *Mufassir* = exegete of the Qur'ān; *Muḥaddith* = collector or narrator of *ḥadīth*.

ABŪ BAKR AL-ṢIDDĪQ ibn Abī Quhāfa al-Taymī (d. 13/634) — 58, 62, 78. Among the greatest of the *Ṣaḥāba* and the first of the Rightly Guided Caliphs. He was a successful cloth merchant in Mecca. When he heard during one of his journeys that Muḥammad had proclaimed his prophecy, Abū Bakr became the fourth person to enter Islam and the first not of the Prophet's family. In the years that followed, he used his wealth the support the fledgling community and for the manumission of slaves.

ABŪ'L-HAYTHAM, ibn al-Tayyihān (d. 37/657) — 31. *Ṣaḥābī* and among the first people of Medina to enter Islam. It is recorded that he was monotheist even before Islam.

ABŪ JAHL, whose given name was ʿAmr ibn Hisham (d. ca. 2 /624) — 114. He was one of the leaders of the Quraysh in fierce opposition to the Prophet ﷺ in Mecca. The name he is known by in Muslim history means "The father of ignorance."

ABŪ ṬĀLIB al-Makkī (see AL-MAKKĪ).

ABŪ ṬĀLIB ibn ʿAbd al-Muṭṭalib (d. 619) — 64. He was the much-loved uncle of the Prophet ﷺ and father of ʿAlī, the fourth of the righteous caliphs. Although he protected Muḥammad ﷺ and was unflagging in his love for him, it is generally agreed that he did not embrace Islam. He died in the same year as Khadījā, the Prophet's wife, which is why that year is remembered as "the year of sorrow."

ABŪ AL-SAʿŪD, Muḥammad b. Muḥammad b. Muṣṭafā al-ʿImādī (d. 982/1574) — 43, 120, 157. *Mufassir*, poet, and Ḥanafī scholar. He was born in Istanbul and became a leading scholar in Arabic, Persian and Turkish. His Quranic commentary, *Irshād al-ʿAql al-Salīm ilā mazāya'l-kitāb al-Karīm*, is still widely studied. He is buried near the resting place of Abū Ayyūb al-Anṣārī in Istanbul. Besides his *tafsīr*, he also remembered as the jurist who issued a ruling that forbade the drinking of coffee in 1543.

ʿALĪ, Ibn Abū Ṭālib (d. 40/661) — 31, 78, 102, 108, 202. Among the greatest of the *Ṣaḥāba*, he was the cousin and later son-in-law of the Prophet through his marriage to Fāṭima. He was also the first male to accept Islam, the fourth caliph, and (according to Shiite doctrine), the first Imām. ʿAlī (and Fāṭima) became the model of austerity, piety, and chivalry (*al-futūwa*).

AL-ʿĀṢ ibn Wā'il (d. 620) — 97, 98. He was among those Meccans most opposed to Prophet ﷺ. It said in several commentaries that after he had referred to the Prophet ﷺ as *abtar*, "cut off because having no male heirs, Sūrat *al-Kawthar* (108) was revealed. Ibn Wā'il's son, ʿAmr, initially followed in his father's footsteps in opposition to Islam, but eventually embraced it and became among the most illustrious of the Companions.

ʿAWF b. Abī Jamīla al-Aʿrābī (c. 146/763) — 41. He was one of the learned of Baṣra is considered a trustworthy *muḥaddith* and figures in the transmission of scores of ḥadīth including many of those in Bukhāri and Muslim. It is also said that he was a *shīʿī* and, thelogically, a determinist (*qādirī*). It is noted in several biographical passages about him that although he was called "al-Aʿrābī" (The Bedouin), he was not a Bedouin, but rather originated from Bandawa, and Assyrian village in the province of Nineveh, in northern Iraq.

AL-BAQLĪ, Ruzbahān (606/1209) — 42, 54, 90, 131, 134, 169, 202, 205. He was a mystic and scholar originally from the south west of Persia and author of the mystical Quranic commentary *ʿArā'is al-bayān fī ḥaqā'iq al-qur'ān*. All references in *al-Baḥr al-Madīd* to "al-Wartajibī" are, in fact, to this work.

BILĀL ibn Rabaḥ al-Ḥabashī (19/640 AD) — 205. A former slave of Ethiopian ancestry, Bilāl became one of the greatest of the *Ṣaḥāba* and was made the first muezzin of Islam by the Prophet ﷺ himself.

AL-BŪZĪDĪ, Muḥammad ibn Aḥmad al-Slimānī al-Ghomārī (d. 1229/1813) — 30, 130. Ah was Sufi shaykh, born and raised in the village of Benslimān, in the Ghomāra region of Morocco near Tetouan. After some years of spiritual journeying around Morocco, he met and became of the disciple of Mūlay al-ʿArabī al-Darqāwī (see below) and was eventually put in direct charge of Ibn ʿAjība's training in the path.

AL-FARRĀ', Abū Zachariah Yaḥyā b. Ziyād (d. 207/822) — notes 37, 99. He was the author of *Maʿānī al-Qurʿān*, one of the earliest *tafsīr*s in existence.

AL-FĀSĪ, Sīdī ʿAbdurraḥmān Abū Zayd (d. 1036/1625) — 41, 74, 103, 194. He was a renowned scholar and Sufi. He was born in Qaṣr al-Kabīr in northern Morocco and studied in Fes with some of the greatest scholars of his day including Yaḥyā Sirāj and Abū al-ʿAbbās al-Manūr. He authored several useful works, among them marginal annotations (*ḥāshiyāt*) to the *ḥadīth* collection of al-Bukhārī, *Dalā'il al-Khayrāt*, and *al-Ḥizb al-Kabīr* of

Imām al-Shādhilī. He also figures as part of chain of transmission (*silsila*) of the *Ṭarīqat al-Shādhiliyya* from the sixteenth century on. His *Ḥāshiya* (Annotations) on the Quranic commentary of Jalāllayn is one of Ibn ʿAjība's main references in *al-Baḥr al-Madīd.*

AL-FUḌAYL, Ibn ʿIyād (d. 187/803) — 161. He was one of the earliest of those who came to known as Sufis. As a youth he had been a thief and is said to have repented while he was climbing a wall in order to rob a house and heard someone reciting the verse *Is it not time for the hearts of the faithful to grow humble at the Remembrance of God...?* He became, thereafter, one of the greatest of the early Sufis, studying *ḥadīth* with Abū Ḥanīfa.

AL-GHAZĀLĪ, Abū Ḥamīd Muḥammad ibn Muḥammad (449- 504/1058-1111) — 62, 89. He was a Sufi, scholar, prolific author, known as *ḥujjat al-islām* ("The proof of Islam"). He was born and died in Ṭūs, in Khorasān. After an illustrious career as teacher and lecturer, he renounced his position at the age of around forty and took up the life of a wandering dervish. The fruits of both his scholarship and efforts in the spiritual path form the basis of his most famous work, *Iḥyā ʿulūm al-dīn*, "The Revival of the Religious Sciences." His works are said to have influenced St. Thomas Aquinas and numerous other western philosophers.

HARAMA B. ḤAYYĀN al-ʿAbdī al-Baṣarī (d. ca 26/647) — 109. Although he lived during the time of the Prophet ﷺ, is considered by most to be among the *tābiʿīn*. He was a commander in certain battles during the caliphates of ʿUmar and ʿUthmān and known as devotee and ascetic. An entry in *Ḥilyat al-awliyā* is devoted to him.

HARAWĪ, Muḥammad b. Aḥmad b. al-Azharī (d. 370/980) — 31. He was the author of *Tahdhīb al-lugha*, an early dictionary of the Arabic language and one of the sources for the renowned *Lisān al-ʿArab*, compiled 100 years later.

IBN ADHAM, Ibrāhīm (d. 165/782) — 161. He was the near-legendary Sufi born in Balkh (in what is present-day Afghanistan) into royalty.

IBN ʿABBĀS, ʿAbdallah (d. 67/687) — 40, 47, 51, 79, 86, 113, 114, 121, 124, 127, 128, 129, 136, 137,

140, 160, 171, 184, 188, 193, 198. Though a child during much of the time he was with the Prophet ﷺ, he is considered to be among the greatest of the *ṣaḥāba*. He was the narrator of thousands of *ḥadīth*, and is considered one of the primary sources for the meanings of words and phrases in the Qur'ān.

IBN ʿARABĪ al-Ḥātimī (d. 638/1240) — 194. Known as *al-Shaykh al-Akbar* (the greatest master), Ibn ʿArabī was born in Murcia in Andalusian Spain, travelled through Morocco, and eventually on to the east. By the time of his death in Damascus he had left behind mystical doctrines in his voluminous writings which had a lasting influence of Sufism nearly everywhere in the Muslim world.

IBN AL-ʿARABI, Qāḍī Abū Bakr Muḥammad ibn ʿAbdallah ibn al-ʿArabī al-Muʿāfirī (d. 543/1148) — 40, 49. He was an Andalusian scholar and *mufassir*, author of *Aḥkām al-Qur'ān*. He was born in Seville, travelled to the east, and died in Fes, where his tomb, in the cemetery of Bab Ftuḥ, is a well-known. He should not be confused with the Sufi, Ibn ʿArabī al-Ḥātimī (see above).

IBN AL-ʿARAFA, Muḥammad al-Warghamī (d. 804/1401) — 40. He was a Tunisian scholar and author of several works on Maliki *fiqh* as well as a Quranic commentary that was compiled by his students after his death.

IBN ʿAṬĀ', Yaʿlā al-ʿĀmirī (d. 120/737) — 71, 174, 196. He was an early *mufassir* who figures in the transmission of scores of sayings concerning the meaning of Quranic verses.

IBN ʿAṬĀ' ALLĀH, Tāj al-Dīn Abū al-Faḍl al-Iskandarī (d. 708/1308) — 28, 119, 195. He was a renowned Sufi and one of the greatest Mālikī scholars of his day in Egypt. He became the spiritual disciple of Abū al-ʿAbbās al-Mursī, the successor of Abū al-Ḥasan al-Shādhilī, and eventually shaykh of the Ṭarīqa in Egypt. He is the author of *Kitāb al-Ḥikam*, The Book of Aphorisms, a compendium of Sufic wisdom which has been the object of numerous commentaries and is one of Ibn ʿAjība's most quoted sources throughout his *tafsīr*.

IBN ʿAṬIYYA, ʿAbd al-Ḥaqq Abū Muḥammad (d. 541/1147) — 46, 71, 74, 154, 178. He was born in Granada towards the beginning of Almoravid rule and eventually became one of the scholars and jurists of Almeria. He is chiefly remembered as the author of al-*Muḥarrar al-Wajīz fī tafsīr al-kitāb al-ʿazīz* an exceptionally concise *tafsīr*.

IBN ḤANBAL, Aḥmad (d. 241/855) — 116. He was a renowned *muḥaddith* and founder of the school of jurisprudence named after him. He travelled extensively in search of Traditions, of which he is said to have committed over three hundred thousand to memory.

IBN JUBAYR, Saʿīd (d. 95/714) — 31, 192. He was a *tābiʿi*. He figures in the transmission of scores of *ḥadīth* and Quranic commentary, particularly from Ibn ʿAbbās.

IBN JUZAYY, Abū ʿAbdallāh Muḥammad ibn Muḥammad ibn Aḥmad Ibn Juzayy al-Kalbī (693-741/1294-140) — 97, 156. *Mufassir* and one of the most renowned Mālikī scholars of Granada. Among his best-known works is his Quranic commentary, *Tas·hīl fī ʿulūm al-tanzīl*.

IBN KHALAF, Ubayy (d. 4/625) — 85. He was one of the leading opponents of Muḥammad and his mission during his life. It is said that he was the one who once picked up a piece of dry bone from the ground, crumbled it in his hand, and said mockingly, "Muḥammad claims that we will be resurrected after we die and have become like this!" a saying that is answered by several verses of the Qur'ān.

IBN MARZŪQ, Muḥammad b. Aḥmad b. Muḥammad, known as *al-Ḥafīd* (the grandson) (d. 842/1438) — 40. He was born and died in Tlemcen, Algeria. He was a renowned North African scholar and mystic and the author of numerous works, including a commentary on *Ṣaḥīḥ al-Bukhārī* entitled *al-Matjar al-Rabīḥ*, and three commentaries on the *Burda*, the best known of which is entitled *Iẓhār ṣiqd al-mawadda fī sharḥ al-burda.*

IBN MASHĪSH, ʿAbd al-Salām (d. c. 565/1355) — 58, 118. He was the near-legendary spiritual master of Abū'l-Ḥasan al-Shādhilī. What is known of his teachings arises from the sayings recorded in the early books of the Shādhiliyya order, notably *Laṭāʾif al-minan*. He is reputed to be the author of a famous prayer of blessing upon the Prophet although there is no direct evidence of this in those books. His tomb atop Jebel ʿAlam in the Rif Mountains of northern Morocco is one of the most venerated shrines in the country.

IBN MASʿŪD, ʿAbd Allāh al-Hudhalī (d. 32/653) — 87, 103, 124. One of the greatest of the Ṣaḥāba, Ibn Masʿūd is said to have been either the third or the sixth convert to Islam. He was particularly well-versed in the recitation and interpretation of the Qur'ān, an expert in matters of law, and the transmitter of scores of important *ḥadīth.*

IBN SULṬĀN, Māḍī Abū'l- ʿAzā'im al-Tamīmī (d. 718/1318) — 87, 103, 124. He was among those early disciples who met Shaykh al-Shādhilī in Tunis and then became his constant companion and servant, travelling with him to Egypt. He is the source of many narrations from al-Shādhilī quoted extensively in *Mafākhir al-ʿAliya*. His tomb is in Tunis.

IBN WAHB, Abū Muḥammad ʿAbdallāh (d. 197/813) — 73. He was a companion of Imām Mālik and instrumental in spreading the Mālikī school of *fiqh* in Egypt and the Maghreb.

ʿIKRIMA b. ʿAbdallāh al-Madanī (d. 105/723-4) — 82, 159. He is said to have been of Berber origin and was the manumitted slave of Ibn ʿAbbās, who taught him the tafsīr which he then passed on to Mujāhid.

JĀBIR ibn ʿAbd Allāh al-Khazrajī al-Anṣārī (d. 78/697) — 87, 88. *Ṣaḥābī*, and notably one of the six of the Khazrajī clan who made the first pledge to welcome the Prophet to Medina. He figures in the narrative chain of many *ḥadīth*, and participated in nineteen of the military expeditions of the Prophet.

JAʿFAR al-Ṣādiq, ibn ʿAlī ibn al-Ḥusayn al-Basṭ (80-148/699-65) — 90, 194. One of the most illustrious and learned of the *tābiʿīn*, he was born and died in Medina where he taught and transmitted *ḥadīth* to both Abū Ḥanīfa and Imām Mālik. He came to called *al-Ṣādiq*, the Honest One, for the fact that he was never known to have told a lie. He is considered by Shīʿi Muslims as the sixth of the twelve Imāms.

AL-JUNAYD, Abu'l-Qāsim b. Muḥammad (d. 277/910) — 67, 116, 195. His family origins were Persian although he was born in Baghdad and is possibly the most famous of the Baghdad Sufis. He kept company with his uncle Sarī al-Saqaṭī (*see below*), al-Ḥārith al-Muḥāsibī, and ʿAlī al-Qaṣāb among many.

KAʿB Abū Iṣḥāq b. Māniʿ, known as *al-Aḥbār* "authority," from the Hebrew *ḥāber* (c. 32/652) — 74, 105, 137. He was a Yemenite Jew who converted to Islam around the year 17 H (638) and is considered one of the principal sources of Judaic stories that were accepted into the *tafsīr* of the Qur'ān.

AL-KALBĪ, Muḥammad b. al-Sā'ib b. al-Ḥārith (d. 146/763) — 35, 49, 56, 71, 87. *Tābiʿī* to whom is attributed some of the earliest exegesis of the Qur'ān which exists presently in quotations from later sources. He should not be confused with the great Andalusian *Mufassir* and Mālikī scholar of Granada Ibn Juzayy (see above), also sometimes referred to as al-Kalbī.

AL-KAWĀSHĪ, Aḥmad Abū'l-ʿAbbās Muwwafaq al-Dīn al-Mawṣilī (d. 680/1281) — 165, 168, 170, 174, 178, 197. He was an eminent Shāfiʿī scholar and the author of a Quranic commentary which exists presently only in manuscript fragments. All Ibn ʿAjība's references to this work are quoted from al-Fāsī's *Ḥāshiya* (see al-Fāsī, above).

KHABĀB b. al-Aratt (d. 37/658) — 96. He had been brought to Mecca before Islam as a captive sold into slavery. As such, he learned the art of sword-making. When the new religion appeared, he became one of the first ten converts to it and was persecuted because of his belief. Later in life, he was granted wealth and became among the most generous of the Companions.

AL-MAJDHŪB, ʿAbd al-Raḥmān b. ʿIyyād b. Yaʿqūb b. Salāma alṢinhājī (976/1568) — 68. He was born in Azemmour on the Atlantic coast of Morocco during the early years of the Saadi dynasty but travelled to Meknes where he lived most of his life and is buried. He is known throughout Morocco as the author of a small book of poetry written in Moroccan Arabic and containing popular wisdom, an attribution which may or may not be correct. His lines of mystical poetry, however, are quoted extensively both in the letters of the Shaykh al-Darqāwī and by Ibn ʿAjība.

AL-MAKKĪ, Abū Ṭālib Muḥammad b. ʿAlī (386/996) — 68. He was a *muḥaddith*, Shafiʿī jurist, and Sufi, known principally for his work *Qūt al-qulūb fī muʿāmalat al-Maḥbūb* (The Nourishment of Hearts in (its) Interactions with the Beloved), a primary source for al-Ghazālī's *Iḥyā' ʿulūm al-dīn*.

MĀLIK, ibn Anas al-Aṣbaḥī (d. 179/795) — 116. The founder of one of the four main schools (*madhāhib*) of Islamic law in Sunni Islam. Born into a family of *ḥadīth* narrators, he studied the recitation of the Qur'ān with Nāfiʿ and heard ḥadīth from al-Ẓuhrī and Ibn al-Munkadir. He taught al-Shāfiʿī, al-Thawrī and Ibn al-Mubārak. His book, *al-Muwaṭṭa'*, is the earliest surviving work of Muslim law, and places great emphasis on the actual practice of Islam in Medina in Imām Mālik's time.

AL-MUJĀHID, ibn Jabr al-Makkī (d. 104/722-3) — 78, 82, 86, 184. A *tābiʿī* known chiefly as being one of the earliest commentators of the Qur'ān. It is said that he read his *tafsīr* to Ibn ʿAbbās thirty times to verify its accuracy.

AL-MUQĀTIL ibn Sulaymān al-Azdī (d. 150/757) — 57, 83, 136, 157. He was a theologian and *mufassir* originally from Balkh in what is now northern Afghanistan who figures in the transmission of numerous hadith in the second generation following the Prophet ﷺ. A Quranic commentary attributed to him exists only as quoted fragments in later sources.

AL-NAḌR B. al-Ḥārīth (d. 2/624) — 91, 114. One of the pagans in Mecca who would stand after the Prophet ﷺ recited some of the verses of the Qur'ān and try to out-do them with lines about Rustam and Persian kings. It was partially to him that Quranic verse *When Our signs are recited unto him, he says, "Fables of those of old!"* ... [83:13-14] refers.

AL-QURṬUBĪ, Abū ʿAbd Allāh (671/1273) — 80. He was a *mufassir* and *muḥaddith*. He was born and grew up in Cordoba but upon its fall to the Spanish in 1236, he travelled to Egypt and spent the rest of his life there. He is best known for his monumental commentary of the Qur'ān entitled *al-Jāmiʿ li Aḥkām al-Qur'ān* which is one of Ibn ʿAjība's main sources.

QUṬRUB, Muḥammad b. al-Mustanīr b. Aḥmad Abū ʿAlī (d. 206/821) — 124. A student of the great grammarian, Sibawayh, and the author of *Maʿānī al-Qur'ān*, one of the earliest syntactical and linguistic commentaries on the Qur'ān.

AL-RĀZĪ, Yaḥyā ibn Muʿādh (d. 258/871) — 208. One of the early Khorasānī Sufis. Many sayings have been attributed to him concerning on renunciation and worship. He died at the age of 41 in Nishapur.

AL-SHĀDHILĪ, ʿAlī ibn ʿAbd Allāh Abū al-Ḥasan (591-656/1195-1258) — 14, 32, 58, 62, 110, 118, 201. The founder of the Sufic order which bears his name. He was born in the Ghomāra region of Morocco near Chefchaouen and studied in Fes. After a discipleship with Mūlay ʿAbd al-Salām ibn Mashīsh atop Jebel ʿAlam in the Rif Mountains of Morocco, he took his spiritual teachings first to Tunisia and then Egypt, where he spent the rest of his life. He died en route to one of the several pilgrimages he made during his life and was buried on the old pilgrims' route, near the Red Sea.

AL-SHĀFIʿĪ, Muḥammad ibn Idrīs al-Qurashī (d. 204/820) — 116. He was the founder of one of the four main schools (*madhāhib*) of Sunni jurisprudence. It is said that he had memorized the Qur'ān by the age of seven and was proficient in the varieties of its recitation and its commentary by the age of thirteen. By around the age of twenty he was living in Medina where he had become the student of Malik ibn Anas, many of whose opinions in *fiqh* he would later adopt. Much of his life after this was spent in traveling—to Yemen, Egypt, Iraq, Syria, and Persia—ever in search of knowledge. He died in Cairo where his tomb is a highly venerated place of devotion.

SIBAWAYH, Abū Bishr ʿAmr b. ʿUthmān al-Baṣrī (180/796) — 141. He was born in Shiraz in what is now Central Iran and travelled first to Baṣra and then Baghdad, where he became established as a grammarian. He is now seen as the father of Arabic linguistics and his main work, al-Kitāb, and one of the first books of Arabic grammar.

AL-SUDDĪ, Ismāʿīl ibn ʿAbd al-Raḥmān (d. ca. 128/745) — 50, 116. *Tābiʿī* and *mufassir*, al-Suddī was originally from the Hijāz, but lived in Kūfa most of his life and was among the major transmitters of Quranic commentary from ibn Masʿūd and Ibn ʿAbbās. Much of what he conveyed was eventually recorded in the monumental work *Jāmiʿ al-Bayān*, by Ibn Jarīr al-Ṭabarī (d. 310/922). His grandson Muḥammad ibn Marwān is also known as a *mufassir*, but is considered less reliable. The two are sometimes distinguished as "al-Suddī *al-kabīr*" and "*al-ṣaghīr*."

AL-THAʿLABĪ, Aḥmad b. Ibrāhīm al-Nisabūrī (d. 383/993) — 51, 124, 143, 160. He was the author of *al-Kashf wa'l-Bayān ʿan Tafsīr al-Qur'ān*, one of Ibn ʿAjība's most often quoted references. He is also the author of *al-ʿArā'is fī qiṣaṣ al-anbiyā'* on the lives of the prophets.

AL-TIRMIDHĪ, Abū ʿAbd Allāh Muḥammad ibn ʿAlī al-Ḥakīm (ca. 255/869) — 71, 89, 90. He was a Sufi, *muḥaddith* and Ḥanafī jurist born in Khorasan, principally remembered as the author of the unique ḥadīth collection

Nawādir al-Uṣūl fī Maʿrifati Akhbār al-Rasūl, as well as *Khatm al-awliyā*, a treatise on the meaning of "The Seal of the Saints." He should not be confused with Abū ʿĪsā Muḥammad al-Tirmidhī (279/892), the compiler al-Sunan, a collection of *ḥadīth* considered to be one of the six *ṣaḥīḥ* collections.

ʿUMAR IBN AL-KHAṬṬĀB (r. 13-23/634-44) — 47, 49, 76. The second of the Rightly Guided Caliphs. At first an enemy of the Prophet's mission, he became one of its staunchest defenders. His conversion is said to have taken place after his own sister had embraced the new religion. Rushing to her house to confront her, he found her with a scroll on which was written a *sūrah* of the Qur'ān which, according to some versions, was *Ṭa Hā*, and others *al-Ḥadīd.* After consenting to wash, 'Umar began to read the page and upon completing it, resolved to enter his sister's religion.

UMAYYA IBN ABĪ AL-ṢALT (d. 05/626) — 188. He was a well-known Jāhilī poet who wrote largely about subjects related to the Next World. He was born in Ṭā'if, spent part of his life in Damascus studying ancient books and returned to Ṭā'if upon hearing about the advent of Islam. It is said that he met the Prophet Muḥammad in Mecca but did not become a Muslim.

"AL-WARTAJIBĪ" (see al-Baqlī)

AL-WARRĀQ, Abū Bakr Muḥammad al-Tirmidhī (d. 240/854) — 141. He was an eminent Khorasānī Sufi and *muḥaddith*. He was born in Tirmidh (in present-day Uzbekistan), and spent his life in Balkh. Although he authored books, none remain, and his words are known only through what later authors quote him as saying.

AL-ZUBAYR, ʿUrwah bin (d. 94/713) — 208. He was a *tābiʿī*, *muḥaddith*, and one of the seven jurists of Medina who participated in the first efforts to formalize Muslim law.

AL-ZUJĀJ, Abū Isḥāq (d. 311/923) — 141. He was an exegete and grammarian. He was born and died in Baghdād and is known principally for his work *Iʿrāb al-Qur'ān.*

Bibliography

Works in Arabic

Abū al-Sa'ūd, Muḥammad b. Muḥammad al-'Imadī. *Irshād al-'Aql al-Salīm ilā Mazāyā al-Kitāb al-Karīm*. Beirut: Dar Iḥyā' al-Turāth al-'Arabī, (undated).

Amrānī, 'Abd al-Nūr al-. *Taqyīd fī tarjumati wa aḥwāli al-Shaykh Abī al-Ḥasan 'Alī bin 'Abdallāh al-shahīr bi al-Shādhilī*, ed. Kenneth Honerkamp. Beirut: Dar el-Machreq, 2012.

Baqlī, Abū Muḥammad Ruzbahān b. Abī Nāṣr al-. *'Arā'is al-Bayān fī Ḥaqā'iq al-Qur'ān*, ed. Aḥmad Farīd al-Mizyādī. Beirut: Dar al-Kutub al-'Ilmiyya, 2008.

Bayhaqī, Aḥmad b. al-Ḥusayn, al-. *Shu'ab al-īmān*, ed. Ḥamdī al-Dammardāsh Muḥammad al-'Adil. Beirut: Dār al-Fikr, 1990.

Dhahabī, Muḥammad Ḥusayn al-. *Isrā'īliyyat fī al-tafsīr wa'l-ḥadīth*. Cairo: Maktaba Wahbah, 1990.

Darqāwī, Mūlay al-'Arabī al-Ḥasanī, al-. *Majmū'a rasā'il*, ed. Muḥammad Bassām Bārūd. Abu Dhabi: Cultural Foundation Publications, 1999.

Fāsī, 'Abd al-Raḥmān (al-'Ārif), al-. *Ḥāshiya 'alā Tafsīr al-Jilālayn*, ed. Dr. Ḥassan 'Azūzī. Fes: Matba'a Umāyma, 2016.

Ghazālī, Abū Hamīd Muḥammad ibn Muḥammad, al-. *Iḥyā' 'ulūm al- dīn*. Jedda: Dar al-Minhāj, 2011.

Ibn 'Abbād, Abū 'Abd Allāh Maḥammad ibn Ibrāhīm *Fatḥ al-Tuḥfa wa iḍā'atu'l-sudfa*. Rabat: Dar Nashr al-Ma'rifa, 2002.

———. *Gayth al-mawāhib al-'aliyya fī sharḥ al-ḥikam al-'aṭā'iyya*, ed. 'Abd al-Ḥalīm Maḥmūd. Cairo: Dār al-Ma'ārif, 1970.

Ibn 'Ajība, Aḥmad. *Al-Baḥr al-Madīd fī tafsīr al-Qur'ān al-Majīd*, ed. Aḥmad 'Abdallāh al-Qurashī Raslān, Cairo: 1999-2001.

———. *Al-Fahrasa*, ed. 'Abd al-Ḥamīd Ṣālih al-Ḥamdā. Cairo: Dar al-Ghadā al-'Arabī, 1990.

———. *Mi 'rāj al-tashawwuf ilā haqā'iq al-taṣawwūf*. Tetouan: Maṭba'at al-Marīnī, 1982.

Ibn 'Aṭā'illāh, Abū al-Faḍl Aḥmad ibn Muḥammad. *Kitāb al-ḥikam*, (lithograph), Morocco, undated.

———. *Laṭā'if al-minan*. Dār al-Ma'ārif, Cairo, 1992.

———. *Al-Tanwīr fī isqāt al-tadbīr*. 'Alam al-Fikr, Cairo, 1998.

Ibn 'Aṭiyya, Abū Muḥammad 'Abd al-Ḥaqq ibn Ghālib. *Al-Muḥarrar al- wajīz fī tafsīr al-kitāb al-'azīz*. Fes: Wizārat al-Awqāf, Morocco, 1977-1989.

Ibn al-Fārid, ʿUmar. *Diwān*, ed. Medhi Muḥammad Naṣr al-Dīn. Beirut: Dar al-Kutub al-ʿIlmiyya.

Ibn Hishām, ʿAbd al-Mālik. *Al-Sīra al-nabawiyya*, ed. Ṭaha ʿAbd al-Raʿūf Saʿd. Beirut: Dār al-Jīl, 1998.

Ibn Qunfudh, Abū al- ʿAbbās Aḥmad ibn al-Ḥusayn al-Qasanṭīnī. *Uns al-faqir wa ʿizz al-ḥaqīr fī taʿrīf bi al-shaykh Abī Madyan al-Ghawth wa aṣ·ḥābihi*. Cairo: Dar al-Muqṭim, 2002.

Ibn al-Ṣabbāgh, Muḥammad ibn al-Qāsim al-Ḥimyarī. *Durrat al-asrār wa tuḥfat al-abrār*. Tunis: 1886.

Iṣfahānī, Abū Nuʿaym, al-. *Ḥilyat al-awliyāʿ wa ṭabaqāt al-aṣfiyāʿ*, ed. Muṣṭafā ʿAbd al-Qādir ʿAṭā. Beirut: Dār al-Kutub al-ʿIlmiyya, 1997.

Kalbī, Hicham b. Muḥammad b. al-Sā'ib, al-. *Kitāb al-Aṣnām*, Ed. Ustadh Aḥmad Zakī Bāshā. Cairo: Dār al-Kutub al-Miṣriyya, 1995.

Kittānī, Muḥammad ibn Jaʿfar al-. *Salwat al-anfās wa muḥādithat al-akyās*. Casablanca: Dār al-Thaqāfa, 2004.

Makkī, Abū Ṭālib, *Qūt al-qulūb*, ed. Bāsam ʿUyūn al-Sūd. Beirut: Dār al-Kutub al-ʿIlmiyya, 1997.

Muʿaskarī, Muḥammad Būziyyān b. Aḥmad al-. *Kanz al-asrār fī manāqib Mawlay al-ʿArabī al-Darqāwi wa baʿḍa aṣḥābihi*. Manuscript d. 2339, Rabat: National Library.

Mundhirī, al-Ḥāfiẓ Zakiyya al-Dīn ʿAbd al-ʿAẓīm, al-. *Al-Targhīb waʿl-tarhīb min al-ḥadīth al-sharīf*. Beirut: Dār al-Fikr, 1993.

Qushayrī, Abūʾl-Qasim, al-. *Laṭā'if al-ishārāt* (*Tafsīr al-Qushayrī*), ed. Dr. Ibrāhīm Basyūnī. Cairo: Al-Hai'atu'l-Miṣriyyat al-ʿĀmma li'l-Kitāb, 2000.

———. *Al-Risālat al-qushayriyya*. Cairo: Dār al-Maʿārif, 1995.

———. *Al-Taḥbīr fī al-Tadhkīr*, ed. Dr. Ibrāhīm Basyūnī.

Cairo: Dār al-Kutub al-ʿArabiyā, 1968.

Talīdī, ʿAbdallāh b. ʿAbd al-Qādir al-. *Al-Muṭrib bi mashāhir awliyāʿi al-maghrib*. Rabat: Dar al-Amān, 2003.

Temsimānī, Muḥammad al-. *Al-Īmām Sīdī Muḥammad b. Aḥmad al-Būzīdī: Tarjamatuhu wa baʿḍa āthārihi*. Beirut: Dār al-Kutub al-ʿIlmiyyah, 2010.

Temsimānī, Muḥammad al-. *Al-Īmām Mawlāya al-ʿArabī al-Darqāwī*. Beirut: Dār al-Kutub al-ʿIlmiyyah, 2007.

Tirmidhī, Muḥammad b. ʿAlī b. Al-Ḥusayn AbūʿAbd Allāh, al-. *Nawādir al-uṣūl fī aḥādīth al-Rasūl*, ed. Dr. ʿAbd al-Raḥmān ʿUmayrh, Beirut: Dār al-Jīl, 1992.

Shawkānī, Aḥmad, al-. *Tuḥfat al-dhākirīn*. Beirut: Mu'assasa al-Kutub al-Thaqāfiya, 1988.

Shushtarī, Abū al-Ḥasan, al-. *Diwān*, ed. Dr. ʿAlī Sāmī al-Nashar, Alexandria: Mu'assasa al-Maʿārif, 1960.

Suyūṭī, Jalāl al-Dīn, al-. *al-Durr al-Munaẓẓam fī ismi Llāhi al-Aʿẓam*, ed. Dr. ʿĀṭif Ismāʿīl Aḥmad, Cairo: Būraṣṣat al-Kutub, 2013.

———. *Ḥabā'ik fī akhbār al-Malā'ik*, ed. Abū Hājar Muḥammad al-Saʿīd b. Basyūnī Zaghlūl. Beirut: Dār al-Kutub al-ʿIlmiyyah, 1985.

———. *al-Itqān fī ʿulūm al-Qurʿān*, ed. Ṭaha ʿAbd al-Ra'ūf Saʿd. Cairo: Al-Maktaba al-Tawfiqiyya (undated).

Ṭabarānī, Sulaymān ibn Aḥmad ibn Ayyūb ibn Mutayr al-Lahkmī al-. *al-Muʿjam al-awsāṭ*. Riyāḍ: Maktaba al-Maʿārif, 1985.

Ḥākim al-Tirmidhī, al-. *Nawādir al-uṣūl fī aḥādīth al-Rasūl*, ed. ʿAbd al-Raḥmān ʿUmayr, Beirut: Dār al-Jīl, 1412/1992.

Zarrūq, Aḥmad b. Aḥmad b. Muḥammad ibn ʿIsā, al-. *Al-Naṣīḥa al-Kāfiya*. Maktaba Imām al-Shāfiʿī, Al-Aḥsā, Saudi Arabia, 1993.

Ziriklī, Khayr al-Dīn, al-. *al-Aʿlām*, 11th edition. Beirut: Dar al-ʿIlm liʿl-Malāyin, 1995

Works in English and French

Darqāwī, Mulay al-ʿArabī, al-. *Letters on the Spiritual Path*. Trans. Mohamed Fouad Aresmouk and Michael Abdurrahman Fitzgerald, Allentown: Al-Madina Institute, 2018.

El-Mansour, Mohamed. *Morocco in the Reign of Mawlay Sulayman*. Cambridgeshire: Middle and Northeastern Studies Press, 1990.

Ghazālī, Abū Hamīd Muḥammad ibn Muḥammad, al-. *The Book of Remembrance of Death and the Afterlife*, trans. T.J. Winter. London: Islamic Texts Society, 1989.

Halman, Hugh Talat, *Where The Two Seas Meet: The Qurʿānic Story of al-Khiḍr and Moses in Sufi Commentaries*. Louisville: Fons Vitae, 2013.

Ibn ʿAjība, Aḥmad. *(Fahrasa) The Autobiography of a Moroccan Soufi*. Trans. from the Arabic by Jean-Louis Michon and from the French by David Steight. Louisville: Fons Vitae, 1999.

———. *The Book of Ascension to the Essential Truths of Sufism (Miʿrāj al-tashawwuf ilā Ḥaqāʿiq al-taṣawwuf)*. Trans. Mohamed Fouad Aresmouk and Michael Abdurrahman Fitzgerald. Louisville: Fons Vitae, 2011.

———. *The Immense Ocean—Al-Baḥr al-Madīd: A thirteenth/eighteenth Qurʿanic commentary on the chapters of The All- Merciful, The Event, and Iron*. Trans. Mohamed Fouad Aresmouk and Michael Abdurrahman Fitzgerald. Louisville: Fons Vitae, 2009.

Ibn ʿAṭā Allāh, Abū al-Faḍl Aḥmad ibn Muḥammad. *The Book of Wisdom*, trans. Victor Danner. New York: Classics of Western Spirituality, 1978.

———. *Laṭā'if al-minan*, trans. Nancy Roberts. Louisville: Fons Vitae, 2005.

Jackson, James Grey. *An Account of Timbuctoo and Hausa.* London, 1820, available on-line through the Gutenberg Project at http://www.gutenberg.org/files/22631/22631-h/22631-h.htm#p156

Lings, Martin. *Muhammad—his life based on the earliest sources.* London: Islamic Texts Society, 1983.

Michon, Jean-Louis. *Le Soufi Marocain Aḥmad ibn 'Ajība et son Mi'rāj. Glossaire de la mystique musulmane.* Paris: Vrin, 1973.

Nasr, Seyyed Hossein (editor). *The Study Qur'an.* New York: Harper Collins, 2015.

Pickthall, Marmaduke (translator). *The Meaning of the Glorious Koran.* London: Allen & Unwin, 1976.

Roberts, Nancy (see above *Ibn 'Aṭā Allāh*)

Rippin, Andrew (editor). *The Blackwell Companion to the Qur'ān.* Oxford: Blackwell Publishing, 2006.

Siddiqi, Muhammad Zubayr. *Hadith Literature: Its Origin, Development & Special Features*, ed. Abdal Hakim Murad, Cambridge: Islamic Texts Society, 1991.

Tustarī, Sahl b. 'Abd Allāh, al-. *Tafsīr al-Tustarī,* trans. Annabel Keeler and Ali Keeler. Louisville: Fons Vitae, 2011.

Winter, T.J. (see above *Ghazālī* and *Siddiqi*).

Software and On-Line Resources

Al-Maktabat al-Shāmila v. 2. distributed through www.waqfeya.net

General Index